THE BIG EIGHT

MARK STEVENS

THE BIG EIGHT

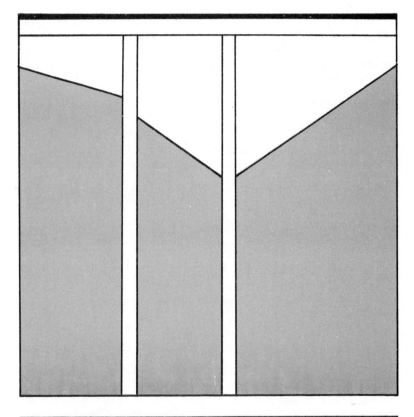

COLLIER BOOKS
Macmillan Publishing Company
New York

Macmillan Publishing Company, 866 Third Avenue, New York, N.Y. 10022
Collier Macmillan Canada, Inc.

Library of Congress Cataloging in Publication Data
Stevens, Mark, 1947–
   The big eight.
   Includes index.
   1. Accounting firms—United States.   2. Big business
—United States.   I. Title.
HF5616.U5S75 1984   338.7′61657′0973   83–18863
ISBN 0–02–008790–X (pbk.)

First Collier Books Edition 1984

10 9 8 7 6 5 4 3 2 1

The Big Eight is also published in a hardcover
edition by Macmillan Publishing Company.

Printed in the United States of America

FOR JUSTIN ARI,
born as my pen hit the paper.

Contents

THE BIG EIGHT

1. Of Armies and Rock Stars

"The Big Eight? Isn't that some kind of football conference ?"
—An account executive at J. Walter Thompson,
the international advertising agency

LIVE FROM HOLLYWOOD—the Academy Awards show. Lights. Action. Music. Oscars. Glitter. Tears. A million "thank you's."

JOHNNY CARSON: And now, to present the award for the outstanding performance by an actress in a starring role, a gentleman who has won two Oscars and tonight is nominated for a third, and a lady who has her own Oscar. They are both remarkable for the unique ability to play comedy as well as drama, and tonight makes the first time they've played together. They are Jack Lemmon and Cloris Leachman.

MUSIC: "Days of Wine and Roses"

(Jack Lemmon and Cloris Leachman come to podium.)

JACK LEMMON: Before we present the first award, we have to explain how the Academy's voting procedure works. All active Academy members may vote on nominations for the five pictures of the year. Other nominations are made by members of each Academy branch. For example, writers nominate the five outstanding writing achievements of the year, actors nominate actors, directors nominate directors, et cetera.

CLORIS LEACHMAN: Later, all members vote on those nominations to select the final awards. Their secret ballots are sent to the Academy's bonded accountants, Price Waterhouse and Com-

pany, for tabulation. Results are known only to Price Waterhouse and Company until the sealed envelopes are opened here
tonight. And guarding those envelopes is Frank Johnson of
Price Waterhouse. Gentlemen—

(He enters to applause.)

The sight of a clean-cut tuxedoed man presenting a sealed envelope to a dashing celebrity is the only vision most Americans have
of The Big Eight at work. Millions, in fact, know only one of The
Big Eight by name—Price Waterhouse—and think it is some sort
of detective agency whose shining hour comes once a year on a
glamourous television show. Something like a corporate Bert Parks.

That the man on the street does not know of The Big Eight, or
that he thinks of it as a football league, is startling. That the only
widely known member of The Big Eight is famous mostly for its
ten-second appearance on the Oscar show is extraordinary. And that
a Big Eighter manages to wrangle a free plug on the most watched
television program in history—and controls the voting for the
world's most coveted film awards—is revealing.

Who are The Big Eight? For starters, they are huge multinational
business organizations, the largest professional firms in the world,
and some of the most influential financial powers on earth. They are
Arthur Andersen; Arthur Young; Coopers & Lybrand; Deloitte
Haskins & Sells; Ernst & Whinney; Peat, Marwick, Mitchell; Price
Waterhouse; and Touche Ross. Working through an intricate network of high-level contacts and special relationships, they operate
at the seat of power and yet are often removed from the public eye.
This influence is pervasive, touching the lives of every human being
and impacting the decisions of governments, corporations,
churches, rock stars, armies, hospitals, universities, museums, peni-
tentiaries, poets, and police. Even those who know of—or even
work for—The Big Eight do not fully recognize the enormity of
their presence. To put it simply, The Big Eight are into everything!
Born into the world as accounting firms, and still widely regarded
as such, The Big Eight have nevertheless defied genetics, assuming
identities never exhibited by their founders. Their scope of practice
is sweeping, offering clients a vast smorgasbord of business services.

Just a brief glance reveals a full menu indeed. The Big Eight are, among other things, auditors, accountants, executive headhunters, merger-makers, tax specialists, consultants, attorneys, lobbyists, expert witnesses, financial planners, actuaries, engineers. They do everything from planning urban medical centers to designing Third World transportation systems. Name a white-collar service and chances are The Big Eight provide it or will find a way to do so.

But how did this all begin? Where did The Big Eight come from? Where are their roots? It all traces back to ancient history, to the very beginning of accounting.

"We all know that the ancient Greeks, while not having an April 15 deadline, utilized accounting as a basic tool," says Walter E. Hanson, former chairman of The Big Eight firm of Peat, Marwick, Mitchell, in an address to the Newcomen Society.

"If you go back to the palace of Nestor in ancient Greece, you'll find not only accounting records, but also records of income-tax computation. So the origins of accounting are as old as civilization itself, because man's need to know and record his inventory position, the grain in his graneries and the flocks in his field, predated his need to write about anything else. . . .

"However, the profession of public accounting or auditing, as we know it, is both young and unique. It began in Great Britain with the company laws and bankruptcy acts passed in Parliament in the 1850s, and you will find, as I thread through this, that most of the advances in accounting came from chaos in business. They did this to safeguard the shareholders of many corporations that resulted from the industrial revolution in Britain. In America, chartered accountants appeared on the scene during the decades of rapid growth following the Civil War. They were mostly Scottish and English who came here to watch over the capital that was surging into the New World from the Old. That's how accounting got started. . . ."

The evolution of Peat, Marwick, Mitchell into a major CPA firm provides a representative example of The Big Eight's rise to power. Peat's roots trace back to both the United States and Great Britain. The firm came to life in England in 1867; in 1891 it was named W.B. Peat & Co. The American ancestor, Marwick, Mitchell & Co., was

fathered by James Marwick and Roger Mitchell in 1897, just a year
after the New York State legislature provided for the designation of
"certified public accountant." Housed in New York's financial dis-
trict at 45 Nassau Street, the firm prospered, built a following
throughout the city, and in 1904 opened offices in Minneapolis and
Chicago, soon to be followed by branches in Winnipeg, Toronto,
Pittsburgh, Philadelphia, and Kansas City. At this time, there were
twelve partners on the letterhead of Marwick, Mitchell & Co.

The year 1907 proved to be an auspicious one for accountants.
Throughout the twentieth century, accountants have greatly expanded their influence and involvement in the business community
in times of economic adversity. In the so-called Panic of 1907, with
banks and businesses failing in alarming numbers, M&M found itself
in the right place at the right time.

"At this point, J.P. Morgan, aware that Marwick, Mitchell had
become specialized in bank auditing, called upon the firm to assess
the solvency of the old Knickerbocker Trust Co., a key bank in the
system," Hanson adds. "The work our firm did contributed, however modestly, to Morgan's strategy for ending the panic and laid
the groundwork for greater business acceptance of the accountant's
role in industry.

"The next important year in our history was 1911, when James
Marwick encountered Sir William Peat during an ocean crossing
from London to New York. Inspired by the bracing salt air and the
superb cuisine, not to mention the fine brandy and cigars, the two
reached a working agreement to combine the strengths of their
partnerships. For a period of fourteen years the firm operated in the
United States as Marwick, Mitchell, Peat & Co. On January 1, 1925,
the firm assumed the name of Peat, Marwick, Mitchell & Co.—
partners on a worldwide basis. The *Co.* in our name represents
copartners, not *company.*

"As you might imagine, Sir William Peat, James Marwick, and
Roger Mitchell all hailed from Scotland, a land that prides itself on
three major exports—accountants, golf, and whiskey. In the meantime, the accounting profession had been given a boost with the
establishment in 1913 of the Federal Reserve Board which resulted

from the 1907 panic. Nineteen-thirteen was also the year that the states ratified the federal income-tax laws. The following year, the Federal Trade Commission was formed. Demands of both the Federal Reserve Board and the Federal Trade Commission as new regulatory bodies led to the adoption of official standards and guidelines for independent accountants, and, obviously, the advent of income tax opened a very broad field for our profession."

So too did the stock market crash of 1929 and the resulting securities laws of 1933 and 1934. In creating the Securities and Exchange Commission and requiring audits of corporate financial reports, this sweeping legislation did more than anything else to foster the enormous growth of public accounting. It laid the groundwork for the tremendous demand for Big Eight services over the past fifty years. Once the role of the CPAs as auditors and tax advisers became well established, the firms grew at an awesome rate. In 1947, for example, Peat, Marwick's revenues were less than $10 million; today they are close to $1 billion.

What has caused this astounding success? Hanson attributes it to "the firm's decision to expand not only into highly specialized industries such as banking and transportation, insurance companies and savings and loans, but also into such areas as nonprofit institutions and government, where independent audits were something of a new idea. The only way this expansion could be achieved was by bringing established experts in each field into our firm. We did this by a series of well-conceived mergers in the 1950s and early 1960s. At the same time, our public company practice was enjoying amazing growth, as were our management consulting services, which date back to the 1920s when PMM was helping its clients install accounting systems. Finally, the fact that our firm was already established in most countries throughout the world put us squarely in a position to move ahead and assist the multinational thrust of postwar American business around the world."

Still, in spite of The Big Eight's evolution as multinational tax experts and management consultants as well as CPAs, the label of "accounting firms" remains accurate, if not complete. The biggest chunk of revenues flowing into The Big Eight comes from what may be broadly defined as accounting services. Most important among these is auditing—the independent review of financial reports by CPAs.

"Basically, the accounting process consists of recording all of an entity's transactions and similar relevant events, grouping those transactions and events in categories with similar characteristics, and presenting them in a set of financial statements intended to meet the needs of a variety of users.

"Accounting then is a means of achieving accountability. In the United States, chiefly through state and federal government agencies, society has used accounting systems and the information they produce as a means of control over a variety of entities. In the areas of income taxation, regulation of banks, insurance companies, and utilities, particularly in matters of rate regulation, government has relied heavily on accounting.

"This reliance usually involves requirements for detailed record-keeping. For example, almost every business, no matter what its size, must keep accounting records for such purposes as income taxes, withholding taxes, social security payments, and wages and hours worked by employees. . . .

"The auditor is an intermediary in an accounting relationship. He is a third party in the relationship between the issuers of financial statements and those who use and rely on those statements. . . .

"An independent audit is necessary because of the inherent potential conflict between the entity's management and the users of its financial information. Since financial statements are one of the means used to evaluate management's performance in operating the entity, management could have an incentive to bias the measurement. The bias could range from unconsciously presenting performance in a better light to outright misrepresentation."*

Although they are engaged in an ever-widening scope of practice, The Big Eight still view themselves as CPA firms in general, auditors in specific. All of The Big Eight chairmen are CPAs and everyone else in the firms is supposed to think and act like a CPA. What's more, The Big Eight labor mightily to classify their practice special-

*The Commission on Auditors' Responsibilities: Report, Conclusions and Recommendations (known as the Cohen Commission Report), 1978.

ties as natural extensions of the CPA's role. Sometimes that takes a major effort: the connections are not always obvious. This is probably true, in part, because laymen are often confused about the accountant's role. They have been ever since CPAs first emerged in our society.

A story on accountants in a 1932 issue of *Fortune* magazine put it this way:

Towards the turn of the century there sprung up in this country a new profession. Already established abroad, it followed English investments to the U.S., watched over them, took root. Today, it is no overstatement to say that there are preeminently three professions upon whose ethics as well as upon whose skill modern society depends: law, medicine, and Certified Public Accounting. Yet this third profession, which is no heritage but a creation of our necessity, is so little known that certainly 100,000 of our free, white, educated American contemporaries will die in A.D. 1932 without ever having the vaguest of what manner of men Certified Public Accountants are. They walk in the shadow of virtual anonymity. So discreet are they that at times it seems as if their aim were to become a disembodied function, almost without proper name. Yet upon the expert opinion of these abstract beings—who pit their judgment against the unbelievably subtle economic forces of this generation—the financial structure of our greatest industries is founded.

Auditing remains the foundation of The Big Eight's practice. It is the center of the action—the land of big bucks. It is here that The Big Eight collect their highest fees, draw their greatest power, and gain entry into the hearts and minds of corporate executives, political leaders, and bureaucrats. Big-league auditing is their private preserve, the one lush and lucrative business market that they alone control. The Big Eight have a lock and key on it.

Among them, the eight professional behemoths audit 90 percent of all the corporations listed on the New York Stock Exchange. This is their exclusive territory because they alone are big enough to serve it. Auditing the likes of General Motors is an enormous undertaking, requiring the skills and talent of fourteen hundred accountants working through offices around the world. The team assembled by Deloitte Haskins & Sells (the auto giant's auditors for sixty years) to conduct the GM audit is larger than 99 percent of all the accounting firms in the world. The vast majority of CPA firms cannot muster the manpower or the facilities to handle a tiny fraction of the GM job. But, for Deloitte, the automaker is simply one of tens of thousands of accounts.

Big business needs big auditors, and The Big Eight are gigantic. Together they employ 150,000 people in 2,500 offices in more than a hundred nations. Each year, The Big Eight interview 160,000 students from U.S. colleges and universities, hire 10,000 and make more than 1,000 new partners. Combined Big Eight revenues approach $5 billion annually, and two of the firms, Peat, Marwick and Coopers & Lybrand, will each cross the $1 billion a year mark in the near future. The largest law firms, by comparison, don't come within 10 percent of this. The Big Eight are in a class by themselves. A study performed by the Congressional Research Service found that clients of the Big Eight account for 94 percent of all sales, 94 percent of all profits, 90 percent of all income taxes paid, 94 percent of all people employed, and 94 percent of all assets owned by New York Stock Exchange members.

But numbers don't tell the whole story. The Big Eight are bastions of information. Many of the world's best financial minds— leading accountants, lawyers, auditors, consultants, actuaries, and tax specialists—are on the staffs, serving clients, writing papers, counseling government, and perhaps most important, making decisions with social, political, and economic repercussions. All of The Big Eight conduct massive educational programs with a curriculum, staff, and student body to rival that of a small college. Arthur Andersen, one of the more aggressive Big Eighters, does in fact maintain its own university complete with a fifty-acre campus. The firms publish thousands of newsletters, booklets, studies, white papers, brochures, press backgrounders, and magazines to educate and propagandize staffers, clients, and opinion leaders with points of view on IRS rulings, tax bills, tariff acts, jobs legislation, regulatory procedures, Supreme Court decisions, social trends, and corporate developments. When anyone wants to know anything about the world of business and finance, they can turn to The Big Eight for the answers.

The scope of The Big Eight's in-house expertise is staggering.

Witness: The tax department at the Big Eight firm of Touche Ross
—which, like its counterparts throughout the Big Eight, provides
specialized tax counsel to corporations, governments, and wealthy
individuals—accounts for only 10 percent of TR's revenues. What's
more, less than half of the staffers in this relatively small corner of
the Touche empire are attorneys. Still, the Touche Ross tax department has enough attorneys to make it qualify as one of the largest
law firms in the world. It fits into the worldwide Touche Ross
organization as Onassis' yacht would fit into the *QE2*. When it
comes to The Big Eight, everything else pales by comparison.

The Big Eight's incomparable array of talent and brainpower, its
armies of attorneys and accountants, its avalanche of reports, booklets, and courses—all are turned, in one way or another, into fees.
When an industrial giant or a well-known institution needs a stamp
of fiscal approval or a new stamping plant, it turns to The Big Eight
for help. No one else—not the government, not the think tanks, not
the old-line consulting firms—can deliver the right talent and experience to so broad a range of problems. "The Big Eight are so large
and influential in relation to other CPA firms that they are able to
control virtually all aspects of accounting and auditing in the U.S."*

Auditing is The Big Eight's foot in the door. A rich and prestigious practice in itself, it is also an entryway into a client's inner
sanctum. Once he is functioning as part of the family—as a trusted
confidant and adviser—the auditor can extend his presence throughout the client's body and soul. One service leads to another and
another and another and. . . .

Take the long-standing relationship between Price Waterhouse
and the Academy of Motion Picture Arts and Sciences. PW, easily
the most prestigious of The Big Eight, made a name for itself as
auditor to Tinsel Town during the heyday of the great Hollywood
studios. Price counted many of the top movie makers among its
clients and still represents the last vestiges of the picture companies,
including Universal, Columbia, and Disney. "We were very well
known in Hollywood during the golden era," says Frank Johnson,

Report of the Senate Subcommittee on Reports, Accounting and Management (known as the
Metcalf Report).

the latest PW partner to supervise the firm's Oscar work and to appear on camera the night of the awards telecast. "I assume that's the reason the Academy first approached us to work for them back in 1927. We were engaged as auditors the year the Academy was formed."

True to form, the auditing job led to additional assignments, including, to name a few, tabulating the results of the Board of Governors election, the Student Film Award balloting, and providing ongoing tax consulting. Most notably, PW was named in 1935 to handle the Oscar balloting. The Academy called on Price to provide a much-needed shot of respectability to the then-fledgling awards. Born in 1929, the Oscar soon came under a cloud of suspicion. A number of controversial awards cast doubt on the legitimacy of the balloting, making it seem as if politics played a bigger role than the vote count in the naming of winners. Mary Pickford's Oscar for the poorly received film *Coquette,* her first talkie, seemed to many to have more to do with the great silent-film star's heavy involvement in the Academy than with her performance in the film. Controversy about the Academy's balloting came to a head with the 1932 dual awards to Fredric March *(Dr. Jekyll and Mr. Hyde)* and Wallace Beery *(The Champ)* after an unprecedented tie vote. Many doubted that the count was actually deadlocked. Rumors were rampant that it was simply a diplomatic way to treat the great stars.

Credit the Academy for recognizing that Oscar would become a truly prestigious award only if perceived as an accurate reflection of the membership's vote. The public and the film community would embrace the awards, providing the balloting were completely honest in fact and appearance. There could not be the slightest hint of backroom wheeling and dealing, of doctoring the vote to favor an Academy pet. To assure this and to send a clear message to the world that the voting would be as clean as a presidential election, the Academy delegated control and supervision of the process to Price Waterhouse. The action succeeded in removing any taint of illegitimacy. Although the Academy membership is often accused of voting with its heart rather than its mind, there is no doubt that the prized statuette goes to the nominee with the most votes.

To this day, Price Waterhouse runs the Academy Award balloting with military precision. The job takes four weeks and more than two thousand manhours. A nice chunk of business that brings in about $150,000. Price Waterhouse staffers in the firm's Los Angeles office literally take the ballots to the post office, check the addresses to confirm that all are Academy members, and mail out the envelopes. When the ballots are returned, about ten days before the popular telecast, Price tabulates the votes, types up cards naming the winners, and places them in the now-famous sealed envelopes. No more than three people know the outcome before the Oscar show goes on the air, and all are on the staff of Price Waterhouse & Co. Earth-shattering, no, but indicative, in one small way, of The Big Eight's pervasive influence and its privileged position throughout the public and private sectors. Whether it is the quarterly earnings report of the troubled Chrysler Corporation, the latest statement on New York City's solvency, the Comptroller of the Currency's policies on bank-lending ratios or the winner of the Best Supporting Actor Award, The Big Eight learns about it before the rest of the world and often plays a role in shaping the outcome. PW's Oscar work is interesting in that it provides a dramatic demonstration of The Big Eight's wide scope of practice. The stereotype of the stiff and formal CPA, locked away in a darkened audit room, surrounded by ledgers, invoices, and receipts, is an accurate reflection of only one part of The Big Eight's work. To be sure, tens of thousands of young audit staffers, many of whom are sorely disillusioned, are relegated to the lonely monotony of backroom adding and subtracting. But there is much more. In The Big Eight's diverse ranks, one finds planners, technicians, administrators, managers, executives, troubleshooters, thinkers, salesmen, and, in the case of Price Waterhouse, on-camera personalities. Some of the problems these men and women have to deal with run far afield of accounting.

"The big problem at the Oscar show is guessing from which door the presenter will enter the stage," Johnson says. "Because there may be six different entrance locations during the show, I'm backstage moving from one spot to another, trying to stay one step ahead of the program. There have been a few close calls. Some of the presenters get caught up in the drama of the moment and forget to wait for the envelope. I have to be alert and literally put it in their

hands. "One of the best things about working on the Oscar engagement is the party afterward. As soon as the show is over, all of the
stars and Academy officials go to a very elaborate bash to celebrate.
It's a lot of fun chatting and mingling with the stars. The thing that
always surprises me, however, is that they are as interested in asking
about my work with Price Waterhouse as I am in discussing their
film careers."

Price Waterhouse—the austere blue-chipper of The Big Eight—
is not too staid to know a good plug when it sees one. PW partners
acknowledge that the firm is best known for this "unusual assignment," and that the high profile it enjoys from the Oscar telecast
provides the winning edge in the competition for a number of
choice accounts.

Even when the firm comes in for some good-natured ribbing by
the stars—as it has a number of times over the years—the fallout is
entirely positive. Everyone is having a good time; the glitter of the
evening rubs off on PW. When Chevy Chase commented extempo-
raneously that the results of the balloting are known only to Price
Waterhouse—and their immediate families, neighbors, etc.—the ad
lib was just another on-the-air promo for PW and another indication
that the firm is part of the glamourous Hollywood community.

Price Waterhouse men are not always introduced on camera. So
when the Oscar's 50th Anniversary Show was scheduled, PW took
no chances on missing out on the free publicity. Frank Johnson
suggested to Academy officials that the firm's introduction would
be in order. Howard Koch, producer of the anniversary program
(and then-president of the Academy's Board of Directors) agreed to
revise the script for this purpose, but not without comment.

"There's a little ham in all of us," he said, in what is certainly one
of the most unusual observations ever made concerning a world-
renowned financial services firm.

There's more to The Big Eight than first meets the eye. Much
more.

2. Behind Closed Doors

"He doesn't work for a living—he's a partner."
—A junior on the Coopers & Lybrand audit staff.

PERHAPS IT'S FITTING that The Big Eight is tied to so glamourous an event as the Academy Awards Show. The world thinks differently about CPAs than it did just a decade ago. Public accounting has shed its lackluster image and has emerged as a sexy profession with more than its share of money and power. Gone are the days of the green eyeshades and the high stools. Today's top Big Eight partners dine at 21, jet the world over, rub elbows with sheiks, princes, and presidents.

The Big Eight are the glamour capitals of accounting. They inhabit a land of prestigious fat-fee accounts and work with an all-star cast of clients the likes of Exxon, TWA, General Electric, Ford, the Hughes empire, Chase Manhattan Bank, ABC, and the Oscars. This association with the high and mighty gives The Big Eight an aura of excitement. Add this to the firms' enormous revenues, the near seven-figure earnings of their chief executives, the tradition of lavish expense accounts, and the resulting image is that of a well-connected, high-rolling group of partners that lives in corporate splendor.

"If you call playing eighteen holes at Winged Foot working, then the partners are hard workers," says an Ivy League graduate and staff member at Coopers & Lybrand. "But I don't call it working; I call it playing golf.

"I've only been here a few months, but that's long enough to understand the system. What you learn is that the staffers do ninety percent of the work and the managers do the remaining ten percent. The partners are rarely here. They're out at the country clubs, the French restaurants, the Caribbean conventions. Their only job is to bring in clients, and that's done at the black-tie balls and tennis matches. For that, they pull down a hundred and twenty-five thousand dollars and a company credit card. "I can't wait to make partner. I don't want to work either."

Adds a garment manufacturer from New York's Westchester County: "My neighbor's a partner with Touche Ross, and I swear I've never seen anyone work the way he does. His life's one big social whirl. He belongs to two local country clubs, he's on the boards of two charities, he's active in the PTA, and he runs the annual Community Day. My wife tells me he's always around town running one meeting or another. Anytime I take a day off, his face is one I know I'll see on the tennis courts. He's a likeable guy—hell, yes—and I guess that's why they pay him so much money: to socialize. He probably brings in a truckload of business. That's all these Big Eight guys have to do."

Not quite. The Big Eight is so secretive about its inner workings that casual observers have distorted notions of what goes on behind closed doors. The images run to extremes. Some think Big Eight partners wile away their days at clubs, golf courses, and cocktail lounges; others see them as an army of Wally Coxes, buried under mountains of ledgers. Although big-league CPAs are no longer the Dickensian auditors of yesteryear, neither are they wheeler-dealers, beautiful people, or social butterflies. World travelers, yes; jet setters, no. The image of glamour that has attached itself to The Big Eight has more to do with the world of their clients than the CPAs themselves. It is a matter of being seen in the right company. And although charm and wit and a penchant for winning new clients are valued traits at The Big Eight, few partners rate high marks at any of these and the vast majority spend more time behind a desk than a putting iron.

What is life really like inside The Big Eight? What do the partners actually do? How do they live? How much money do they make? How much power do they have?

To begin with, the firms are structured as partnerships—of a sort.

"They are hybrid business organizations," says Wallace Olson, former president of the American Institute of Certified Public Accountants (AICPA). "Combinations of partnerships and corporate forms. What's different here from most partnerships is that much power rests in the hands of a few."

For those whose perception of a partnership is two or three people united in some form of cozy business arrangement, partnerships Big Eight-style take a little getting used to. The partners don't know all the others' names, or what they look like, or how much they earn. Many could bump into each other on the street and never know they had anything in common. Being in business with near strangers is enough to give the partners of more traditional companies waves of anxiety and many sleepless nights.

But at The Big Eight, no one flinches. These are enormous partnerships—the behemoths of the species—with enough principals to populate a small town. At Peat, Marwick, Mitchell, for example, the list of partners numbers more than a thousand. Even the fastest talkers wouldn't find enough time in the day to greet them all.

"I used to be able to greet every partner by name just a few years ago," says Russell Palmer, managing partner of The Big Eight firm of Touche Ross. "But lately I find myself groping for a name now and then. It's embarrassing."

For the flavor of the earlier days at the firm (then called Touche, Niven & Co.), long before men in Palmer's position had to jog their memories for partners' names, we can read this correspondence between George Touche and J.B. Niven, Scottish accountants who entered into a partnership to practice in the United States and England. The following excerpt of a letter, written in 1905 from Touche (based in London) to Niven (stationed at 30 Broad Street in New York), reflects the tenor of a simpler time, the warm relationship between the founding partners and the development of The Big Eight partnerships:

My Dear Niven:
   I am in receipt of your long letter of the 7th May with regard to the expiration of the present arrangements, and plans for the future.
   Before proceeding to discuss these, let me congratulate you on the

fact that Miss Gordon has fixed the day on which you are really going to begin to live. I sincerely hope it will be the red-letter day of both your lives.

I had given careful consideration to everything you say in your letter, and I need not tell you that I am by no means unmindful of your own interests. I quite recognise that you might easily have been earning a bigger income elsewhere, although I think it would have been a mistake for you to take an official position, or one outside the profession. On the whole, therefore, I have satisfaction in feeling that although the establishment of Touche, Niven & Co. has done nothing for me from a monetary point of view, it has given you an opportunity of establishing yourself in business, free from some of the difficulties and disadvantages which assail a fellow when he commences on his own hook.

The crucial point in your letter is that relating to the future division of profits. I agree that the old arrangement should now be reviewed; indeed, if the business had become more rapidly profitable, it was never my intention to interpret our agreement in any strict way. In a business like ours, I believe in a generous recognition of individual effort, without too close a regard to the precise provisions of the Articles of Partnership.

With this preliminary, let me say that when I read your suggestion that you should have the first $2,500 and two-thirds of the surplus (with the exception of $150), I felt that you were shaping well as a business-getter for the firm. The impulse of the natural man in me would be to promptly accede to your suggestion, but having regard to the whole position I hardly think this would be quite a businesslike arrangement. It would put me on little better than agency terms. You must bear in mind, too, that out of my share, when it becomes productive, I ought to make some provision for Tait, who never misses an opportunity of endeavoring to steer business into your office. . . .

The alternative proposition which I would therefore make is:

1) That your time, valued at $2,500 per annum, rank pari passu with my capital, valued at 5 percent;

2) That the profits in excess of these two items be divided between us in equal shares.

If this arrangement had been in force last year, you would have received $3,873, and I would have received $1,523.

Let me say again, in conclusion, that I feel no dissatisfaction with what you have already accomplished, and I believe that we are now nearing the realisation of far better results than anything you have hitherto dreamt of in your sober moments.

All our thoughts be with you on the 1st June. I only wish I could be present on so eventful an occasion.

Believe me,
Yours always,
George A. Touche

(Niven himself later attributed much of his success to his marriage to Susan Gordon, which took place soon after this letter was written. The Tait mentioned in the letter (Andrew Wilson Tait) later became a partner in the firm.)

Today, in spite of their size, The Big Eight are, in the most important matter, legitimate partnerships—that is, the firm's profits are passed through to the partners. Unlike a corporation, the firms' earnings are reported to the IRS on the partners' own personal income tax returns. When the firm has a banner year, the partners share in the bounty; when things turn sour, the partners take their lumps together. Not that all partners earn the same amount of money. Not by a long shot. Here again, The Big Eight differ from "traditional" partnerships. Some senior partners earn more than ten times as much as their most junior colleagues. That too doesn't sit right with partnership purists. At The Big Eight, partners' earnings are evaluated annually by an executive committee. Just how much a partner earns is based on the individual's overall performance, level of responsibility, quality of client service, and volume of new business brought into the firm. Although The Big Eight deny it, the last criterion is the most important. When it comes to corralling the big bucks, there's no better way to hit the jackpot than to cultivate new clients or to substantially expand services to existing accounts. The Big Eight are engaged in a hotly competitive market, clawing at one another for every new client that springs loose in the marketplace. Partners blessed with the right skills for this "professional war" come in for the biggest paychecks.

"They've got a guy over at one of the Arthurs that the top people there call 'Superman,' " says a corporate controller. "He's their top salesman. The Big Eight say they don't have guys like that, but that's just so much bull. Whenever a plum account is up for grabs, they put a bow tie on this guy and march him out to the client's offices. I've seen him in action, and let me tell you, he really is super. The guy just has a winning way about him. He's a fast learner about the prospect's business, can recite facts and figures like Robert McNamara used to when he was secretary of defense and, best of all, he can charm the pocket watches off those stiff corporate types. CEOs also take to him right away—they want to hire the guy."

All of The Big Eight have a few "Supermen" they call on to go after the big accounts. But this is not a popular topic of conversation. None of the firms like to talk about it. Why? Simply because it is deemed unprofessional for CPAs to wind up sales robots and send them off, smiles flashing, to pitch for accounts Madison Avenue-style. Still, management does admit that when the heat is on—when competitors are verging on a new prospect from all directions—survival of the fittest demands that the best account getter go into battle.

"It's embarrassing for us to talk about it because these guys are often the worst accountants," says one Big Eight managing partner. "We all know that there's that tiny percentage of partners that get by on their smiles or their country-club etiquette. We know it, we accept it, and I for one am delighted that we have a few solid salesmen around here. But I'll be damned if I want to sit around and talk about them. Not when we have a small army of skilled and talented CPAs, consultants, and tax attorneys. Who deserves the attention? Don't forget, this is a professional firm. I've got a guy two floors below who's probably the world's leading authority on corporate tax. The secretary of the treasury calls on him when he needs advice. What would he think if I spent my time boasting about some partner whose best skill is bellying up to a bar?"

Salesmen may not get the publicity but they do get the money. The biggest share of the profits goes to those partners who consistently land big accounts for the firm. Also high on the earnings scale are partners-in-charge: those with management responsibility for major audit accounts. A single audit client can generate fees of more than $5 million. Partners skilled at keeping clients of that magnitude loyal and content are valuable assets and are well paid, to be sure. An elite corps of Big Eight partners manage to pull down top earnings without any flair at all for client relations. They do it simply by being the best CPAs in the world. Known as "technicians," these guys are encyclopedic. Name an accounting or auditing problem and chances are good that they have the answer or know where to find it. With thousands of partners engaged in complex transactions around the world—many of which involve the firm's professional reputation—it is crucial to have a few resident geniuses around to field the tough ones, to know the rules inside out.

You can spot the technicians a mile away. Just walk through the halls of The Big Eight and peek inside the offices. You'll see all kinds of men and women. Technicians are the ones who look as though they've been locked in a library ever since puberty. It's a strange breed: Introverted, glazy-eyed little men, they dress in sober fashion even by Big Eight standards, stare at their shoes, and carry themselves with an icy formality. Social clodhoppers though they may be, most can nevertheless talk incessantly about the one thing in life that really turns them on. When the subject is accounting principles, this group can put the memory of Hubert Humphrey to shame. They are steeped in a bewildering maze of rules, opinions, decisions, standards, precedents, and pronouncements concerning the proper preparation and presentation of financial statements. With this group, the old image of the accountant with his head stuck in the stacks of ledgers—the Caspar Milquetoast with an obsession for numbers—rings true. Technicians are surrounded by charts, directories, reports—an arsenal of professional literature. Accounting probably produces more paperwork than any other profession: It's the technician's job to keep track of the enormous flow of data, to make sense of it, to isolate the key factors and to communicate them to partners throughout the firm. Most Big Eighters are too busy pitching new business, servicing pesky accounts, or grinding out field work to keep an ear to the ground for new developments and to formulate professional policies. They leave that up to the technicians.

This is not a lowly group of back-office toilers. Top technicians can rise to the highest management levels. They are among the most senior people in the firm. Earnings scale up to a solid $250,000 a year, and that's matched by an equally heavy dose of executive clout. It's E.F. Hutton time: When top technicians talk, partners listen. They alone must steer the firm through a labyrinth of laws, regulations, and ethics. Professional credentials as well as firm-wide reputations are at stake.

Most chief technical guys play the resident genius role to the hilt. They rarely talk; they lecture. Imbued with an embarrassing amount of self-importance, they regard themselves as brilliant men, pillars of the economy, and, most important, guardians of the profession. Public accounting Big Eight style has been subject to sharp attacks in recent years, including calls to break up the firms and to bring them under the control of a new regulatory agency. In many cases, accounting techniques are at issue. The very criticism of the status quo is viewed by the technicians as some sort of socialist heresy. They lead their partners throughout The Big Eight in viewing any outsider's remarks about the profession as stupid, ill-informed, and somewhat dangerous. To this bent of mind, stockholders, government regulators, politicians, and even corporate executives are not qualified to talk on the subject of accounting and should keep their mouths shut. There is an us-versus-them mentality at work here, one that is deeply ingrained.

"I'll never forget seeing the movie *The Alamo,*" says one technical honcho, a squeaky-voiced man whose teeth clench and temples twitch when accounting critics are discussed. "Not that it was a great movie or anything. I just recall that scene where the sharpshooters are perched on the Alamo walls, picking off the enemy as they approach. That's what it's like for us. We sit in our offices trying to do honest work and we're surrounded by forces from the SEC, Congress, the FTC, the Senate—and they're all trying to break through the fort. We're the outnumbered sharpshooters of today. We have enemies around every corner. Why? Because we do things wrong? Of course not. It's because we're successful, powerful, and rich. That combination makes for an irresistible target. The do-goodniks have to take it out on us. But we'll hold our ground. We'll overcome."

That Big Eighters talk in military terms is fitting. They do perceive a war; they do see an enemy. Tucked away in their offices, they bring to mind field officers, holed up in concrete bunkers, cursing the opposition with every breath.

"My biggest mistake was having lunch with one of those technical guys," says a reporter for a business magazine. "He takes me out to Mamma Leone's of all places. Even the tourists know that place is the pits. I'd heard that the guy violates The Big Eight code and brown bags it most days, but I didn't believe it until I saw his choice of restaurants. Only a New Yorker who rarely eats out would pick Leone's—that's my opinion. Imagine having a huge expense account and never using it. That's the technicians for you.

"Anyway, he starts off all tongue-tied and we can't seem to sustain a two-minute conversation. I mean it was deadly. That's until he downs a whiskey sour. Suddenly he's ripped—high as a kite and running at the mouth. Amen to the power of alcohol. Never underestimate it.

"The guy's whole personality changes. He starts talking like a teamster, ranting on and on about a Puerto Rican receptionist he wants to grab and says his secretary has the best cleavage in the office. The sexual fantasies go on for about ten minutes, then he suddenly stops, thinks a moment, and tears into his clients. He hates them. Why? 'Because most are not CPAs!' So? 'So, you can't trust them. I've gotten to the point,' he says, 'where I can't trust anyone who's not a CPA. I don't socialize with anyone else and, except for my family, I really don't like anyone else. That's just how it is.' "

Technicians and salesmen are at the opposite poles of The Big Eight. The latter are personality boys, out for a buck, using public accounting as a means to an end. The former don't know how to smile, aren't allowed within a hundred miles of a prospective client and genuinely love the profession more than the money. Salesmen and technicians repel one another: They have little contact in or out of the office and, when referring to one another, the word *partner* sticks in the throat like a malignant polyp.

In between these two extremes are the bulk of The Big Eight partners. As a group, they are hardworking, sincere, intelligent devotees of the Protestant ethic. Most are intelligent but colorless, competent but unimaginative, honest but highly competitive. One is impressed with the solidness of The Big Eight partners. It is difficult to find one who is not competent at what he does. That is a considerable accomplishment and is testimony to the calibre of individual that makes it to the partner level.

Still, there are few flashes of brilliance. While the bulk of the partners are not disappointing, neither are they impressive. Here and there one finds an exceptional individual—an extraordinary mind or striking personality—but this is not the norm. At The Big Eight, the old-fashioned notion that salesmanship, hard work, and persistence lead to success still applies. You don't have to be great to make it to partner. You have to be competent, dedicated, and hard-driving. The rigid atmosphere of The Big Eight—the emphasis on conformity—actually screens out the brilliant, innovative, and unorthodox minds.

There is no such thing as a "typical" Big Eight partner. The group is a mixed bag of personality types, religions, ages, skills, educational backgrounds, and regional identities. The impact of affirmative action has seen to that, putting an end to the genteel WASP club that once was The Big Eight.

"They really were the good old days back when I was an active partner," says a retired Big Eight auditor who still dresses in white shirt and tie every day to go shopping or putter around the house. "It was a gentleman's business, that's what I liked about it. Now, it's like the UN there. I wouldn't be with the firm today, not under these conditions. You don't have anything in common with your partners.

"I drop in to see the fellas every once in a while—a few of my contemporaries are still around—and it's a shock every time that I do. I just can't get used to it. I mean, in my day lunchtime was a relaxed affair. A good meal and good conversation with men of your own ilk. Now if you want to tell a joke, you have to look around the table first. One of your partners may be Negro, Spanish, a Jew, or a woman. You know how sensitive they are."

Still, the majority of Big Eight partners are white Anglo-Saxon Protestants, mostly from the Midwest. Although affirmative action has brought some mix to the ranks, it is still worlds away from the

UN. A composite picture of the predominant group of partners shows a forty-five-year-old man, bespectacled, balding and slightly paunchy. A native of a rural Michigan town, he attended Michigan State, joined a fraternity, went directly to a Big Eight firm upon graduation, and married soon after. He has three children, looks rather pale, favors classic business suits in sober grays or dark browns. He works in a major city outside of his home state, lives in a suburban split-level, and builds model airplanes in his spare time. He earns $130,000 a year, is comfortable but not rich, enjoys his work, is proud of his profession, feels a genuine sense of camaraderie with his partners, and is exceptionally loyal to his firm. It will be his lifelong employer.

Women in The Big Eight exhibit similar traits, lifestyles, and attitudes. Although still a distinct minority in the partnership ranks, they are gradually filtering into positions of importance. With women now accounting for 30 percent of The Big Eight's college recruits, it is likely that they will command 20 percent of the new partnership slots by 1990. Although one still hears much antiwomen chatter among older male partners ("They'll probably all leave and have babies," says one recruiter), the calibre of the women coming into The Big Eight is exceptional. They are too good to hold back. What's more, most appear to be team players: quiet, serious, lackluster—very much like their male colleagues.

"I'm sympathetic to feminine goals but I don't wear them on my sleeve," says a twenty-five-year-old woman audit manager. "There's respect for ability here, not for rabble-rousing. I want to make partner badly—and before I'm thirty. The only way is to do your stuff better than anyone else and leave the politics at home. To tell you the truth, I'm happy with it this way. I've never been a wavemaker; I've always been too busy for that."

There is an everyman quality about The Big Eight partners that belies their material success. Professionals and executives with similar earnings—doctors, attorneys, architects—usually develop a sense of style, a personal flair, that goes with the upper-middle-class lifestyle. There sport stylish hair combs, designer eyeglasses, Mercedes convertibles, sharply tailored suits. But Big Eighters abstain, rarely exhibiting color of any kind. Most look like $20,000-a-year bank supervisors or insurance adjusters. Tastes are undeniably bland; the emphasis is on the practical. This is a money-in-the-bank Toyota crowd. The rare partner with a penchant for fashion sticks out like a showgirl in a church. One middle-aged vice-chairman, a handsome graying man with a year-round tan (courtesy of health-club sun lamps) sports Georgio Armani suits, a heavy gold watch, and a star sapphire pinky ring. In the blah confines of The Big Eight, he looks out of place—like a riverboat gambler. In an advertising agency, he'd be just another tight-vested conservative type.

Hats off to the partners with the gumption to go counter to the prevailing styles or lack of them. There are unwritten laws at The Big Eight designed to keep everyone looking and acting like everyone else. The partnership exerts a collective pressure on those who stray from the norm, ostracizing the more adventurous souls or cutting back on their share of the profits. This is not conformity for conformity's sake: It is a conscious effort to measure up to the clients' image of what a prominent CPA should look like. The consensus is that he should be a clean-cut, three-piece suiter, with a white shirt, wing-tip shoes, and heavy brown briefcase.

Image has much to do with The Big Eight's success, and partners don't want to tamper with that precious asset. When the controller of a prospective *Fortune* 500 client walks into the Price Waterhouse national headquarters at 1251 Avenue of the Americas in New York, he expects an atmosphere of quiet dignity. And he gets it. As the most tradition-bound of The Big Eight, Price works hard to retain its image as the gilt-edge CPA firm. Understatement is the byword. The place looks and feels like an Ivy League university—properly aged, hallowed by time. Partners have to look as if they match the surroundings, and at Price Waterhouse & Co. that means Brooks Brothers all the way.

"The talk is that Big Eight partners make a lot of dough, but believe me, they earn every penny," says a Pepsico marketing executive. "My next-door neighbor is a partner with one of the firms, and what he takes for the sake of money I wouldn't put up with for a million a day. Last summer he was riding his lawn tractor in front of the house. It's a broiling hot day so he's stripped to the

9-10
Friday
27th

to measure for

Bowers Carpet

settle deposit

waist, wearing only Bermuda shorts and chugging a Löwenbräu. "Don't you know that the next day he gets called in on the carpet. An executive partner happened to be in the neighborhood visiting a relative, spotted his colleague doing the lawn, and got madder than hell. He tells my neighbor 'not to make crude public displays.' That he should never be seen around the house with less than a golf shirt and that he should confine his 'use of alcoholic beverages to the indoors.' The executive partner was afraid that a client might see my neighbor·and 'the firm would be disgraced.'

"Well, my neighbor was livid! Angry, upset, ashamed—he was literally torn between crying and screaming. The guy was treated like a grade-schooler. Imagine a boss telling you how to dress at home! But you know what? As defiant as he felt when the incident occurred, you'll now find him on the hottest Sundays clean-shaven, hair styled, and sporting a freshly laundered Izod.

"Word has it he leaves his shirt on to make love. Never know who's under the bed."

It's not the infamous pink slip that Big Eight partners worry about. At most of the firms, it's terribly difficult to axe a partner.

"Firing a partner is the hardest thing to do around here," says Joseph Connor, chairman of Price Waterhouse. "I cannot do it alone. In fact, ninety percent of the firm's policy board must approve the action. Only one partner in the history of Price Waterhouse has ever been forced out this way. Some have been pressured to leave for various reasons, including some cases of alcoholism, but they left without formal action by the firm."

It is clear that partners who, for one reason or another, are viewed as liabilities are ostracized. The isolation, the feeling of collective anger, is terribly difficult to withstand. Everyone tries desperately to avoid that fate. There is, therefore, great pressure to play by the rules. The burdens of partnership Big Eight style also come in the form of heavy workloads. The country-club image held by junior staffers and those outside the profession is way off base. This is not an easy life. Most partners who meet with clients on the links or the tennis courts do so only after logging in a heavy schedule in the office or on the road. Precisely because the Big Eight are partnerships—because the profits are shared—it is difficult for slackers to hide out in closed offices watching the clocks tick. There is great peer pressure to do *more* than one's share. Add to this the positive inducement that the more money the firm makes, the more the partners pull down. Both factors combine to keep Big Eighters working very hard.

"I think of our business in terms of the hotel industry," says Harold Haddock, financial administrator for Price Waterhouse. "If a room is not rented for one night, you can't make that money up. The same goes for our staff. We can't inventory idle hours. If the people are not working, they're not working, period. The billing opportunity is lost."

Most Big Eighters are in the office by 8:30 A.M.; few make it home for the network news. Putting in sixteen-hour days is not unusual: twelve hours in the office, two hours of homework, and two hours trying to drum up business at clubs, charities, and assorted social functions.

"Home? Where's that?" jokes a weary DH&S partner. "I've been going till midnight the last four days or so. Haven't even seen my family. I've been sacking out at the Princeton Club, and I must say that I'm much better acquainted with the facilities there than I'd like to be."

A fair share of the overtime can be attributed to social work, Big Eight-style. Partners are expected to be joiners, to land seats on boards, committees, organizations, groups, and clubs. The purpose is twofold: to spread the firm's influence where it counts most, and to drum up new business. Price Waterhouse boasts that a partial listing of its partners' affiliations includes:

AICPA Board and Council
AICPA Accounting Standards Executive Committee
AICPA Executive Committee on Management Advisory Services
AICPA Committee on FASB Interpretation and Amendments
AICPA Practice Review Committee
AICPA/SEC Relations Committee
AICPA Federal Tax Division
AICPA Technical Standards Committee of Ethics Division
AICPA Task Force on Employers' Pension Costs

AICPA Task Force on GAAP Codification
SEC Advisory Committee on Oil & Gas Accounting
AICPA, IIA & CICA Joint Task Force on Audit Implications
and Data Base Systems
National Tax Association—Tax Institute of America
Chamber of Commerce of the United States—Taxation Committee
National Association of Manufacturers Tax Committee
International Fiscal Association
Institute of Management Consultants

Says the firm's 1980 annual report, "A complete recitation of the full involvement of PW people would take volumes."

There is strong evidence of a direct relationship between the number of outside activities on a partner's résumé and his rank in the firm. Russ Palmer's personal credits include:

International Federation of Accountants—United States
AICPA—Board of Directors and Council Delegate
Financial Accounting Foundation—President
Accounting Hall of Fame—Trustee
Beta Gamma Sigma—Directors' Table
Business Committee for the Arts—Executive Committee
Carnegie Hall Corporation—Trustee
Joint Council on Economic Education—Director
New York University Graduate School of Business—Advisory
Board
United World College—Board of Directors
Greenwich Country Day School—Trustee
Salvation Army—Vice-Chairman, National Advisory Board
United Nations Association of the United States of America—
Economic Policy Council
Membership in the following clubs: Links
Union League
Merion Cricket
Field Club of Greenwich
Round Hill Club
New York Athletic Club
Seaview Country Club

"Under the code of professional ethics, an accountant is barred from going to see the chief executive of a company or the financial vice-president, trying to persuade him to switch auditors. But nothing prevents the accountant from socializing with potentially useful contacts or participating with them in civic or charitable activities —at the country club, on the local United Fund Committee, and so forth. Sometimes it pays off."*

All of this meeting and greeting and handshaking and backslapping and toasting—fitted around performing a complex job—takes time. Every waking hour.

Talk of long hours is one of the staples of conversation at The Big Eight. Partners pride themselves on burning the candle at both ends. Although most bellyache about the lack of leisure time and of precious few moments with the family ("I hardly know my kids," is a familiar refrain), this is just camouflage. The truth is that work is their real love: Everything else can and will be sacrificed. The kind of person The Big Eight attracts and keeps—the kind that rises to partner—is a workaholic, happiest when he's busy striving for more money and greater career success. He likes the direction, the discipline that organized work provides. Everything in his world puts great value on this. It's part of the system and the system has done him well.

"The bottom line is that to rise to the top, you must give your heart and soul to the firm," says a former Big Eight auditor still in his early thirties. "It's easy to fall into that trap. You come in all psyched to make partner and you tell yourself that nothing will stand in your way. Nothing.

"I started coming home at 10:00 P.M. and then putting in a few hours of paperwork before going to bed. My wife complained, our marriage and sex life were deteriorating, but I kept at it because I had to make partner. The incredible thing is that after working for the firm for a few years, I didn't even know why I wanted to make partner. The partners I met weren't my cup of tea—not the kind of people I could relate to. I found myself making all sorts of excuses just to get out of lunching with them. What's more, I discovered

*Peter Bernstein, "Competition Comes to Accounting," *Fortune*, July 17, 1978.

that they didn't have the leisurely way of life you hear about in college. The crazy hours never stop. In fact, they can be worse once you're part of the inner circle. I didn't want to live my life that way. But you know what, even though I felt this way, even though I no longer understood why I wanted to be a partner, I kept ignoring my wife, neglecting my kids, letting my marriage slide and pushing, pushing to make partner. It just gets into your blood. It becomes automatic.

"Luckily, a series of incidents, all occurring within a two-week period, made me face up to the madness and helped me break the cycle. It was June and the names of new partners were due to be released. I was told by my superiors that I'd be on the list. To celebrate, I was taking my wife on a vacation to the islands. This was to be the trip of a lifetime. I'd booked the best hotels, first-class seats, the works. We'd have a ball, get our marriage back on an even keel, and I'd return in triumph, as a partner.

"I called the office from Kennedy Airport minutes before boarding time. I just wanted to relish the official news of my appointment before we blasted off. Well, I got the shock of my life! My name wasn't on the list. It was like getting slammed in the solar plexus.

"The vacation was a disaster. I didn't enjoy a single minute of it. In fact, I was itching to get back, to find out what the hell happened. I couldn't relate to my wife, to the salt air, to the ocean, to anything on that damned island. I felt like a failure.

"When I got back to the office, pale and tired from lack of sleep, I was ushered into a meeting with the powers that be. Apologies, apologies—I got them by the dozens. Wait till next year, that was the message. My work was fine, I was told, but my commitment to the firm was in question. Some of my partners were concerned that I never put in Saturday hours.

"Suddenly I stopped hearing what they were saying and just saw their mouths moving. I realized what they were doing. That it was all a sham, a scheme designed to make me work even harder. It wasn't enough that my personal life was near ruin and that I was on the brink of exhaustion. By dangling the carrot very close and then pulling it away, they hoped to wring a bit more out of me. In an instant, I saw through it all and that was all I needed. It was a revelation. I excused myself, left the meeting, and went home. The next day, I resigned. What frightens me is that if I'd been made a partner, I'd probably have been sucked in for life."

Now a partner with a much smaller CPA firm, the former Big Eighter claims to be happy with his new affiliation. He insists that his exodus from The Big Eight saved his marriage and restored his peace of mind. He now lives and works in an affluent suburb, gets home by 6:00 P.M., and is never tempted to put in a few hours on Saturday. He can't: They lock the doors Friday night.

Many of the dropouts who've never made it to The Big Eight partnership ranks appear to be envious of their former colleagues. Sometimes, sour grapes are to blame. Although our former auditor does appear to be genuinely pleased with his career, it is a common reaction for others who've failed to get into the big leagues to say they didn't want it anyway. Some of the most vociferous critics of The Big Eight are former staffers who've parked their careers with the small, obscure CPA firms at the base of the accounting pyramid.

The reward for enduring The Big Eight's heavy politics and punishing work load is the superior compensation—a solid 50 percent above the average for small CPA firms. But this too is not without some mitigating factors. Because they are partnerships, most accounting firms require that all those admitted as partners contribute an amount of working capital of from 25 to 50 percent of the individual's annual earnings. At The Big Eight, that can be a substantial sum.

"Like any other company, we need capital to finance our business," says David Moxley, national director of operations for Touche Ross. "Our partners provide this, each contributing an amount based on their earnings. As a partner's earnings increase or decrease, the capital requirements rise and fall accordingly. A partner whose earnings drop from one year to the next is entitled to a capital refund.

"At Touche Ross, the partner's compensation has two components: basic compensation—determined at the start of the year—reflects the individual's performance in the prior year; a bonus, based on the firm's current revenues and figured at year's end, is added to the basic figure. Because this is a partnership, all the partners benefit when the firm has a good year."

At Touche, a partner's capital contribution is computed solely on the basis of ordinary earnings. The bonus does not figure into the equation. The capital formula is earnings minus $25,000. Newly appointed partners earning about $50,000 a year must, therefore, pay in about $25,000 in capital. Typically, this rises a few thousand dollars a year as the partner's income grows. After ten years, the Touche partner can figure on earning about $110,000 basic income and paying in about $85,000 in capital. The capital figure is a sum total of smaller contributions made over the years.

"It gives you a healthy respect for the meaning of partnership," says Russ Palmer, TR's dynamic managing partner. Elected to the top spot at age thirty-seven, Palmer was the youngest man ever to run a Big Eight firm. Now only forty-six, he has already served nine years as Touche's top executive.

"When I became managing partner, my income took a big leap forward. But I wasn't newly rich—not by a long shot. I had to come up with a huge sum of capital to reflect that big earnings rise. It takes a few years, at least, to catch up and enjoy some of the fruits."

Palmer, who claims to earn about $500,000 a year (others put the figure closer to $800,000), undoubtedly has a heavy capital investment in the firm. Coming up with the big bucks upon his election to managing partner obviously took a heavy toll on his newly fattened paycheck. But the burden is also great on junior partners who must shell out $25,000. Most take out personal bank loans and pay them back in three to five years.

At Price Waterhouse, partners' earnings and capital requirements are handled differently. Income is based on a single factor, called shares, which are determined at the start of a fiscal year. The number of shares allotted to a partner determines his percentage of the firm's total earnings. Put simply, if there are three partners and ten shares outstanding, a partner awarded with four shares would be entitled to 40 percent of the earnings. At PW, which boasts the highest average earnings in The Big Eight, new partners start at about $75,000, rise to about $100,000 in five years, and then $150,000 in fifteen years. Executive partners are said to earn slightly more than $200,000, and up to about $250,000 for Chairman Joe Connor. The ideal of a traditional partnership remains strongest at PW. There are fewer partners than at the other firms, and much less of a disparity between the earnings of partners and managing partners. PW provides an internal financing mechanism enabling partners to have capital contributions deducted from annual earnings. Although some partners prefer to plunk down capital contributions in lump-sum cash payments, most choose the financing alternative. Throughout The Big Eight, a partner's full capital contribution is returned to him at retirement. It is, in effect, a kind of forced savings.

"Yes, but we never earn a penny of interest on the money," says a Big Eight tax partner, an offensive, irritable man, who makes microscopic doodles on his note pad. "When the self-appointed critics complain that The Big Eight partners make too much money, they should stop to consider all of this cash we have to tie up in capital. There's no yield on it at all."

Complain as they will, contributing capital is another aspect of partnership Big Eight-style that the partners secretly enjoy. There's an entrepreneurial feel to it; something like being in business for oneself. What better way to feel important to the firm than to participate in its financing. It's like owning "a piece of the rock." Partners love to dwell on it, to boast and bitch simultaneously.

"It kills me to see all this hard-earned money that I have to near kill myself to make just lying fallow in a capital account," says a Price Waterhouse auditor. "But I'll tell you one thing: That money proves that I'm no mere employee. Some people think that because we have so many partners, we all just work here. Bullshit to that. I finance this firm. I damn well own it."

An exaggeration, to be sure. Each partner's interest in a Big Eight firm is only a tiny fraction of a percent. What's more, they can be reprimanded, shifted from client to client, and relocated across the fifty states, often against their will. This is hardly the kind of treatment "business owners" have to tolerate. The truth is that Big Eight partners are more like vested employees than owners. They get a piece of the action and a voice in management, but it's a tiny piece and in most cases a soft voice.

The real power at The Big Eight, much as at their corporate clients, rests with the firms' chairmen (also known as "managing" or "senior" partners), vice-chairmen, and executive committees.

These forces establish current and long-term policies, set procedures, approve partner earnings, and make life miserable for those who violate the firms' rules or standards.

Partners do have considerable power, however, when they rise up and act in unison. Collectively, they can press their will on the executive committees, either rebuking management or demanding that it act in a manner acceptable to the majority. This ganging up on the establishment, once a rare occurrence in The Big Eight, is now bordering on a trend. The natives are restless—worried about the state of their profession, the direction their firms are moving in, and the speed with which they are going. With their incomes, their personal status, their careers at stake, the partners are less willing than in the past to sit back and accept management's actions as infallible. They are challenging the guy in the corner office—and they are winning some of the bouts.

A case in point is the Peat, Marwick revolt of 1979. In what *Fortune* magazine dubbed the "Battle of Boca Raton," Peat's partners rejected management's choice for the best slate of officers to run the firm in the promising but highly problemsome 1980s.

A little background is in order. Like the rest of her seven sisters among the CPA superfirms, PMM had some tough sledding throughout the 1960s and deep into the '70s. Astronomical growth —a sevenfold increase in revenues from 1965 to 1979—and the cultivation of new practice areas had a disrupting effect on the staff and partners. Add to this an intensive scrutiny by governmental bodies; criticism of PMM's accounting practices for such troubled companies as Penn Central, Sterling Homex, and National Student Marketing; and an official reprimand by the Securities and Exchange Commission—and you have serious problems of morale and image. Peat had grown to be a mammoth professional organization, but at what price? A fine old reputation was tarnished. According to *Fortune,* one count showed the firm lost a total of sixty-three major clients in 1974–75.

Under former chairman Walter E. Hanson, PMM moved headlong into a multifaceted growth strategy. A firm believer in offering clients a wide range of services, Hanson placed great emphasis on expanding beyond the traditional audit market. From a pure marketing perspective, this made all the sense in the world. Slugging it out for *Fortune* 500 audit accounts alone is a good way to get nowhere fast. With all The Big Eight competing vociferously for these choice clients, all are bound to win some and lose some. Just as soon as a firm picks off a fast-food king, it loses a public utility. With all the time, money, and talent it takes to woo a plum account, this kind of trade-off can be a costly and frustrating experience. It is also bad business.

Aggressive CPAs, men of Hanson's ilk, quickly recognized that to sustain their extraordinary growth, the big firms had to adopt classic marketing techniques. Positioning and market segmentation came very much into vogue. The Big Eight consciously moved away from the limited sphere of auditing and transformed themselves into a hybrid: part professional firm, part supermarket. They became—with Peat, Arthur Andersen, and Coopers leading the way —purveyors of a varied smorgasbord of financial services. The marketers among them saw, quite clearly, that the rich veins to be tapped were in general consulting, taxes, small-business counseling, government work, executive recruiting, feasibility studies, and actuarial services. Put simply, whatever clients requested, providing it was remotely related to the CPAs' role, The Big Eight provided it. It was time to grow, grow, grow. The firms were in perfect position to expand.

"Of course, they could sign up clients for a host of services," says Abraham Briloff, an accounting professor and The Big Eight's best-known critic. "They were already part of the family under the guise of independent auditors. It's easy to capitalize on this privileged position. The point is, is it right?"

Briloff clearly doesn't think so. Nor do like thinkers in Congress, the SEC, and investor groups. Although there is no arguing that The Big Eight have the skill and the resources to perform all of their practice functions quite competently, critics contend that this conflicts with their central role—the one they are licensed to perform —as certified public accountants and objective auditors.

"The CPA's written opinion of a public company's books must be completely objective in fact and appearance," Briloff adds. "It must be beyond reproach. But that's impossible when that so-called independent auditor has its hands in the clients' pockets for a number of profitable services."

The firms don't take this argument lying down. All dismiss the aging warrior as a man with a worn-out message. Officially, they have persuasive rebuttals for all of his points, and they take pride in voicing the party line to the press, civic groups, professional associations, and congressional committees. Still, many partners, especially those in the more aggressive firms, believe that controversy of any kind is bad for the profession. Fearing government regulation, a gradual loss of prestige, and perhaps a legal ban against nonaudit work, they have shown a clear preference in recent years for a return to a more traditional CPA practice. One which grows, yes, but by natural forces rather than hard sell; and one which remains focused, although not exclusively, on the more conservative fields of audit and tax work.

Thus the "Battle of Boca Raton." When the partners gathered in the great hall of a posh Florida resort hotel to elect a successor to Hanson, they rebuked the outgoing chairman's handpicked choice for the job. After fourteen years of razzle-dazzle leadership, the partners of Peat, Marwick opted for dark-horse candidate Thomas L. Holton. A conservative CPA, an authority on auditing and SEC matters, Holton's surprise election was a sure sign that the partners yearned for a return to more traditional ways. Concerned with the mounting problems rapid growth was bringing to the firm, they wanted to pause for a while, to collect their thoughts, to establish new priorities. By working together, by voting as a block, they were able to utilize the power of a partnership to bring about the majority will.

A shocked Walter Hanson gave testimony to that power on the evening following his candidate's stunning defeat at Boca Raton.

"We are a partnership, and there are one thousand and forty-four persons who have the vote."

Thomas Holton, the newly elected chairman, said, in part, "The partners have expressed their will, and we are very well unified. Everyone is committed to going forward in the cooperative spirit that has been a big factor in making this firm great over the years."

Holton, the victor in what was closer to a white-collar brawl than a cooperative event, obviously felt the need to soothe injured egos and to heal the divisions within the firm. Still, he could not resist what appears to be a poorly concealed slap at the previous administration.

"Peat, Marwick, Mitchell does not need a major overhaul and change in direction. We'll be moving forward with pretty much the same philosophy we've had in the past. We will just *work harder at doing our jobs better.*"

3. In the Looking Glass

"The chairman's going off the deep end. This morning he summons me to his office, on the double. I get there breathless, certain that we lost a big one to Coopers. But no, he wants my opinion on wallpaper. He's redecorating the conference room and can't decide between beige or brown."

—A Big Eight partner.

THE CONTROVERSIAL changing of the guard at Peat, Marwick clearly illustrates the high value Big Eighters now place on matters of image. Above all else, PMM's partners did not want the firm viewed as a reckless or shoddy outfit hell-bent on achieving growth alone. In The Big Eight's competitive battles, size alone is not sufficient to win position and keep the plum accounts. All of the firms, each in its own way, must project images of unswerving independence, thorough professionalism, noble traditions, high quality, and superior customer services. These are the classic standards accounting firms have used to sell themselves on the open market.

But today, The Big Eight need more—more than the holier-than-thou attributes that look good on press releases. Modern marketing practices have come to CPA-land and with them the need to segment the market, position the product, find the USP (Unique Selling Proposition), and promote like crazy. This, after all, is the Pepsi Generation. Positioning a CPA firm, much like a soft drink, requires establishing its unique appeal: one that is either prestigious, adventurous, innovative, flexible, perfectionist, aggressive, or elite.

Big Eight senior partners spend more time fine-tuning their firms' images than they care to admit. It is for some an obsession, involving them in everything from the selection of official stationery to the color of conference-room wallpaper. One chairman spent five weeks at New York's famed Decoration & Design (D&D) Building, interior decorator in tow, choosing sofas, lamps, and bric-a-brac for the firm's national offices. Perhaps he was mindful of A.C. Ernst's (founder of what is now Ernst & Whinney) visionary statement that "Without personality, a public accountant may be likened to a nourishing food without flavor."

Visits to The Big Eight's New York offices—six of which serve as U.S. headquarters (Arthur Andersen is based in Chicago; Ernst & Whinney calls Cleveland home)—reveal that much attention is paid to creating personality through decor. This is the wrapping on the package, the label on the tube of Crest. The Big Eight clearly believe that the look of the executive suite is a meaningful reflection of their firm's professional style. Before exchanging a single word with its partners, a visitor to a Big Eight headquarters can gain a fairly accurate insight into the kind of image the men and women inside want to project. The surroundings make a clear statement, much like the lobby of a hotel.

The preoccupation with image-making is symptomatic of the competitive frenzy that is rumbling throughout The Big Eight. Firms with celebrated histories and noble traditions have suddenly traded all of this in for a new look. Some appear confused as to who they are and what they want to be. Although there are differences among The Big Eight's assorted images, forces now at work may soon change that. The firms are moving, en masse, away from their traditional postures and toward a centrist position. All are trying desperately to evoke some elusive image of a 1980s CPA firm. For some, it is a shocking change.

Take the case of Price Waterhouse. Step from the elevator at PW's national headquarters in a modern office tower and you enter a world of quiet dignity far removed from the crowds, the cars, and the crime on the streets below. Price exudes the heavy-handed look of tradition: the kind of sober surroundings one finds in a Wall Street investment bank. Enormous mahogany desks, portraits in oil, deep brown rugs, and quaint reading lamps set the tone. Thick, floor-length drapes block out the sunlight; coffee is served in fine china cups; partners converse in hushed tones.

The setting fits the Price Waterhouse mystique. As *Fortune* put it in a story on accounting a half century ago:

22 25

22.25
12
4450
2225
26700
2 1
04

$285

17 50

17.5
12
350
175
210.0

$285

$225

The accountants who certify that, in their opinion, the balance sheet of U.S. Steel is properly drawn up so as to present a true and correct view of its financial position are to accounting what Steel is to business, what sterling is to silver. Price Waterhouse is easily the world's foremost accounting firm in size, reputation, and number of clients.* Price Waterhouse is as unapproachable as royalty, entrenched in tradition and pride, as well as professional ethics.

The PW image can be traced back to its roots. Founded in England in 1860 by chartered accountants S.H. Price and Edwin Waterhouse, the firm attracted distinguished partners, including four K.B.E.'s (Knights of the British Empire), and quickly landed a roster of impressive accounts.

Fueled by galloping industrialization, the accounting profession expanded greatly throughout the world. By the mid-1930s, there were fifty-seven PW branches around the world boasting twenty-five hundred employees. The New York practice—which came into being when the firm of Jones, Caeser & Co. joined with PW at the turn of the century—grew to be the largest and most powerful Price office. An illustrious group of partners deserved much of the credit. Joseph Edmund Sterrett, an early partner at Price's American firm, rendered monumental services to the profession and to the nation. Sterrett, at the behest of the U.S. government, helped to investigate the finances and the economy of Mexico, served as adviser to the Treasury on tax matters, took part, in 1919, in the organization of the Reparation Commission, was appointed American member of the Transfer Committee for Reparation Payments under the Dawes Plan, and was honored with the Order of Leopold of Belgium, the First Order of the German Red Cross, and with the Crown of Italy.

Fortune noted:

His career is prophetic and foreshadows the larger and larger part accountants' brains, training, and imagination will and should play in a society which is perforce overhauling its economic system.

The "sterling" image that Price Waterhouse garnered in its early days helped it to woo, as audit clients, the bluest of the blue-chip

*PW has since been surpassed in revenues and number of clients.

corporations. Most notably, big oil and big steel moved into the PW fold, becoming showcase clients and prompting a stampede of choice accounts to follow suit. As PW became known as the elite accounting firm, big business stood in line to buy some of its cachet. It became, at the time, prestigious to hire PW.

Throughout the twentieth century, the blue-chippers came in droves. So much so that by the 1970s, PW had lined up about 100 of the *Fortune* 500, including among its clients General Foods, U.S. Steel, and Exxon. And it is precisely this type of client that has helped to further shape PW's image. Of all The Big Eight, PW has been most adept at winning favor with the legendary names in business and industry. There is no denying that Price has won a special place for itself in The Big Eight hierarchy. Not the biggest of the big, it is nevertheless the most prestigious. Although competitors carp and bitch about PW's "stuffy, arrogant air," all would trade their Hewlett Packard calculators for a sprinking of the Price Waterhouse mystique.

"When I was a young staffer here we had a training session one Saturday morning," says Frederick Werblow, a PW partner and marketing director. "The speaker said the other firms' partners were Fords or Chevies and PW's partners were Cadillacs. I felt he was wrong. I believed Price Waterhouse was the Rolls-Royce of the profession, and that's why I joined the firm." "We have the finest reputation in the business, there's no doubt about that," adds PW's Joe Connor, a mild-mannered man who looks like the stereotype of a CPA but is relaxed, confident, and self-assured. The man garners high marks for his professional and managerial abilities. "Some of the other firms have good reputations too, but we have the best. A number of our clients go back a hundred years with the firm."

Connor, like his counterparts at Touche Ross and Deloitte Haskins & Sells, can talk nonstop about his firm, his profession, and the changing nature of both. Immensely proud of PW and of his leadership position in the partnership, he appears, nevertheless, to be disturbed and troubled by the changes that are sweeping through The Big Eight. Seated in his elegant, tastefully appointed offices—furnished in a brighter and softer style than the standard PW setting—Connor seems at times like a man sadly mourning the past, the end of an era.

There is good reason for this. PW's genteel image is not holding up well in today's rough-and-tumble markets. The white gloves are off; Big Eighters are aggressively competing for business with hard-sell techniques, expanding their range of services, and promising clients a long list of extras. What's more, they are cutting fees, courting accounts by shaving millions of dollars from bid proposals. The classic Price Waterhouse formula of offering high-quality work, maintaining a gilt-edge image, and charging premium fees is out of step with the times. More and more clients are balking at big fees and at the aloof and haughty attitude of Big Eight firms. A growing number of today's clients want competitive rates, extra services, and efficiency. Modern corporate managers are more concerned with the audit budget than with notions of grandeur. For a firm like PW, which obtains 75 percent of its fees from audit practice —more than any other Big Eight competitor—this can be a problem of major proportions.

Sadly and belatedly, Price Waterhouse has acknowledged that it can no longer sit on its lofty pedestal, charge the highest fees, and simply wait for new accounts to come knocking at the door. Today, Rolls-Royce must advertise, Mercedes must talk fuel efficiency, and Price Waterhouse must come out of its stately abode and sell. Sell, sell, sell.

"We have an image of forthrightness and conservatism," Connor says. "This removes us from consideration by some of the companies that are seeking an auditor. Those that don't want a conservative firm stay away from us.

"We worry that our image is too stodgy. We have always been the blue-chip firm, and so people believe that we are interested only in big business. But that's not true. We are very active in developing our practice with small business as well."

In an era when The Big Eight must expand well beyond huge audit accounts in order to meet their insatiable appetite for growth, the image of blue-chip auditor can be damaging. Mid-size and small businesses, even those attracted to the PW image, fear that the great Price Waterhouse is really interested in serving only the biggies. It's the old small-fish-in-the-big-pond phobia. But PW is working overtime to dispel this notion. It is collaring the press, industry associations, and trade groups, telling one and all that PW is now a flexible giant, ready and willing to serve small business, to perform a wide range of consulting work, and to bid for fee-sensitive jobs. In no way a lowballer, PW is nevertheless learning to compromise: It is shaking off some of the dust, but isn't quite sure how far to go. Although competing more vigorously, the firm is still somewhat gun-shy: It still views the CPA as an austere professional, removed from the competitive fray. PW, it seems, wants to do it all: to retain its royal image while at the same time mixing it up in the streets, prowling for business with the best of them. That is hard to do. Can Tiffany's open a discount shop?

"We are conservative but innovative," Connor says. "Conservative in deciding what is acceptable professionally but innovative in our approach to serving clients.

"Price Waterhouse will compete for clients, yes, but any chairman who says you can sell this service like toothpaste or cereal does not understand the profession. An audit is not a commodity. You cannot sell a professional service like a packaged good." The firm faces a tough balancing act, but Connor appears capable of pulling it off in the PW tradition.

Price Waterhouse's neighbor at 1114 Avenue of the Americas, Deloitte Haskins & Sells, has a number of similar strengths and problems on its hands. Known throughout the profession as the "auditors' auditor," DH&S is also saddled with a very fine image that simply doesn't generate business in the new accounting marketplace. Its reputation for solid, extremely thorough audits has a conservative ring that turns off many potential clients. Today, perfectionism takes a back seat to innovation, aggressiveness, speed, and economy. Those auditors deemed likely to spend thousands of hours of billable time double-checking every minor transaction frighten the hell out of budget-conscious controllers. They are more likely to go with a Big Eight speed demon that whips through audits with high-powered computer programs and that does the work for half the time and half the fee.

Another Johnny-come-lately to The Big Eight's promotional wars, DH&S has, like Price Waterhouse, recognized that it must shed its stodgy suit and pocket watch and emerge as a more vibrant personality. Unlike PW, however, Deloitte appears to be going at it with naked enthusiasm, even leading the pack in a number of marketing tactics.

Charles Steele, DH&S's senior partner, is responsible for this. A born-again CPA, a product of the old school who has changed his outlook on the profession, Steele knows full well that quality alone may win brownie points but it no longer puts money in the partners' pockets.

"To be successful today, a major CPA firm like ours must combine quality with aggressiveness," says Steele, a handsome, gregarious man who looks the part of a successful WASP banker or corporate executive.

"Like it or not, the nature of the profession has changed. You must sell yourself and demonstrate a wide scope of practice, innovation, and leadership. We'd like to move away somewhat from the image of being the auditors' auditor to something that more adequately reflects our well-rounded and responsive practice. Quality is important, no question about that, but you've got to have more today. You don't want to be seen as stodgy."

Michael Chetkovich, DH&S former managing partner, called it "a whole new world of competition. . . . The big accounting firms have not yet taken to the streets with sandwich boards to hawk their services, but a fierce competitive struggle is transforming their once-staid behavior. Long accustomed to having clients seek them out, they are now vigorously pursuing potential customers. . . ."*

Deloitte Haskins & Sells' executive offices reflect this "new world's" sought-after image of a dynamic practice tempered by tradition. Charles Steele's expansive office is formal but not heavy; comfortable but not cozy. Lots of polished woods, elegant fabrics, plush rugs. The aura is one of confidence, success, stability. Fitting for the auditors of General Motors.

Steele exudes self-confidence. Not a boisterous self-confidence but one evidenced by forthrightness and a willingness to discuss the good and the bad. Unlike some of his counterparts throughout The Big Eight, Steele is not defensive about the profession. He is charming, intelligent, and quite candid.

*Bernstein, "Competition Comes to Accounting, *op. cit.*

"We were the first Big Eight firm to use hard-sell advertising. Arthur Young did some institutional ads before us, but we were the first to launch a national hard-sell campaign. One of the reasons we did this was to change our image. Historically, our firm has been recognized as one of the most conservative in The Big Eight. We felt the need to revise that."

DH&S launched its ad campaign in 1979 soon after the AICPA, under pressure from the FTC and the SEC, dropped its ban against professional advertising. In an opinion poll by Reichman Research, Deloitte found that although it got high marks from its clients, it was not as well known in the business community as its sister Big Eighters. That kind of low profile is a definite no-no in today's competitive market.

The campaign, produced by the well-known agency of Needham, Harper & Steers, communicates DH&S' wide scope of practice and its willingness to go the extra mile to service clients. The ad slogan "Beyond the Bottom Line," neatly sums up the firm's new outlook and image. For the most part, the ads are attractive and tasteful without the sleepy quality one might expect from a blue-chip CPA firm. The professionalism of the campaign is indicative of the fact that The Big Eight usually buy the best. When management focuses on a priority, money is no object: Lots of green get thrown around. In addition to an advertising agency, a charity consultant, and a research firm, DH&S also hires public relations counsel and corporate identity advisers. Taken together, it all shapes up into a well-funded, high-powered promotional machine.

"In the past, we had always believed that if you did a better audit you got more business—the better mousetrap theory," Steele adds. "But we found that that old stance is no good in today's environment. Clients want what they perceive as more agressive firms because they think that's who will deliver more services.

"Our advertising is designed to give us an image of a more alert and more with-it firm that is hungry for business and is service oriented. The profession has changed greatly. Our image of being quiet and conservative used to reflect the style of the business. No more. Fifteen years ago if a prospective client called and asked you to propose for their account, you would first call the existing auditors as a courtesy. Now we go out and try to lock up the account before the other guy knows what the hell hit him."

One of the ways DH&S is seeking "to get to new accounts first" is by building its market exposure through the organized approach to philanthropy. In order to polish the image of the firm's Atlanta office, for example, a paid outside charity consultant was hired to develop and implement a program of corporate philanthropy designed to produce maximum goodwill for DH&S. The accent is on encouraging the partners' personal involvement in those local charitable organizations that promise to do the most for the firm's prestige and public relations. The goal is to obtain a trade-off between giving and receiving.

"The outside groups that depend on volunteers have come to realize that we are willing to commit these resources," says the DH&S consultant, "but we expect a reasonable degree of recognition of our contributions, and here degree is the operative word. All it might take, for example, is an individual's affiliation with Deloitte Haskins & Sells noted on a dinner program or in a press release. . . .

"Certain organizations have a higher prestige factor, a higher profile in the volunteer community than others. As a consequence, the better groups often have a more select membership, and so these are the groups we would recommend that DH&S people join. After all, if you're going to invest the time and effort, you might as well go with the best."

DH&S is trying to find a middle ground—to be viewed as somewhat of a swinger but one with class, finesse, and a tradition of quality. It is willing to waltz for business, but it's not quite ready to disco. It leaves that dance to Touche Ross.

TR hears a different drummer. Its problem is having too much of what the grande dames of accounting crave: too much rhythm, too little etiquette. When the critics turn to TR, the talk is of poor quality, weak standards, and lowballing. There's no denying that Touche Ross comes up short on tradition, hallowed halls, and "rah! rah! rah!"

Touche Ross is the one firm its newly aggressive competitors love to hate. That's because TR is an imaginative and energetic CPA firm with its sights set squarely on today and its mind focused more on tomorrow than on yesterday. It is a street-smart, gutsy firm with few formalities, a top-notch staff, intelligent and innovative partners, and hot prospects for continued growth. If Price Waterhouse is at one end of The Big Eight spectrum, Touche Ross is at the other: PW with its Brahmin pedigree, TR with its feet on the ground prowling the city for business.

That Touche Ross is the only Big Eight firm with national offices on New York's Broadway is symbolic. The others, housed in gleaming office buildings along the corporate boulevards of Park Avenue, Third Avenue, and Avenue of the Americas, have chosen the prime territory of the city's big-business community. These pristine thoroughfares lined with steel-and-glass towers have little in the way of urban color and electricity. The Touche Ross domain, just blocks away but across the city's Sixth Avenue DMZ and into the deep West Side, is surrounded by a more typical New York collage of cheap bars, fine old restaurants, street vendors, sidewalk musicians, ptomaine parlors, massage parlors, pizza joints, porno shops, whores, hustlers, pimps, drug dealers, pickpockets, and muggers. This is nitty-gritty New York—a pulsing, threatening, challenging world that never slows down, never sleeps.

Touche Ross is to big-league public accounting as Broadway is to Park Avenue. It is intimidating, ill-mannered, informal, hungry, and aggressive. The product of numerous mergers, Touche is eager to climb to the top of The Big Eight. It does not, however, plan to wait in line. TR has blazed the way in adopting modern marketing techniques, in trading in the white gloves for boxing gloves, in clawing at competitors for loose accounts, and in slashing fees to win business. Touche Ross plays for keeps.

TR's very willingness to challenge tradition, to do things its own way, has brought it considerable criticism from the accounting establishment. Old-timers—card-carrying members of The Big Eight Club—consider Touche Ross to be a whorehouse of poor standards and low fees. So-called generally accepted accounting principles (GAAP), on which CPA firms base their audits, permit a range of acceptable procedures and therefore leave substantial room for interpretation. TR's critics claim that the firm uses this leeway not to design the most accurate audits but instead to give clients the greatest freedom in computing the bottom line. An illustration in *Fortune*'s excellent article on The Big Eight ("Competition Comes to Accounting") pictured a TR man wearing a sandwich board reading WRITE OFF THAT LOSS WITH HELP FROM TOUCHE ROSS.

TR's reputation for fancy pencilwork is not fair. The image stems from the firm's association with a number of controversial entrepreneurs and troublesome accounts like the Chrysler Corporation. Although TR has had some serious run-ins with the SEC and has been involved in its share of questionable audits, so too have its competitors. Today, Touche Ross is a vibrant, modern-thinking firm, out for the big bucks but also highly concerned with the quality of its practice.

As a group, TR's partners are different from those at Peat, Marwick; Coopers; Arthur Young; and the like. Touche people tend to be more casual, relaxed, and candid. There is greater diversity here: One does not get the feeling that a stamping machine turns out TR partners according to a master plan. At a single meeting at Touche's national office, one finds a brash, cigar-chomping New Yorker, a gesturing Japanese, a reserved Texan, and a jovial, toothy Midwesterner. There's a Jew, a Jap, a Catholic, and a WASP.

The paranoia that haunts much of The Big Eight is not evident at Touche Ross. Partners are not afraid to be themselves, to take positions, to speak freely: They are willing to take on tough questions asked by the press, to admit some wrongdoing in the profession, and to let the chips fall where they may. This candor extends all the way up through the ranks to managing partner Russ Palmer. Such widespread willingness to open up is unusual and quite refreshing.

"This profession is nowhere near being perfect," says Tom Presby, TR's partner in charge of marketing. A charming man with a continental flair, Presby discusses the business-getting side of The Big Eight's activities with none of the hush-hush, top-secret shenanigans engaged in by the others. "When a big client is up for grabs, we all fight tooth and nail for it. Sometimes standards are bent

—nothing unethical or illegal, but not always the ideal way of doing things. This is a business. You have to be somewhat flexible. The trend is clear: Those who think public accounting has been competitive in recent years haven't seen a thing. The future is going to make the past look like child's play."

Presby's very presence on a Big Eight staff is revealing. To find marketing men sharing the executive suite with auditors, tax specialists, and consultants would be enough to make the gentlemen founders of The Big Eight turn in their graves. More and more the giant CPA firms think and act like Procter & Gamble, spinning the complex marketing plans once reserved for the makers of deodorant and breakfast cereals. TR's Presby is a skilled practitioner at this increasingly important activity. Like his counterparts throughout The Big Eight, Presby uses the concept of industry specialization as the centerpiece of his marketing program. The idea, simply stated, is to acquire categories of clients, to invest heavily in special services for these accounts, and to become a source of information to them. In today's complex and fast-changing environment, the *Fortune* 1000 corporations want auditors who are thoroughly familiar with the latest industry regulations, SEC positions, and IRS rulings impacting their operations.

The Big Eight firm with a host of prominent bank clients is deemed to have significant experience in the banking field and stands the best chance of snaring a new bank account that comes up for grabs. When the teams of Big Eight salesmen troupe into the prospect's offices to make a rousing pitch for business, the partners that can tick off the names of fifteen major bank clients are the ones most likely to walk away with the prize.

"There are two points of view to defining the market for a professional service. On the one hand, a market can be defined in terms of a prospective client universe that can be served by a firm's existing personnel, capabilities, and services. On the other hand, a market can be defined in terms of the marketplace itself—its configurations and needs—within the framework of a firm's ability to adapt to those needs. The classic example might be the piano player in the cocktail lounge. Some piano players will play anything you want to hear, so long as all you want to hear is "Melancholy Baby." Others recognize the taste and demands of their clientele and use their piano-playing skills to play the kind of music the patrons want. Clearly, it's the second piano player who works more regularly."*

Incredible as it seems, the same corporation that shies away from an advertising agency because it dreams up jingles for a single competitor will gladly select an auditor that already services half that corporation's industry. Fears of potential conflicts are mitigated by the auditor's expertise in the field: This is valued above all else. Thus, the marketing clout of industry specialization.

Once a small corps of bank, health care, insurance, airline, retail, or energy clients is assembled, marketers within The Big Eight go about building up these specialized divisions. Partners are assigned to coordinate all services to the client groups, combining tax, audit, and consulting into an integrated program. The goal is to make the client dependent on the firm for the widest possible range of services. Once the CPAs establish a reputation in the field and get their foot in the client's door, they become the natural choice to fill this central role. If not The Big Eight auditor—the powerhouse of financial services—than who else?

To enhance their reputations as industry specialists, The Big Eight spend millions producing libraries of booklets, pamphlets, newsletters, position papers, brochures, and comprehensive reference works on subjects of interest to the industry groups. Just a sampling of the DH&S literary output includes the following:

Cash Management—A Practical Guide: A reference book for municipal managers.

Public Utilities Manual: A guide to the special regulatory and accounting aspects of the industry.

Serving Government—for More Effective Public Administration: A booklet describing our services to government.

Questions at Stockholder Meetings: An annual booklet containing examples of questions that may be expected at annual meetings.

---

*Bruce W. Marcus, Director of External Communications, Arthur Young & Co., *Marketing an Accounting Firm.*

Replacement Costs: A guide for complying with SEC requirements.

System for Hospital Uniform Reporting: A booklet describing our recommendations for a better approach to uniform reporting systems for hospitals and other health-care institutions.

Clearly, the goal is to become a source of information; to prompt clients to rely on The Big Eight to decipher the meaning of the latest 100-page tome cranked out by the federal bureaucracy. The equation etched into the minds of Big Eight marketing executives looks something like this:

GREATER CLIENT DEPENDENCE=GREATER VOL-
UME AND SCOPE OF SERVICES=GREATER FEES

Not that industry specialization is window dressing, the showy equivalent of a soup-can label. Not at all. The Big Eight put a tremendous amount of money and effort into developing expertise in a broad cross section of industries. The literature produced is, for the most part, well written, and enlightening to the corporate subscribers. Partners assigned to service industry group accounts have to earn their stripes before they can parade around as an expert in anything. This means putting in up to 100 hours a year in continuing education—far beyond the AICPA's forty-hour requirement for SEC Practice Section members. Price Waterhouse, a leader in energy clients, lists among the in-house courses and seminars available to its partners:

Audit/Introductory Industry and Special Services Program
Introduction to Petroleum Industry
Petroleum Industry Conference
Introductory Public Utility Seminar
Update Public Utility Seminar
MAS/Consulting on Energy Matters for Government

TR's Tom Presby has no doubts that continuing education and the related efforts that go into industry specialization pay off handsomely. In terms accountants can easily understand, he indicates that there's a good return on the investment.

"Developing expertise in a field makes it easier to get clients in that industry," Presby says. "If you get known as the widget-business accountants, you'll get the widget clients.

"We built our health-care specialization group from scratch, making it a strong force in the field in less than ten years. It was about 1970 when we identified health care as an emerging growth market we should be involved in. To get started—to motivate our people in this direction—we used the old Louis B. Mayer star system. We'd say to young staffers here, 'How would you like to be a partner?' When they said they'd love it, we'd say, 'Learn the health-care business.' With that kind of motivation, you get action. We now have about three hundred health-care clients, mostly hospitals. We start off by doing feasibility studies for these facilities before they are even built and then we graduate to auditing, forecasting, and other financial services."

A good marketing program, Big Eight-style, has an interlocking practice grid that draws clients into an ever-wider net of professional relationships. One service feeds into another. Such is the thinking behind TR's Inbound Investment Program.

"There's a lot of hand holding here," Presby explains. "Let's say a Tokyo-based bank client of Touche Ross wants to open a branch in New York. Our Inbound Investment Program will help the bank through the entire process of setting up a subsidiary here. We'll introduce them to the U.S. market, help scout for office space, find qualified employees, arrange for the necessary legal clearances—just about everything. Once the client gets established, we hope to provide auditing, tax, and other services in this country. Our New York office alone has fifteen Japanese accountants serving the U.S. arm of a Japanese client. The program works exceptionally well: Each Touche Ross office with a major inflow of international business has an Inbound Investment Program."

The IIP is further evidence of TR's aggressive approach to marketing. The program attracts foreign clients to its U.S. practice and then locks them up as captive accounts, serviced well and insulated from competitive maneuvers by the other accounting wolves baying at the door.

No one doubts TR's willingness to go head to head with the competition or to bend over backward to serve clients. Touche's image problem is that the firm is viewed as too aggressive, too middle-class, with too little of the prestige that is Price Waterhouse's stock in trade.

"We know we don't have the gilt-edge, Rolls-Royce image," Palmer acknowledges, "but we've matured as a firm and we're considered a high-quality, capable, superservice-oriented practice."

This is the irony of The Big Eight today: All of the firms are running in the same direction, trying to stake out a middle ground. Price Waterhouse and DH&S, for example, want to put a little sex in their lives; Touche Ross wants a little religion.

A stroll down TR's executive row is revealing. The decor reflects the eclectic image Touche Ross is trying desperately to cultivate: that of a sharply modern practice with a proud, impressive past. Furnishings are contemporary in design, featuring earth tones, laminates, and exotic fixtures. This is balanced by a sober gallery of oil paintings, the traditional founders' portraits, placed prominently in the clients' reception room.

The driving force in planning and presenting this dual image— and in making Touche a Big Eight firm to reckon with—is managing partner Palmer. The youngest man to ever head a Big Eight firm, Palmer's rise to power is interesting from two perspectives: First, it is a classic example of the young man who enters a large organization, finds a high-ranking sponsor, and is rapidly propelled through the ranks over the bodies of his former superiors; second, it reflects the fact that most of The Big Eight's top executives have their roots in the plain-folk towns of Middle America.

"I didn't grow up in modest circumstances, I grew up poor," says Palmer, with the up-by-the-bootstraps pride that is abundant among Big Eighters. "My family was on welfare. You don't get much poorer than that. Not that I'm complaining: Mom surrounded me with love, so I never felt deprived. It was a happy childhood. It's just that there was never any money."

Palmer—a handsome, fit, likeable man—is an all-out extrovert, a full-throttle talker, and a friendly, high-spirited, self-confident human being who comes off like a born salesman. No backslapper, he simply has a dynamic quality that is attractive and wins clients.

Palmer wants to be viewed as a senior statesman of the profession, a prominent authority in the field of public accounting. But you don't get that kind of portrait in oils by being perceived as a hot-shot salesman with a Hollywood smile.

"If I'd been just a salesman, I'd never have made it to this desk," Palmer asserts, comfortably seated in his posh office suite, imaginatively divided into work, studying, and meeting areas. "There are too many outstanding people here, and there are too many responsibilities in this position for a salesman to hold the leadership reins. I don't want to sound immodest, but I got here by being a well-rounded professional, a first-class auditor, client-service specialist, and salesman.

"The problem is, I don't look like an accountant. I never did. I remember back in the early days when I first joined the firm—then Touche, Niven, Bailey and Smart—right out of Michigan State. I worked in Detroit and lived as a bachelor in Ma Parker's Boarding House. This was a quaint, comfortable place inhabited by a sort of family of young accountants.

"One night we're all seated around the dinner table, and Ma Parker asks to see me in her apartment. When we were alone, she said 'You told me a falsehood. You said you were an accountant.' When I protested that I was, in fact, an accountant, she said, 'Why you don't look or act like any accountant I've ever known.'

"It's this kind of impression of me—the fact that I don't look like a CPA—that makes people dub me a salesman. But it's inaccurate, and it's not why I was elected to head this firm."

There is truth to Palmer's claim. As a young staffer, he was called to the army and found himself dressed in fatigues while his peers at Touche Niven were moving up the ladder in Brooks Brothers suits. When Palmer returned to civilian life, he had a long way to catch up at the firm. An extremely competitive man, he begged and bothered superiors for a chance to make up for lost time. When the opportunity came along to take a growth spot in Touche, Niven's Denver office, Palmer jumped at it.

"Within ten days of the offer I was in my new office in Colorado, busy at work. My wife was still back in Detroit, sewing up our affairs. But I didn't waste any time. I saw a chance to play catch-up ball in Denver and I went for it."

Palmer has run Touche Ross the same way: coming from behind, seizing opportunities, invading new markets, doing the unorthodox. It's the Touche Ross style, based to a great extent on the chairman's own run for daylight. He learned a lot from the Denver experience. It confirmed his belief that swift decisive action pays off. He has called on the strategy again and again—once at the most critical time in his career.

"By age twenty-seven, I was a supervisor running the audit department in Denver. I was the only nonpartner in the whole firm signing opinions. A little-known provision in the firm's manual allowed for that. The Denver office grew rapidly, and I garnered a good deal of exposure. Most notably, I came into favor with the then managing partner Robert Beyer, who asked me to move on to the even-greater challenge of running the Philadelphia office. This made my star shine even brighter. Again I grabbed the opportunity to prove myself and it paid off: The office's revenues doubled a year after I took over."

Palmer became the heir apparent sometime around the midpoint of his five-year stint in the City of Brotherly Love. Nearing the end of his term in office, Beyer nominated Palmer to fill his shoes.

"It was a controversial thing to do," Palmer recalls, relishing the memory of it all. "I was only thirty-six years old, nominated for the top office above so many distinguished senior partners. My opponent in the balloting, a well-established partner with a distinguished career, seemed to traditionalists in and out of the firm as a much more fitting choice for the job. But, tradition aside, I won."

Still, a crisis loomed just ahead. A month before Palmer was to go to New York to officially take command, Beyer suffered a stroke. Incapacitated, he was unable to conduct the firm's affairs. For several weeks, Touche was rudderless.

Most important, there was serious question as to whether Palmer's election was still valid. Voices in the corridors were whispering that a new succession process was in order, a new election. Fearing that his narrow victory could be snatched away in the eleventh hour, Palmer opted for his quick-strike strategy.

"I just told my secretary to gather my papers and I went to New York. I had Beyer's desk cleaned and I moved right in. The firm needed a leader, and I felt it was my duty to take command. I don't mind saying that I also acted in order to prevent the election from being invalidated. I wanted to put an end to any talk of that. I knew that decisive action and strong leadership would do the trick."

Aggressive, cocky, unorthodox. That's the Palmer style; that's the Touche Ross style. Is it right for now? Is it right for the eighties? Yes and no. The toughness required to ferret out and win new accounts must be tempered with a quality image that impresses audit committees and stockholders. For all its new competitiveness, public accounting is not the vacuum-cleaner business. Going from door to door for new business is unbecoming of a first-class firm. To be highly successful, a Big Eighter must draw a substantial flock of clients simply because it is what it is. Prestige, although not the trump card of the past, is still important. Touche Ross needs a dash of finesse—a year at a finishing school. That's what it is getting: The firm hosts a series of elegant dinners with the likes of John D. Rockefeller, Al Ullman, and Tip O'Neill. And Russ Palmer, the former welfare case from Jackson, Michigan, tends to an elaborate wine cellar in the basement of his Greenwich, Connecticut, mansion. He talks of touring the Bordeaux region, inspecting vineyards, and collecting rare bottles. Very *de rigueur*.

Palmer's days at TR are numbered. His ten year term as CEO/CPA expires in 1982. Unless he mounts a last-minute campaign to change the firm's bylaws, he'll be out to pasture by age forty-seven. Although the man is worshipped in much of the Touche Ross organization, and it is likely that his stamp will be pressed on to the TR personality for years to come, there's no telling what kind of prescription the new managing partner will write for the Touche image. Things are up in the air.

Not so a few blocks away at Peat, Marwick. With a new slate of officers installed at the infamous "Battle of Boca Raton," the firm's management posture is likely to remain constant throughout the 1980s. The operating style will be set by Chairman Holton and Vice-Chairman Sloan. Considering the circumstances of their election, the duo will undoubtedly opt for tighter quality controls and more cautious growth in the nonaudit practice. PMM's image still bears some of the stains of the past two decades. Cleaning that up will be a top priority. Holton and Sloan have their partners' mandate to do so.

PMM's greatest strength and weakness is its size. A colossus of The Big Eight—locked with archnemesis Coopers & Lybrand in a silly numbers game, with each claiming the highest revenues in The Big Eight—PMM has a vast array of talented people in its ranks, mixed, however, with what to one observer appears to be mediocre hangers-on. There is no arguing with the principle that the bigger a business organization, the more room for slackers to hide out.

Everything about Peat exudes bigness. The executive suite is expansive. The furnishings are grand pieces, mostly modern in design but solid and subdued. A perfect reflection of the Peat, Marwick image.

Not surprisingly for a firm that has been under the gun for years, the atmosphere at PMM appears rather tense. One is reminded of an ocean liner on the high seas, listing lightly after a rough storm. There is a sense that the captain has things under control, but also a deep-seated fear that perhaps—just perhaps—there's a slight leak in the bow. No one's jumping ship, but everyone knows exactly where to find the life preservers.

PMM brass come across as defensive. Perhaps that's because Peat views itself as the symbol of the accounting establishment. As such, it takes any hint of criticism as conspiratorial and dangerous. Don Sloan holds that many critics are simply misinformed snoopers.

"If damage to our reputation that occurred in the 1970s still lingers, it's because the files of *The New York Times* and the *Wall Street Journal* still have stories about our problems. Anyone can pull them out."

Sloan boasts of Peat's grandiose size, proclaiming over and over again that PMM is the largest CPA firm in the world.

"We are the largest, and I think it's important to be the largest. If we weren't the largest, than I wouldn't strive to reach that. But since we are the largest, I want to retain the top spot."

That Peat likes to go after the big engagements, even if for a relatively low fee, is evidenced by its taking on the mammoth challenge of auditing New York City. In a three-year contract with the city (signed in 1977), Peat was guaranteed slightly less than $1 million per year for an audit project so great in scope and so complicated that some Big Eight competitors put the cost for such an engagement at $4 million or more. Clearly, Peat sought the job to build its credibility as a municipal auditor and to garner the publicity and the prestige of serving the greatest city in the world.

Others wanted no part of it. "I take a dim view of municipal audit work," says Joe Connor. "That's $5-per-hour work. I have better ways to allocate this firm's resources."

Peat, Marwick obviously took a more positive view. It tackled the engagement with gusto and with the resolve to perform it well. But PMM's eighty-five-man New York City audit team had its hands full the first year.

"One problem we had right off the bat was how to define the city," says Bob Happ, highly competent Peat partner in charge of the audit. "It's made up of so many different entities providing different services like transportation, health care, and the like. We had to determine which of these entities would be included in the city's numbers.

"The Transit Authority posed a typical problem. That's really a state agency, but the city makes up its deficit. The city owns the subway cars, even though the state operates the cars. To make matters even more complex, some transit workers are state employees, and others work for the city. We had to look at every entity, and each part of every entity, to see what should be counted with the city.

"Some real crazy questions came into the audit. The city owns parcels of land. How do you value them? Some suggested that we value the city's land at the $24 price that the Indians were paid for Manhattan, because we use cost as the basis for assets in municipal accounting."

Adding fuel to the fire, PMM's auditors were greeted with the clenched fists of a frightened bureaucracy, worried that the outsiders would somehow cut budgets and have them fired.

"To help with this problem, the mayor and the controller held a big meeting with the leaders of all city agencies," Happ says. "Our role was explained. People were assured that we were not there as detectives."

In spite of the chuckling by Peat's competitors about this lowest of lowball engagements, PMM has performed admirably on the job, has won the respect of the city's financial brass, and has taught the bureaucrats lessons that may well help to stabilize New York over the long term. The presence of financial pros blowing the dust off centuries of poor bookkeeping and sloppy fiscal controls has, by most accounts, proven beneficial. Peat has also garnered its publicity coup and has emerged with its banners flying.

What bitterly annoys Peat's management, however, is that this excellent performance cannot be rewarded with continued work on the engagement. After PMM signed with New York, it was discovered that the city's charter calls for the rotation of CPA firms every fourth year. Peat partners admit that they were looking to future years as the city's auditors to make substantial profits on the engagement. Once the initial costs of an audit are absorbed—those expenses involved in getting to understand a new client—more of the fees can then filter down to the bottom line. But Peat will have to be satisfied with the image benefits. Certainly a giant public accounting firm cannot be seen crying about a charter provision designed to assure high levels of independence and objectivity.

Although Peat holds fast to its claim to be the largest accounting firm in the world, many contend that Coopers & Lybrand has surpassed PMM in revenues and is now in the number one slot. As one of the fastest growing of The Big Eight—and one of the most aggressive—C&L poses a major challenge to PMM on all fronts. It is a determined competitor in the audit market and an unabashed proponent of diverse practice specialties.

Sloan angrily dismisses C&L's claim to the top spot. "We question some of the figures C&L is publishing in their financials. They say that they include only the revenues of Coopers & Lybrand firms, but they really include their Swiss firm too. That's not C&L; it's a correspondent firm."

Russ Palmer takes a swipe at those involved in the revenues race this way: "What the hell does size alone mean? When I first started in this business, I was told I was going to work on a $50-million account. Well, I was tickled pink. 'Wow,' I thought, 'they know my worth.' When I asked how long it would take, they said, 'Two weeks.' 'Only two weeks?' I asked. 'Yes,' they said, 'the business is a slaughterhouse.' So what does size tell you? It can still be a slaughterhouse!"

The size question is a matter of debate because of the complex nature of Big Eight's overseas affiliates. Some foreign branches are legitimately part of a Big Eight firm's international organization; others are completely independent outfits or correspondent firms which serve as local auditing representatives for some or all of The Big Eight. The Philippines SVG Organization, a good-sized CPA firm for that part of the world, does auditing work for a number of The Big Eight. Just how its revenues should be counted is a matter of controversy. Some observers say that a few of the firms are claiming the identical revenues in their own worldwide figures; others say that the fees of correspondents should not be counted at all. The argument is indicative of the petty carping that now colors Big Eight competition. *Forbes,* noting Coopers's first announcement that it was in fact the new revenues champion, had this to say about it:

The result was an immediate brouhaha of claim and counterclaim among accounting's Big Eight about who ranked where, a debate that sounded and probably was about as meaningful as an argument about a third-strike call. . . . So, as Costello used to ask Abbott, "Who's on first?"—and who cares?

Obviously, there is no love lost among The Big Eight. All compete vigorously; all are out for themselves. As private businesses, they seek to grow, in part, by taking business from the others. In the constant head-to-head competition, bad feelings develop among the rival firms. Winners gloat in public; losers seek revenge. It is all part of the game. In this context, however, there are pockets of animosity that go beyond the norm. Here bad feelings intensify, rise to the surface, and embroil the dueling CPAs in ugly mudslinging. It is bad for the profession.

"There's a tremendous amount of open competition and hostility among The Big Eight now," says Sloan. "I guess if we went too far we could wind up damaging the reputation of The Big Eight and the profession as a whole."

The leadership of Coopers and Peat share some striking similarities. Norman Auerbach, Cooper's opinionated chairman, is a staunch defender of his firm. Conservative, polished, almost genteel in appearance, Auerbach nevertheless appears to relish The Big Eight's competitive brawls and grabs every opportunity to sing the praises of C&L.

When asked about the widespread notion that Coopers wins accounts by lowballing, Auerbach contracts his face and body in a controlled rage.

"Our reputation as a price-cutter is ugly. It's just a way for the competition to excuse our growth. We have never been a price-cutter and we never will be.

"My image of C&L is that of a firm with a complete service concept. We are not interested in being only auditors. We see and understand the tremendous interaction between auditing, tax, and the computer revolution."

This appears to be an ethical way of saying that Coopers & Lybrand sees a huge, lucrative market out there for a smorgasbord of services. It wants to sell much of what the market will bear. C&L is one of the leaders in The Big Eight's movement away from the limited role of certified public accountants and toward that of a broad-based financial services firm. This is their business objective and their chosen image. The emphasis is on growth and diversity. It is not proper, however, for CPAs to sound greedy or salesy. Their marketing strategies must be couched in austere terms. Accounting, after all, is a profession: Partners want to preserve the special status and privilege that goes along with that. For this reason they play at being boy scouts, claiming in official announcements to respect competitors and to refuse favor at another's expense. This is just a show, a kind of silly game. No sooner do the noble statements pass from their lips, than the partners are behind closed doors, attacking competitors with vicious, underhanded comments.

Peat and Coopers are not the only ones that like to take potshots at each other. Partners at Touche Ross love to snipe at Arthur

Andersen, DH&S takes pleasure in belittling Touche, Ernst & Whinney gets nasty about Coopers, and Andersen looks down on everyone.

In some circles, especially a number of major Midwestern corporations, Andersen is considered to be the premier CPA firm. It does enjoy a reputation for competence and aggressiveness, expanding ahead of the pack into sophisticated tax and consulting services. That aggressiveness has, however, caused problems internally, resulting in the partners' revolt against former chairman Harvey Kapnick, Jr. and his subsequent resignation (October 1979) after nearly a decade of dynamic leadership. A flamboyant executive, Kapnick propelled Andersen deeper and deeper into nonaudit work, with consulting engagements accounting for more than 21 percent of the firm's revenues. When the chairman suggested separating the consulting arm from the audit practice in order to avoid a possible conflict with the Securities and Exchange Commission (which has shown increasing concern about the scope of practice by public accounting firms), Andersen partners cast him out, preferring to install the more conservative audit-oriented Duane Kullberg in the chief executive's office. Andersen has been busy ever since attempting to stabilize itself and to re-emphasize its traditional strengths while still developing nonaudit services at a measured pace.

The other Arthur in The Big Eight—Arthur Young—is a strange firm, the only real eccentric among The Big Eight. It appears to be stuffy, dated—somewhat like a once-grand hotel. It is still uncomfortable as a huckster and yearns for the good old days when things were done in a more gentlemanly fashion.

The firm gets high marks for its thorough audits, exacting standards, and total professionalism. Deep down it still clings to the old traditions, valuing prudence and perfectionism over today's zestier attributes of aggressiveness and innovation. The fortress mentality —the fear that others want nothing more than to destroy Arthur Young—appears to be strong in the firm's executive offices. When approached for this book, a senior staffer said, "There is a terrible espionage system in The Big Eight. People who pose as writers of books and articles are really spies."

Arthur Young competes in the modern marketplace with great reluctance. It does not like selling itself as a package good and it performs poorly at the task. Image-making is not its forte. Once again, office decor is revealing. The reception area at AY's executive suite is a drab-looking tacky little space that looks like a combination Howard Johnson's and Holiday Inn. No other Big Eight firm would show its face in public without a little makeup. Arthur Young is different: It does not appear to have a master plan for presenting itself to the world.

AY seemingly prefers to bury its head in the sand—to ignore the changes that have reshaped the profession in the past two decades and to follow its own piper. But it cannot. The demands of the marketplace are such that to remain in the exclusive circle, each Big Eight firm must achieve enormous growth year after year. Huge multinational corporations need huge multinational CPA firms. As clients expand, so too must their auditors, their tax advisers, their consultants. It is an indisputable rule of business that a company cannot stand in place: It must actively move ahead, or it will inevitably fall behind. Competitors will see to it.

"When, a few years ago, the code of ethics was changed to allow straightforward marketing by professionals, there came into play a new configuration of circumstances and activities that will reverberate throughout the accounting profession for years to come.

"For generations, concepts of probity have pervaded public accounting. Accountants were to be, not merely independent, but well beyond the fray of public quarrel or exposure. The sword of the CPA has always been independence, and, it was long felt, independence is compromised by public debate. And now comes marketing, the crux of which is visibility.

"Now, after all these generations, public accountants may advertise, may compete for one another's clients, may sing their own praises, may discuss publicly differences that once had been solely family affairs. This is how marketing has come to public accounting.

"No longer do accountants compete solely on the strength of their capabilities. Today, every accounting firm—and not just The Big Eight—competes with every other accounting firm in its market area for clients present and future, for attention, for exposure. Accounting firms compete with one another presentation for presentation, press release for press release, speech for speech, seminar for seminar, and, increasingly, ad for ad."*

With this in mind, AY has come kicking and screaming into the competitive arena, taking steps to assure its place among The Big Eight. It is beefing up its international presence, adopting some modern marketing tactics, and taking steps to dust off the old image. But one gets the feeling its heart is not in it. While Young's lanky, square-jawed chairman William Kanaga tries to muster up enthusiasm for the challenges of the future, it seems the firm would really be more comfortable with the advertising slogan penned for it by *Fortune:* "Arthur Young—Old Reliable."

All of the firms, regardless of their place on the aggressiveness curve, stress over and over again that quality service is deeply rooted in their history and tradition. Ernst & Whinney's well-respected head partner Ray Groves—who looks and holds himself like the accountant's accountant—stresses the quality theme more than any of his colleagues. It is hard to budge the man from the topic.

"There is no fast track here at Ernst & Whinney," he says. "New people can't come in here and expect to be made a partner quickly. You have to earn it through a record of consistent, top-quality work.

"We feel that we cannot simply say that we stand for quality and professionalism, because the market perceives that as dull. But the truth is that ours is a long tradition of fine quality."

Regardless of past performance, however, The Big Eight are faced with an increasingly difficult problem: the maintenance of quality controls in ever-larger firms with an ever-wider scope of practice. The senior partners' second biggest concern (after that of landing accounts) is to insure that the quality of their firms' practices remains high across the globe and throughout the various professional disciplines.

With tens of thousands of professionals serving hundreds of thousands of clients, this is no mean feat. It is also complicated by the fact that competition among the firms is forcing down fees and prompting management to seek shortcuts.

*Marcus, *op. cit.*

"It's not the lack of competition but possible excess competition that appears to be a problem to the public accounting profession today. Time and budget pressures frequently cause substandard auditing. Time pressures are often the result of unrealistic and unnecessary deadlines for completion of audits. However, there are substantial, sometimes destructive pressures to reduce the total time to complete audits, without regard to particular deadlines. One probable cause of time and budget pressures is excessive price competition, that is, excessive competition among firms to offer lower fees."*

Adds Arthur Young's Chester Vanatta, in a speech to the Financial Executives Institute: "Competition in any industry in our free enterprise system has its advantages and disadvantages. The advantages are obvious. If we compete by improving the quality of our service, than you are a beneficiary of that competition. If we compete, on the other hand, by tactics that are deleterious to our profession, then nobody benefits. And we've certainly seen some unusual things recently, such as giving away television sets for new accounts or dinners and theater tickets to staff members who bring in new clients. Times have certainly changed. It gives rise to questions as to what is now "professional," or "gentlemanly." These words have been used by public accountants, and to many of us have had real substance over the years. Perhaps these concepts are old-fashioned, and some of us just haven't gotten the message."

Says DH&S' Charles Steele, "My perception of the biggest problem of the 1980s is that in the competition for growth, there is a certain amount of competitive bidding. In the process, fees are going down. If that does not level off or stop at a reasonable level, we will lose our ability to hire and retain the kinds of people that we need.

"I hope the profession will be smart enough not to continue in a gas war to the extent that our finances are damaged." Steele, who speaks his mind freely and who is willing to admit what others in his position believe but will vent only in private, adds that "if fees are lower, we cannot motivate these bright, hardworking people to put in the grueling hours they put in to provide the kind of service

*Cohen Commission Report.

they give clients. It's a pressure-packed, demanding life: heavy travel, away from family, scurrying to service clients every time the phone rings. I was traveling 180 days last year (1979). We can't motivate people to do this if the money is not adequate.

"I admit that we have been partly responsible for the low-bidding problem. We are not angels here."

4. Avarice in Audit Land

"Professionalism has been completely thrown out in favor of the business aspects (time budgets and fees) in the practice of public accounting."
—From a survey of CPAs conducted for the Commission on Auditors' Responsibilities.

MUCH OF THE IMAGE-MAKING that preoccupies The Big Eight is designed to attract the lush audit accounts that dot the business landscape. This is the land of milk and honey—where The Big Eight turn for their bread-and-butter fees. Giant corporations pay from $1 million to $6 million each for annual audits; many retain the same firm year after year and fork up an additional 50 percent in fees for related services. The best audit accounts are like annuities: They just keep on paying off.

Audit work has made The Big Eight the behemoths they are today. When the Securities Act of 1933 mandated independent reviews of public companies, it gave birth to the modern accounting profession. With an act of Congress, virtually every major corporation in the land became a major consumer of auditing services. CPAs were enlisted to help carry out the sweeping financial reforms of the postdepression era. Charged with checking the accuracy of corporate financial statements, they were to protect the investing public from erroneous information. In principle, accountants were supposed to serve as a check and balance on management's natural inclination to put a pretty face on financial reports. This role as a built-in buffer between business and the public gave the CPAs the opportunity to extend their services and their influence throughout society.

"The former humble quill pusher with a green eyeshade today dominates the crossroads of economic movement, charged as he is by the Securities Act of 1933 to monitor the financial position of public companies as those are reported to the shareholders. He owes his not inconsiderable livelihood to reforms of the 1930s that sought to reassure an investing public bruised and disillusioned by the Great Crash. He audits transactions and verifies assets and liabilities; then, if all is well, he issues a report proclaiming that these corporate annual accounts of profit and loss conform to 'generally accepted accounting principles.' The company publishes this certificate in its annual report."*

Publicly owned companies do not decide whether or not to have an audit. There is no choice in the matter: That's the law. Big Eight partners will quip, now and then, that their paychecks are guaranteed by Uncle Sam—a sort of white collar welfare.

What clients can decide is who shall have the honor of doing the audit. For huge multinationals, the field is limited to the handful of CPA firms big enough to service them, mostly The Big Eight. Just which one gets the nod is not so simple, however, and is often the cause for extended deliberations and heavy promotional spending by the candidates. Lined up like finalists at a beauty pageant, these pillars of the financial world parade around trying to impress the judges. The problem is, they don't always know what it takes to win. Will the vote be based on talent, wit, intelligence, or sex appeal? How about a wink at the MC?

Although the securities laws never intended it to be this way, every client selects its auditors on a different basis. To many observers, the fact that corporations can choose and compensate their own "independent" auditors makes a mockery of the entire process. Although this seems true enough at first glance, there is simply no better way to accomplish a limited test of corporate financials. Bringing in the federal government to tackle the job, as some propose, is a nightmarish prospect. Imagine, Son of Post Office. Still, there is no denying that a goodly number of companies seek out auditors who will play ball, will be flexible, and will apply those accounting principles that make management look like heroes to the shareholders.

"Even if auditors reason by analogy properly, different auditors

*John Thackray, "Auditing the Auditors," in *The Nation*, May 14, 1977.

may neverthess conclude on occasion that different accounting principles are appropriate in similar circumstances. This has sometimes led to the selection of auditors on the basis of their acceptance or rejection of a particular accounting principle. Selection of auditors on this basis could result in a deterioration of accounting principles and a tendency for auditors to abstain from judgments they are competent to make. Such a result can only serve to erode users' confidence further, and modification is needed in the means by which independent auditors are appointed."*

Abe Briloff tells the story of a corporation shopping for an auditor:

"The president figured he'd make the rounds, asking CPA firms how much is two plus two. Invariably, they all said four. Finally, when he gets to the last firm on his list, he poses the question again: How much is two plus two? This time the response is more to his liking, 'What did you have in mind?' "

This kind of loose ball is played today but it is clearly the exception rather than the rule. The machinations of the 1960s and 1970s, which brought a cloud of bad publicity to the profession, have given way to tough new standards for audit work. Although long-time critics like Briloff insist that there is still a good deal of monkey business going on, there is little hard evidence of this. The impression one gets of Big Eight audit partners is that they are an honest lot, sobered by the controversies of recent years and determined to perform their jobs in an ethical and professional manner.

"Audit partners are under a tremendous amount of pressure," says a former Big Eighter, now a client controller. "They really live in fear—make that *terror*—that there will be an audit failure, their name will be caught up in the scandal, and they'll be accused of foul play on page one of the *Wall Street Journal.*"

This pervasive fear may bring auditors to accept an unwritten version of Briloff's somewhat overdramatic proposal to "impose a Nuremberg Code on each of us engaged in our professional pursuit, a code whereby we commit ourselves to implement a standard of fairness even though a contrary result could be subsumed under

*Cohen Commission Report.

GAAP. And we should adhere to the code in spite of superiors' orders or clients' directives."

Big Eight audit divisions are the ruling fiefdoms of the firms. They are enormous professional organizations in their own right, spanning the globe, servicing clients through a blurring range of cultures, languages, and monetary systems. Amazingly—dispersed and dislocated as they are—these divisions remain taut, coordinated, and tightly controlled. They can be whipped together on a moment's notice to perform with the precision of the Israeli army. This happens when a big account is up for grabs.

A prospective client on the loose brings out the best and the worst of The Big Eight. Witness the scramble to snare Caltex Petroleum, a large oil company jointly owned by Standard Oil of California and Texaco. Arthur Andersen, long the Caltex auditor, also served Texaco in this capacity. The increasing focus on audit integrity in the 1970s prompted the boards of both parent companies to seek new auditors for Caltex. Texaco and Standard Oil of California decided as a matter of policy that an auditor of a joint venture in which they were involved should not also be the auditor of one of the partners in the venture. As a result, Arthur Andersen got the boot.

"A change was sought because of the greater sensitivity about auditor independence both in the business community and the SEC," says Harold R. Wiggins, controller of Caltex. "We felt that since we had the choice, we were better off having a different auditor than Texaco.

"Not that we weren't pleased with Arthur Andersen. We were, in fact, quite happy with the quality of their work and their overall professionalism. The change was simply a matter of wanting to have a different auditor than Texaco."

Caltex is the kind of client that makes The Big Eight drool. A multibillion dollar giant, it is highly profitable, has conservative management likely to stick with its auditor for many years, and is in a key industry crowded with prospective clients. Establishing a larger beachhead in oil and gas is the best way to pick off fat new clients in this lucrative field.

Caltex batted its eyes at three Big Eighters: Peat, Coopers, and Ernst. All three boast a strong international network, a real plus for a client with Caltex's global operations. More and more, bidders with the strongest presence in all the world's commercial centers win the multinational accounts. For this reason, there is great pressure on The Big Eight to expand internationally by pouring money and talent into overseas offices or by merging with established firms in Europe, Asia, and the Americas.

"All of our business, except the headquarters office, is located outside the United States," Wiggins adds. "It is therefore imperative for us to work with an auditor that has a strong representation worldwide. That is why we asked the three candidates to propose for our account."

That's when The Big Eight's marketing operations really swing into action. The competition for a major audit account is waged on several fronts, involving dozens of partners and thousands of dollars. Most of the time, the money and effort go into producing a "proposal," which is simply a document used by a firm to sell itself. Running up to several hundred pages, the proposal outlines the client's audit needs, describes how the auditor will go about fulfilling them, and generally touts the CPA firm's "glowing reputation, wide experience, and uncompromising professionalism." It is not uncommon for $200,000 to go into a proposal, most of which is money down the drain. Even the fastest-growing Big Eighters lose more audit competitions than they win, and, what's more, there is good reason to believe that, formalities aside, accounts are won on the basis of personality contests, not weighty documents. New business teams fielded by the competitors to land accounts can have much more of an impact on the auditor selection process than the most thorough and comprehensive proposal. Just how The Big Eight audit partners and client management hit it off can be the decisive factor. It is all very human—clients pick people they want to work with.

Still, proposals do play a role in deciding some competitions and are a necessary formality in others. The most important thing is to prove to prospective clients that the auditor has made an effort to learn its business and to find out what it will take to provide good service. This is a crash course—a hectic immersion in the account's operations, visiting remote locations, meeting managers and employees, touring facilities, digesting an enormous amount of information. It is a Herculean task: nothing less than learning the ins and outs of a century-old firm in a matter of weeks. The fact that The Big Eight submit to this brand of torture with only a slim chance of picking up business reveals how hungry they are for audit accounts.

The Caltex competition was especially rough, waged as it was in a tight three-week schedule. Within that period, the firms had to assemble teams of partners both to be responsible for the account (engagement teams) and to supervise the presentation (presentation teams). Others had to outline the presentation, do field research on the client's operations, compile the resulting information, write the proposal, print it, deliver it, and then be prepared to make an oral presentation to the client's selection committee.

Peat, Marwick won the Caltex account, thanks, in good measure, to the leadership of Don Sloan. Then managing partner of the New York office, he was named client partner for the Caltex competition and was granted full responsibility for PMM's presentation. After the first meeting with Caltex management on April 24 to establish guidelines for the proposal, Sloan prepared a plan of attack and gave marching orders to key partners and managers throughout the Peat, Marwick organization. John Flack (New York participating manager) was asked to take charge of the day-to-day activities; Bill Cummins (New York engagement partner) was assigned to schedule and coordinate the project.

Central coordination is crucial because most of the work of a good proposal is done in the field. A tremendous amount of information about the prospective client must be gathered, organized, and relayed to the head office. For this reason, travel assignments were handed out immediately to PMM staffers and requests for information were sent to the firm's offices in Singapore, Kuala Lumpur, Bahrain, Johannesburg, Capetown, Tokyo, Sydney, and Nairobi. Partners from around the world found themselves jetting off to visit the far-flung Caltex facilities. Bob McGregor, head of Peat's Los Angeles office audit department, was, in the space of three days, asked to return to New York to serve as Caltex engagement partner and to board a plane heading for Singapore, Jakarta, and Tokyo.

When a Big Eight firm sets its sights on winning a new client, personal schedules are disrupted, routine work is cast aside, all parties are swept along in a team effort.

The mission of the field group is clear: to come up with the kinds of information that make for an impressive proposal. This means discovering the firm's audit concerns and trying to find creditable ways to improve the system. A substantial amount of homework is in order.

As raw data came in from Peat's local offices and its traveling partners, the administrative team in New York started piecing the puzzle together. By May 4, Sloan had decided on the structure of the printed presentation and on the use of charts, illustrations, and the like.

The proposal was designed in fourteen sections. Key segments covered the greater glory of Peat, Marwick International, the firm's oil industry experience, an overlay map of Peat and Caltex locations worldwide, a review of the audit scope, and a description of PMM's consulting and tax services.

Typically, this flurry of proposal activity proceeds with one eye on the client and one on the competition. Like commando units planning a raid, new business teams gather up-to-the-minute intelligence from strategic locations, checking on the competition's maneuvers in all key cities. Knowing what the others are up to—trying to find a weakness in their plan—is considered vital to a successful offense. As Peat's headquarters captains were drafting the proposal, intelligence reports alerted them that both Coopers and Ernst had already visited a number of Caltex facilities. It was clear that everyone was playing hard ball. The pressure mounted. Even before the final draft was inked, presenting partners rehearsed the oral presentation. Professional delivery is as important to a Big Eight sales team as it is to a Broadway actor. Performances are videotaped, played back before an independent panel, and critiqued as to smoothness, credibility, tone, style, flow, and eye contact. With a plum account hanging in the balance—one that can generate up to $50 million in total fees over a decade—nothing is left to chance.

Still, things can go wrong. By Friday, May 11, all the traveling partners were back in New York—a weary and exhausted bunch wiped out by multiple jet lag. Gathered together at 5:30 P.M. on Sunday, the scheduled time for reviewing a completed draft of the proposal, they had little to do but sit and wait. After all the jets and telexes and snap decisions and meetings and scheduling and rehearsals and writing and editing, a technical snafu threatened the timely completion of the project. With three days left to deadline, the word-processing system went on the blink, coughing up only brief passages of the report. It wasn't until 3:30 A.M. Monday that technology turned in the firm's favor, and a full text came spitting out of the machine. In spite of additional technical difficulties over the next few days, a finished report was delivered to Caltex headquarters by 5:00 P.M. on May 16.

After another week of rehearsals the Peat presentation team headed by Hanson and Sloan made the big pitch to Caltex at 2:00 P.M., Monday, May 21. It was payoff time. The grueling effort that had gone on behind the scenes now took the form of a masterly planned and executed presentation of a major CPA firm's professional capabilities, its understanding of a prospective client, and its well-thought-out strategy for servicing that client's diverse needs. The Caltex people were duly impressed. By May 25 Sloan received a confidential call informing him that PMM had been recommended to the Caltex audit committee.

"We were impressed both with Peat, Marwick, Mitchell's preparation and with their selection of an engagement partner," Wiggins says. "The proposal process gave us a chance to see the firm in operation, and we liked what we saw. Most important, we had confidence in their abilities. We did not feel that the problems Peat, Marwick had in the early 1970s made the firm unacceptable to Caltex. The people at the firm we would be dealing with were of the highest calibre. The firm's earlier troubles would not impact on us."

Peat's victory was especially sweet because Caltex is a rarity in the audit market in that it does not nickel-dime its CPAs. Officials at the oil company made it clear from the start that they weren't shopping for bargains. Fees would not be a factor: The new auditor would be compensated at the same general level as Arthur Andersen, but with an inflation kicker. At a time when Big Eight chairmen complain bitterly that they are forced by competitive bidding to accept marginally profitable business, a sporty outfit that still treats CPAs like professionals is a much-beloved client indeed.

Peat savored the victory but courted controversy by publishing a slick flyer recounting its version of the battle for the Caltex account. Looking much like a business-magazine story, the piece is headlined "Worldwide PMI Effort Wins Caltex Engagement—A behind-the-scenes look at the intense, complex process of winning a new client." The complaint is that Peat identified the losing contenders by name and took a swipe at their alleged shortcomings in terms of geographic representation.

This ruffled some prominent feathers. "For Peat, Marwick to try and belittle its competitors in print is a disgrace," barks Coopers' chief Norman Auerbach. "It's cheap, it's vulgar, and it's a sign of a troubled firm that's unsure of itself. It's one of the few big accounts they've won in ten years. Only those who believe that they can't compete on an equal footing feel the need to tear down others. We just took a big insurance account away from Peat, Marwick. We wouldn't think of naming Peat in any announcement of that."

For his part, Don Sloan insists that the flyer was produced solely for distribution within the Peat, Marwick organization. "I have no apologies for that article. It was for internal use only—a harmless device used to inform our people of a job well done and to give credit where credit is due. No one ever saw this as a promotion piece. It was for Peat, Marwick eyes only."

Asked why the flyer was distributed to a journalist, Sloan responds that "mistakes happen—we weren't trying to get it in the papers."

Bitch and bicker as they do about each other's policies and procedures, The Big Eight are remarkably similar in their auditing practices. It is safe to say that a client who substitutes the formal proposal process with good old "eenie, meenie, minie, mo" would not suffer one iota of difference. When it comes to auditing, Price Waterhouse and Touche Ross—two Big Eighters at the opposite ends of the spectrum—go about their work in much the same way. The distinctions they draw are more a matter of marketing tactics than substantive technical procedures.

What is an audit? What is this service for which The Big Eight

all the subsequent activities. Ideally, the audit scope must be wide enough to cover all aspects of the company's operations that can materially affect the accuracy of its financial reporting without being so comprehensive as to result in unduly burdensome fees. The call is for a delicate balance, one that will provide the users of financial reports with reasonable assurance and that can also be justified in cost/benefit terms.

Defining the audit scope is not a hit-or-miss affair. There's more to it than checking a bit here, a bit there, and an extra this or that for good measure. Modern auditing is based on rules, laws, and theories of its own. Much is now computer-based, with complex programs sizing up a behemoth the size of Exxon, isolating its audit risks, planning the audit scope, and automatically performing many of the audit calculations. Add to this the CPAs experience—his human instinct and professional know-how—and the full dimension of the audit comes into play.

As in most practice areas, the great bulk of the audit is performed by staff accountants. These underlings—most of whom are green recruits a year or two out of college—do 90 percent of the interminable grunt work that goes into an audit. Their days are spent much like those of the squinty-eyed bookkeepers in Dickens' novels—the old handwritten ledgers replaced by computer printouts. Poring over reports, checking and rechecking calculations, they are near robots, forced to adhere to an exacting audit plan and to perform a long list of set chores. The Young Turks who turn to accounting with dreams of fiscal wheeling and dealing quickly take their leave after a few months on the audit staff. Some depart in weeks.

"It's no joke—I went through a severe depression after about ten days or so on the job," says a former Price Waterhouse staff auditor now with a small CPA firm. "The work is for cretins. You don't get an inch of room to apply your own ideas. The best way to describe it is like painting by numbers. I'm no Picasso but I'm not seven years old either. I don't want to be told what color to paint a tree. Give me a break!

"I turned to Price Waterhouse to gain entree into big business, to be in the thick of it. So where did it get me? I had less action than a gas station bookkeeper. To make it on a Big Eight audit staff, you have to be willing to put your brains on the back burner for a couple of years."

Commenting on this attitude, a Touche Ross audit partner says, "The bellyachers will always bellyache, but that's probably healthy. It shakes out the ones who don't really want to be auditors and leaves us with the best of the crop. The young staffers must conform to the system; we can't change it for them. I get palpitations just thinking of these kids going off and doing an audit the way they want without following the plan. You know what would happen? The audit would cost six times the projection, it would never be completed, and there'd be no assurance whatsoever about the company's financials. Like it or not, an audit is a team effort, and each player has to do his assigned job. No one can play whatever position they choose. If that happened in baseball, there'd be nine pitchers."

The next level up on the audit staff hierarchy are the "seniors." Performing as low-ranking field officers, the seniors supervise the work of staff or junior accountants, participate in the audit planning, and do a considerable amount of audit work. The senior keeps the grunts in line, defines for them the objective of the audit, and makes certain that the engagement moves along on schedule and according to the master plan. He also serves as the eyes and ears of the responsible partner, alerting him of any difficulties in performing the audit or in protecting the accounting firm's professional standing.

Managers (or supervisors) claim the next rung on the organizational ladder. Most are five-to-seven-year veterans of the firms and are good bets to make partner. Their job is to manage the audit on a day-to-day basis, planning the scope, dividing up the work load, assigning the appropriate staffers, checking the progress, and keeping the work on target and on schedule.

The role of the top man or woman on an audit—that of the partner in charge—is limited to providing executive direction for the work, approving the audit scope as well as the ultimate findings, meeting with client management, signing the auditor's opinion, and billing the client. He retains full responsibility for the audit regardless of where in the world the activities are being conducted. The partner in charge rarely gets involved in the performance of audit procedures except to review critical staff work and to sort out major problems. This makes all the sense in the world: Clients don't want $120-per-hour partners playing around with pocket calculators, and the audit firms themselves cannot afford to have their most valuable resources bogged down in Mickey Mouse work. The partners are there to provide leadership, assure quality control, get the job done, protect the firm's reputation, and keep the client happy.

Even partners are not, however, the stars of today's audits. The introduction of hard-sell marketing tactics to big-league public accounting has prompted The Big Eight to give brand-name status to their auditing systems. In true Procter & Gamble fashion, they have pasted catchy little labels on their audit procedures. Like any number of shampoos or toothpastes, the goal is to achieve greater brand identification and market share. The names have a futuristic ring, evoking images of speed, accuracy, and technical prowess.

Coopers & Lybrand has so many accounting and auditing time-sharing programs in-house that it publishes a directory just to keep track of them. Just how complex these computer programs can be —and how valuable they are to The Big Eight and their clients— is evidenced by C&L's LEASEPAK program (as described in the firm's directory):

The Financial Accounting Standards Board Statement of Financial Accounting Standards No. 13 *Accounting for Leases,* November 1976, establishes standards of financial accounting and reporting for leases by lessees and lessors. The new accounting and reporting requirements involve computations that differ considerably, both in number and complexity, from those previously required.

The LEASEPAK programs perform the computations required by FASB Statement No. 13, *Accounting for Leases.* These programs provide management with answers to questions such as:

How will the including in the financial statements of assets qualifying as capital leases affect the consolidated balance sheet and statement of income and retained earnings?

What are the asset and accumulated amortization balances of leased property under capital leases by major classes?

What are the current and noncurrent obligations under capital leases?

What are the future minimum lease payments under all noncancelable leases?

What does the present value of net minimum lease payments for capital leases amount to after deducting estimated executory costs (taxes, maintenance, and insurance) and imputed interest?

What is the total interest and depreciation expense for all capital leases?

How will the requirements affect budgeting and planning for the future?

Other C&L programs include Oil Refiner Cost Reports for Department of Energy (DOEREF), Multi-Level Financing Calculations (MORTG$AG), Random Sample Generator (RANDG$), and Inventory Analysis (INSAM$).

Most of The Big Eight have similar programs and all rely on computers to handle a growing share of the work load.

"I think it's safe to say that the basic audit function doesn't differ much from firm to firm," says Arch Schmeiser, an accounting fellow serving with the SEC's Chief Accountant's Office. "They try to draw distinctions, but there are really more similarities than differences."

The promotional razzmatazz aside, auditing a major corporation is a complex process. A closer look at one of the firm's audit techniques is revealing. At Touche Ross, the job is broken down into three major phases involving a total of about twenty key interrelated procedures. Before the audit even begins, the CPAs must define a number of key terms as they apply to the engagement at hand. These serve as guidelines for the audit:

Auditability: "The existence of an audit engagement and reliable sources of evidence, together with client personnel who act in good faith and with integrity."*

Put simply, this means that the CPAs must feel confident that the client is auditable. Poor financial recordkeeping or sloppy internal controls may make it impossible to audit the client with any measure

*Touche Ross Audit Manual.

of accuracy. Auditors do not creat financial controls, nor do they set up bookkeeping systems. On the contrary, they rely on these internal mechanisms to accomplish the audit. Controls are checked to test their reliability, but they are not built from the ground up. All The Big Eight firms have consulting arms that do design and implement financial controls, but this is not the work of the auditor.

Another test of auditability is the integrity of client management. Contrary to charges made by the profession's critics, Big Eighters will not accept engagements where there is ample evidence that the client is engaged in fraudulent activities and is using illegal tactics to deceive the IRS and the SEC or the investing public. A quality audit is difficult enough with a cooperative client; dealing with devious parties greatly increases the odds of audit failure. This means that the auditor is more likely to sign off on a set of books that do not represent the client's true financial status. For auditors, this can lead to lawsuits, problems with the SEC, and, most important, damage to their reputations.

"We frequently turn down engagements because they appear to be nonauditable," says Joe Connor. "Critics charge that big accounting firms will take any large audits that come their way, but that's not true at all. The partners of this firm would never let the Price Waterhouse reputation get damaged because some dishonest corporation wanted to pull the wool over the public's eyes. No one could ever pay a fee big enough to tempt us in that regard."

This attitude—which appears to be genuine—applies throughout The Big Eight. Even the king-size audit clients, the likes of General Motors and General Foods, account for less than one percent of the auditors' revenues. Smaller corporations, which are the ones more likely to be involved in questionable activities, can account for less than 1/100 of one percent of the auditors' total fees. Certainly only a fool would jeopardize a sterling reputation for a few grains of salt.

Not that every Big Eight client is purer than the driven snow. No way. Theirs is a mixed bag of accounts, including a healthy helping of fast talkers and shady operatives who approach the law much the way a tennis ace toes the base line. But the outright con artists have a hard time attracting The Big Eight auditors unless they cleverly disguise their true intentions. They must pass the auditability test, and the standards have become much tougher what with the scandals of the past two decades. At Touche Ross, three factors will result in failure of the test:

A computer system which does not provide sufficient controls and "audit trail" to audit a sample of transactions by examining source information.

Management's refusal to allow the examination of significant documents, such as the minutes of the board of directors' meetings, to corroborate their representations.

Finding evidence of management intentionally failing to record a material transaction.

Once the pre-audit questions are answered—providing the client is not rejected—the audit begins in earnest. At Touche Ross, phase one involves the design of the audit approach based on information gathered about the client, including an evaluation of its internal controls. Auditors must gain some familiarity with the client's business in order to identify the key types of transactions and their importance in overall financial reporting.

They must also determine how these transactions are processed and accounted for. Much of this information gathering is accomplished through interviews with client employees. Sometimes the auditors learn more or less than they need to.

"A few employees may think that this is a good opportunity to grumble about their supervisors; others may be reluctant to admit that they do not work strictly 'according to the book' if they think such admissions may be used against them; some may not think to explain certain special types of transactions because they instictively take the attitude that 'everybody knows about that.' We must be both tactful and firm in keeping the interview in the right direction and on the right subject."*

Much of the preparatory work is dispensed with when the audit involves an existing client. The CPAs already know the firm, understand its operations, and can therefore move quickly into the heart

*Touche Ross Audit Manual.

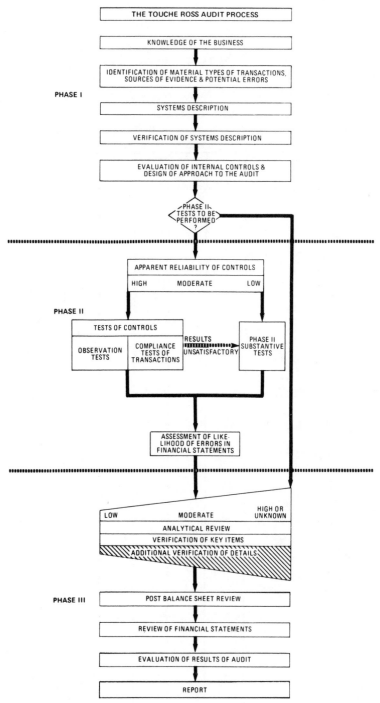

THE TOUCHE ROSS AUDIT PROCESS

KNOWLEDGE OF THE BUSINESS

IDENTIFICATION OF MATERIAL TYPES OF TRANSACTIONS, SOURCES OF EVIDENCE & POTENTIAL ERRORS

PHASE I

SYSTEMS DESCRIPTION

VERIFICATION OF SYSTEMS DESCRIPTION

EVALUATION OF INTERNAL CONTROLS & DESIGN OF APPROACH TO THE AUDIT

PHASE II TESTS TO BE PERFORMED?

APPARENT RELIABILITY OF CONTROLS

HIGH   MODERATE   LOW

PHASE II

TESTS OF CONTROLS

OBSERVATION TESTS | COMPLIANCE TESTS OF TRANSACTIONS

RESULTS UNSATISFACTORY

PHASE II SUBSTANTIVE TESTS

ASSESSMENT OF LIKELIHOOD OF ERRORS IN FINANCIAL STATEMENTS

LOW   MODERATE   HIGH OR UNKNOWN

ANALYTICAL REVIEW

VERIFICATION OF KEY ITEMS

ADDITIONAL VERIFICATION OF DETAILS

PHASE III

POST BALANCE SHEET REVIEW

REVIEW OF FINANCIAL STATEMENTS

EVALUATION OF RESULTS OF AUDIT

REPORT

TOUCHE ROSS AUDIT PROCESS
ILLUSTRATIVE WORKING PAPER No 1 (1 OF 2)

SCHEDULE _____
PREPARED BY _____
                    DATE
REVIEWED BY _____

IDENTIFICATION OF TRANSACTION TYPES AND
SOURCES OF EVIDENCE

MATERIAL TRANSACTION TYPES	AVAILABLE SOURCES OF EVIDENCE					
	PROCESSED BY FORMAL SYSTEMS					OTHER
	BOOKS RECORDS REPORTS	SALES BILLINGS RECEIVABLES COLLECTIONS	PURCHASES PAYABLE PAYMENTS	WAGES AND SALARIES	COST AND INVENTORY RECORDS	
SALES:						
1 PRODUCTS		✓			✓	
2 SCRAP		✓				
3 MARKETABLE SECURITIES						BROKERS VOUCHERS & STATEMENTS
4 FIXED ASSETS						VOUCHERS, DOCUMENTS & MINUTES
COLLECTIONS:						
5 ACCOUNTS RECEIVABLE		✓				
PURCHASES:						
6 RAW MATERIALS			✓		✓	
7 FIXED ASSETS			✓			MINUTES, BUDGETS, VOUCHERS & DOCUMENTS
8 SERVICES AND SUPPLIES			✓			
9 MARKETABLE SECURITIES			✓			MINUTES, BROKERS VOUCHERS & STATEMENTS
PAYMENTS						
10 ACCOUNTS PAYABLE AND NON PAYROLL ACCRUALS			✓			
11 PAYROLL AND RELATED ACCRUALS			✓	✓		
MOVEMENT OF INVENTORY:						
12 RAW MATERIALS TO WORK-IN-PROCESS					✓	
13 WORK-IN-PROCESS TO FINISHED GOODS					✓	

DIAGRAM OF PHASE I

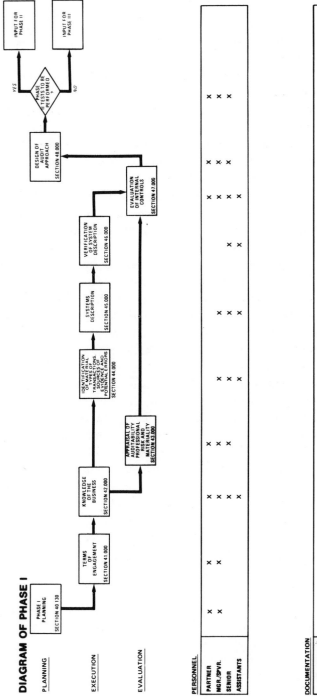

PLANNING

| PHASE I PLANNING SECTION 40.130 |

EXECUTION

| TERMS OF ENGAGEMENT SECTION 41.000 | → | KNOWLEDGE OF THE BUSINESS SECTION 42.000 | → | IDENTIFICATION OF MATERIAL TYPES OF TRANSACTIONS, SOURCES OF EVIDENCE AND POTENTIAL ERRORS SECTION 44.000 | → | SYSTEMS DESCRIPTION SECTION 45.000 | → | VERIFICATION OF SYSTEM DESCRIPTION SECTION 46.000 |

| APPRAISAL OF AUDITABILITY PROFESSIONAL RISK AND MATERIALITY SECTION 43.000 |

EVALUATION

| EVALUATION OF INTERNAL CONTROLS SECTION 47.000 |

| DESIGN OF AUDIT APPROACH SECTION 48.000 |

PHASE II TESTS TO BE PERFORMED?

YES — INPUT FOR PHASE II

NO — INPUT FOR PHASE III

PERSONNEL

	TERMS OF ENGAGEMENT	KNOWLEDGE OF BUSINESS	APPRAISAL OF AUDITABILITY	IDENTIFICATION	SYSTEMS DESCRIPTION	VERIFICATION	EVALUATION OF INTERNAL CONTROLS	DESIGN OF AUDIT APPROACH
PARTNER	X	X	X				X	X
MGR./SPVR.	X	X	X	X	X		X	X
SENIOR		X	X	X	X	X	X	X
ASSISTANTS		X		X	X	X	X	X

DOCUMENTATION

AUDIT PROGRAM		X			X			X
MEMORANDUM		X	X		X		⊗	X
DETAILED W/P	X			⊗	X	⊗	X

of the audit. This is one reason why long-term clients can be more profitable.

The Touche Ross engagement partner uses the phase one period to gear up his own team. He obtains staff allocations, informs overseas offices of work that will be done in their markets, and prepares time and cost budgets. The latter is a tricky business. Budgeting is vital to completing the audit on time and within the bounds of the set fee. The Big Eight are, after all, in this game to make money. Black ink will be on the bottom line only if the man-hours, travel bills, telephone calls, duplicating, computer time, and related costs do not exceed the fee. Simple as this sounds, it is easy for a big audit to get out of hand, to lose direction, to pile up tremendous bills that far exceed the sum being paid for it. With many audits now being let on the basis of competitive bids, fees are dropping. Lowballers —those firms willing to accept new business for slim profits or to even lose money in the early years—are forcing The Big Eight to shave margins on many audits. With little padding built into the fee, it doesn't take much to put the engagement into the red. Five hundred staffers working on a big audit in fifty offices across the globe generate expenses at an alarming rate.

Budgeting the amount of time audit team members can spend performing various procedures, and controlling the number of client facilities they may visit, helps to keep the audit moving along briskly and profitably. The problem is that audits are supposed to be planned and performed on the basis of accuracy and thoroughness, not the accounting firm's profit goals. And although The Big Eight vehemently deny that they ever limit or rush an engagement in order to make budget, there is little doubt that they do just that. The pressure to keep the job in the black—to get everything done within the established time frame—is relentless. Something has to give, and that something is often the quality of the work.

The Cohen Commission found:

Although there are other factors, the Commission believes that excessive time pressures are one of the most pervasive causes of audit failure. These excessive time pressures stem from a number of sources, some in the business environment and some within public accounting firms. They appear in a number of forms, some of which may seem to reflect other causes but which are ultimately traceable to time pressure. The term *time pressure* denotes both influences and attempts to reduce audit time. Time pressure may be the result of an effort to reduce the total hours devoted to an audit regardless of when the work is done. It may also be the indirect result of the imposition of a deadline date for completion. Of course, there are always some time pressures in an audit. An audit is conducted in a business environment; the service is performed and paid for by profit-making entities. Rational considerations of economy and efficiency will dictate attention to reasonable limits on the time expended in performing the audit without, however, impairing the quality of assurance desired and provided. The concern here is on *excessive* time pressures, conditions under which the reasonable concern with efficiency is exaggerated to the point that the quality of the audit is adversely affected.

The Cohen Commission report draws the picture of a partner "supervising fifteen or twenty engagements, many with identical year-ends, working considerable overtime, unable to find adequate time to review work papers, and faced with several crucial decisions, some of which were ultimately made incorrectly."

Even more damaging, Cohen found that 58 percent of the CPAs responding to a survey admitted having signed off on audit steps when they had not really performed the work:

When a budgeting system induces behavior such as signing off for work not performed, or performing work but not recording the time for billing purposes, the budgeting system is producing conduct that is the opposite of the goals of a budgeting system and is inconsistent with professional auditing standards.

Going a step further, the commission traced reasons why audit staffers would neglect their responsibilities, violating professional ethics for the sake of time budgets:

The ability to meet time budgets is believed by the majority of the respondents to the Commission survey to be necessary for an individual to advance within a firm. The survey shows that the auditor's ability to use audit techniques to keep time charges low, his ability to meet time budgets, and the quantity of work produced, as measured in billable hours, are considered very important to personal success.

Good budgeting strikes the delicate balance between quality and profit. It ranks among the most crucial phase-one procedures.

Also of tremendous importance is the evaluation of the client's internal controls. Well-managed corporations do not rely on auditors alone to determine that fiscal transactions are being properly handled and recorded. They have intricate control systems in place throughout the organization, checking and rechecking cash, credit, sales, profit and loss measurements on a regular basis. This is vital for keeping the firm on target businesswise and for spotting internal fraud, waste, or emerging problems of many varieties. Financial controls are an indispensable management tool.

The quality of internal controls, however, varies across the lot. Some are excellent; others are mostly window dressing. Where controls are good, the auditor's job is measurably easier. He can rely on the controls as the foundation of the audit. In evaluating internal controls, the auditor looks for evidence that they can be relied upon to prevent, detect, and correct potential errors. Controls are grouped into three major categories:

Those that insure completeness of the transaction processing and recording.

Those that insure proper authorization for all transactions.

Those that insure accuracy. Transactions must be properly valued, classified, summarized, and recorded in the correct accounting period.

In phase two of the Touche Ross audit process, the team assesses the likelihood of errors in the client's financial statements. This is achieved by performing tests of controls. These tests are of two types: observation, and compliance tests of transactions. Observation tests are performed where there is no documentary evidence of the performance of a control.

Examples of controls that can be subjected to observation would include segregation of duties, controls over the distribution of wages, the opening of mail, the punching of clock cards, physical controls over inventory, the quality and timeliness of internal management reports, and the reconciliation of control accounts.

DIAGRAM OF PHASE II

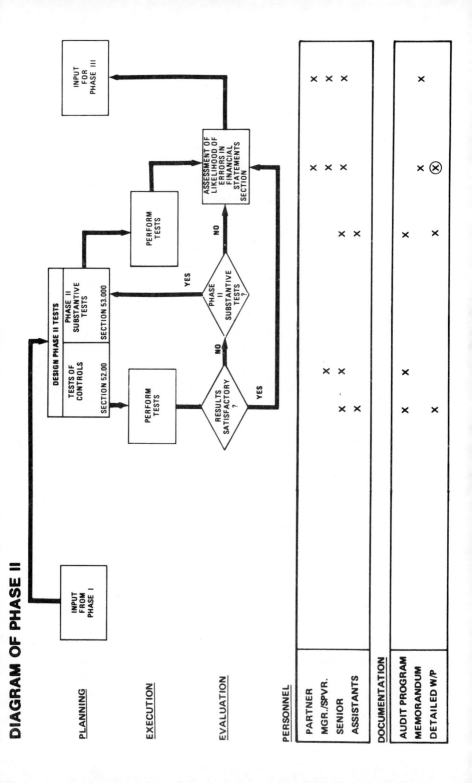

PLANNING

EXECUTION

EVALUATION

| INPUT FROM PHASE I |

DESIGN PHASE II TESTS	
TESTS OF CONTROLS	PHASE II SUBSTANTIVE TESTS
SECTION 52.00	SECTION 53.000

PERFORM TESTS

RESULTS SATISFACTORY ?

PHASE II SUBSTANTIVE TESTS ?

PERFORM TESTS

ASSESSMENT OF LIKELIHOOD OF ERRORS IN FINANCIAL STATEMENTS SECTION

INPUT FOR PHASE III

NO

YES

NO

YES

PERSONNEL				
PARTNER		X	X	X
MGR./SPVR.	X	X	X	X
SENIOR	X	X	X	X
ASSISTANTS	X	X	X	X

DOCUMENTATION				
AUDIT PROGRAM		X	X	
MEMORANDUM	X	X	X	X
DETAILED W/P	X	X	X	⊗

Where there is documentary evidence, compliance tests are performed. In designing a compliance test of transactions, the auditors must define what will constitute a compliance deviation for that particular test. For example, if a test is being made of the control which matches shipping documents to sales invoices and checks that all goods shipped have been billed, the definition of a compliance deviation will include a lack of evidence of the check, both an unmatched shipping document and a shipping document matched to the wrong sales invoice, since in each case the control would not have operated reliably.

If the tests indicate that the controls are in fact reliable, the auditor will conclude that the likelihood of errors in the financial statements is low. If the controls prove to be unreliable, the initial evaluation of them must be corrected and the audit scope adjusted accordingly. More substantive tests will have to be performed.

All of the work performed in phase two of the Touche Ross system is directed at making a sound assessment of the likelihood of errors in the financial statements. The phase concludes with the making of this assessment and with a preliminary report to client management identifying areas where improvements can or should be made in the effectiveness or the efficiency of the firm's system. It is particularly important to make management aware of serious weaknesses in internal controls if a large number of errors are occurring. Sophisticated audit clients look to The Big Eight for this kind of advice. Top managers see the audit as more than a mandatory compliance process but also as a way to obtain expert information on the firm's internal controls.

"We get our money's worth," is the way one *Fortune* 100 controller rates his Big Eight auditor. "They can tell us things we just wouldn't see on our own. I view the audit as a wonderful opportunity for annually updating and improving our controls."

Adds John Mullarkey, a TR audit partner, "Sometimes we have to enlighten clients about their own businesses. We'll say something like 'Excuse me, but you say you're making all sorts of money, but have you ever noticed you don't have a dime? Why? Yes, there are sales being made but people aren't paying. Bad credit risks are being accepted, invoices not sent—whatever.' We tell them what they need to know."

DIAGRAM OF PHASE III

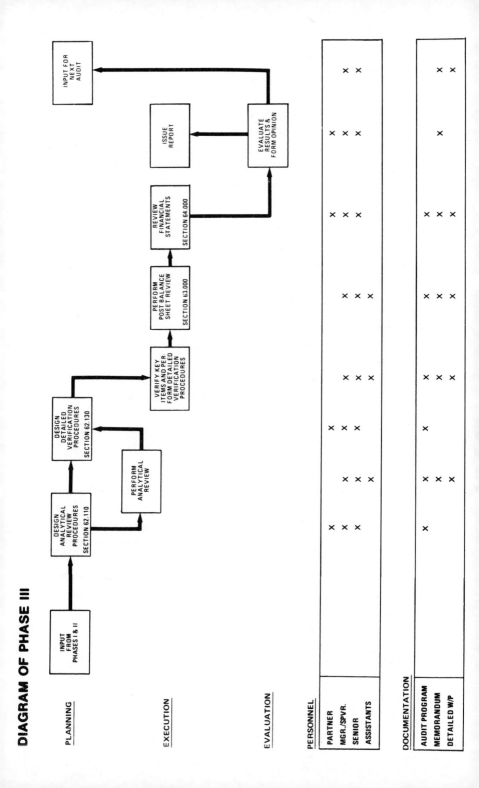

PLANNING

INPUT FROM PHASES I & II

DESIGN ANALYTICAL REVIEW PROCEDURES
SECTION 62.110

DESIGN DETAILED VERIFICATION PROCEDURES
SECTION 62.130

EXECUTION

PERFORM ANALYTICAL REVIEW

VERIFY KEY ITEMS AND PERFORM DETAILED VERIFICATION PROCEDURES

PERFORM POST BALANCE SHEET REVIEW
SECTION 63.000

REVIEW FINANCIAL STATEMENTS
SECTION 64.000

EVALUATION

ISSUE REPORT

EVALUATE RESULTS & FORM OPINION

INPUT FOR NEXT AUDIT

PERSONNEL

	Design Analytical Review	Perform Analytical Review	Design Detailed Verification	Verify Key Items	Post Balance Sheet	Review Financial Statements	Evaluate Results	Input for Next Audit
PARTNER	X		X			X	X	
MGR./SPVR.	X	X	X	X	X	X	X	X
SENIOR	X	X	X	X	X	X	X	X
ASSISTANTS		X		X	X			

DOCUMENTATION

	Design Analytical Review	Perform Analytical Review	Design Detailed Verification	Verify Key Items	Post Balance Sheet	Review Financial Statements	Evaluate Results	Input for Next Audit
AUDIT PROGRAM	X		X	X	X	X		
MEMORANDUM	X		X	X	X	X	X	X
DETAILED W/P		X		X	X	X		X

Phase three of the Touche Ross audit involves a review of audit evidence and procedures conducted in the first two phases and a series of decisions as to the extent of additional testing required. The findings of the earlier phases have a great bearing on the amount of work required in phase three. The overall objective here is to be able to reach an appropriate opinion on the client's financial statements.

Nine specific audit objectives must be satisfied before the audit is complete:

Existence:
All recorded amounts are valid.
All amounts are recorded.
Ownership—assets are owned.

Valuation:
Recorded amounts are accurate.
Changes of circumstances are reflected in the accounts.
Classification—amounts are recorded in the correct accounts.
Cutoff—amounts are recorded in the proper period.
Mechanical Accuracy—amounts are correctly posted and summarized.
Adequate Disclosure—all pertinent information is set forth in accordance with appropriate accounting principles and statutory requirements.

After a final verification of all audit areas, including key items that require intensive scrutiny, the auditors issue an opinion and a full report on their findings. The engagement partner has full responsibility for the report although he may simply check the work of subordinates.

To insure some measure of quality control, the firms often build in redundant checks on the work of each audit-team member. At Touche, for example, each person's work during an audit engagement is subject to a review by his supervisor or higher staff level. In many cases, a second partner checks the work of the engagement partner. This serves as an added technical review and also dissuades the engagement partner from taking a lax approach to long-term accounts.

In spite of its technical grounding and highly structured format, a major audit demands a great deal of subjective decision-making. Good auditors bring judgment, experience, and intuition to the job.

Precisely because an audit is a sampling of transactions rather than a blanket review, judgment comes into play at the outset—the very design of the audit scope. Just where to train the audit spotlight is a decision based partly on established principles, partly on instinct.

Much the way a master detective can swiftly isolate the key suspects in a crime, top auditors can deftly identify the categories of transactions that are integral to the overall veracity of the financial statements.

A key concern in setting the audit scope and in performing the subsequent tests is the concept of "materiality." Put simply, this holds that the auditor can limit his concern to those items that will likely influence the users of financial statements. In other words, errors or inconsistencies will be discovered in every audit. Just how far the auditor goes in tracing them down to their origins, and just how much he allows them to influence his overall opinion depends on whether or not they are deemed to be material.

The difficulty in applying this criterion is that materiality must be measured differently for various users of financial statements. Stockholders, the largest group of users, are most interested in measures of profits, the ability to pay dividends or to generate cash for reinvestment. These are the factors which often have the greatest impact on stock prices. Banks and others providing short-term credit use financial statements to measure liquidity and the coverage of debt. Secured long-term creditors look to financial statements to see if the creditor can generate sufficient funds to make interest and principal payments.

The failure to uncover material errors can leave the auditor open to legal claims by users of financial statements who act on the basis of erroneous information and subsequently suffer losses that can be traced to this. The most common form of litigation against The Big Eight is, in fact, class-action suits brought by corporate stockholders claiming stock market losses attributable to audit failures. While most of these suits are unsuccessful, the firms are extremely wary of this exposure. With suits running in the hundreds of millions of dollars, a single major loss here could potentially wipe out a Big Eight firm, extending beyond its liability insurance and seizing its capital.

"Most of The Big Eight are organized as partnerships," says Richard Murray, Touche Ross's general counsel. "There is no immunity against the assets of the partners. If a judgment is entered against the firm that our liability insurance can't cover, the partnership assets would be at risk. First to go would be the $110 million capitalization of the Touche Ross partnership. If that were not enough, the personal assets of the partners would be at risk. Plaintiffs could force the firm to liquidate its assets. Such a tremendous settlement does not seem likely, but the threat of bankruptcy does exist."

Just to be safe, The Big Eight have between $60 million and $100 million liability insurance each, with the individual policies actually paying double the face amount if the extra coverage should be required. But the Supreme Court's landmark "Hochfelder" decision confirmed the difficulty of winning a massive suit against a public accounting firm. In the case of *Ernst & Ernst** v. *Olga Hochfelder* (March 30, 1976), the court held that "scienter—the intent to deceive, manipulate, or defraud—is a necessary requirement of any private action for damages under the fraud provisions of the federal securities laws. Thus, independent auditors are apparently liable to damaged individuals only when it can be proved that they intentionally performed a faulty audit or certified incorrect information. Independent auditors would not be liable for negligent or incomplete audits which result in damages to innocent investors relying on certified corporate financial statements."**

The firms also use the concept of materiality as a legal defense for their audit procedures. For the most part, an item or group of items that will affect the financial statements by 5 percent or more are deemed to be material. But errors of less consequence can qualify as well. "Generally, the materiality factor for individual substantive tests will be less than the total materiality guideline established for

---

*The predecessor of Ernst & Whinney.
**Metcalf Report.

the measurement base. This is because errors of less than material amounts in different account balances or transaction streams may accumulate and exceed the materiality guidelines. For example, if our materiality guideline is $50,000, we could not accept errors of $49,000 in each of four account balances, even though the error in each account balance is immaterial, because the total exceeds materiality. We would reduce the $50,000 for individual substantive tests to a lower number on a judgmental basis."*

The absence of hard-and-fast rules gives The Big Eight more leeway in defining the audit scope—and therefore greater freedom in limiting audits to accommodate time pressures—but also confuses the issue of legal responsibility. The need to balance thoroughness with quickness, professionalism with profitability, makes The Big Eight audit partners a jittery bunch. Decisions on audit scope and materiality—often made under pressure and without the time for careful deliberation—can damage personal and firm-wide reputations, jeopardize professional standings, and cause financial losses resulting from legal actions.

In the course of his work, every engagement partner leaves a trail of decisions that can come to haunt him at any moment. Those prone to second-guessing are known to start lunches with an "auditor's cocktail": a Librium and a bloody mary.

"You know the old B-movie scene where the guy wakes up in the middle of the night, drenched in a cold sweat, screaming aloud about some nightmare he's had," says one Big Eight audit partner. "Well, that really happens to me. I'm frankly worried all the time that I might have made a mistake on this or that decision. Although I can live with the fear under most circumstances, at night it turns into sheer terror. I guess that's because I dream about the possible repercussions of making a really bad mistake.

"The thing of it is that people expect auditors to be perfect. We're expected to know things no other mortal would ever be held accountable for. Let's take just one of the tricky parts of a *Fortune* 100 audit. Let's say the company's a manufacturer whose products are warranteed for two years. What will warranty claims cost the firm

---

*Touche Ross Audit Manual.

in future years? Will they threaten the corporation's very survival? It is possible! With established products we can look to performance to date and make a fairly accurate guestimate. But what about new products? A small amount of claims may not be material, but what if it is an indication of an avalanche of claims. Who on earth can tell? Only the auditor is expected to!"

"Accounting results—the financial statements—cannot be more accurate or reliable than the underlying accounting measurement methods permit. For example, no one, including accountants, can foresee the results of many uncertain future events. To the extent that the accuracy of an accounting presentation is dependent on an unpredictable future event, the accounting presentation will be inaccurate. The audited accounting presentation can be no more accurate, for the auditor cannot add certainty where it does not exist. . . .

"Uncertainty about the outcome of future events affects the measurement of both an entity's earnings for a particular period and the measurement of its assets and liabilities at a particular date. . . .

"For example, assets normally include accounts receivable, for which an estimate of the amount that may be uncollectible is required. Liabilities often include estimates of claims to be paid under warranties and similar obligations. Many matters that affect financial statements cannot be resolved until some future date. Lawsuits must await judicial determination or settlement, and assets in a foreign location may be jeopardized by political unrest or a threat of expatriation. The resolution of such uncertainties must await the outcome of future events, but financial statements are traditionally issued on a periodic basis, at least annually. Financial statement amounts often must be determined on the basis of the best estimates that management can make at the time."*

In an excellent article on the complexities of corporate audits, James K. Loebbecke, former director of auditing programs for Touche Ross, writes, "Audits are constructed like icebergs: What is visible—the auditors' report—is a minor portion of the total bulk. . . . But few nonauditors realize the extent of the activities required for the auditor to deliver his opinion.

*Cohen Commission Report.

"From the auditor's perspective, an audit is a method by which he becomes reasonably satisfied, at an acceptable cost, that the economic events that represent the client's operations have been properly reflected in its financial statements. The balance between reasonable satisfaction and acceptable cost is important. For although the auditor must perform all work necessary to reach a proper opinion, there are economic limits to the scope of his work. Thus a series of judgments must be made about trade-offs between audit costs and the valuable information to be obtained."*

Clearly, the auditors' favorite theme is that the end product of all their work is by no means a guarantee of the corporate financials. In one of the classic contradictions in American business, The Big Eight insist that their audit services are indispensable to the orderly functioning of the economic system, but in the same breath deny any responsibility for the accuracy of the statements they audit. In effect, they say that audits are essential for the users of financial statements, but that the users had better not rely on the auditor's opinion as the gospel. Reading between the lines, the message is clear: Reports are better than having nothing, but don't bet your last dollar on them.

"The concepts of reasonable satisfaction and acceptable cost also give a clue to what an audit is not," Loebbecke adds. "It is not a guarantee that there are no misrecorded transactions, incorrect accounting judgments, omitted disclosures, or committed frauds. However, the chances of these conditions existing in a material amount are greatly minimized through the audit process. They are minimized to the point where only a small fraction of all auditor's opinions have been found to be incorrect when professional standards were diligently followed."

It is true that auditors cannot be expected to provide absolute assurance on financial statements. There are simply too many variables—too many opportunities for mistakes or deceptions—for an outsider to check, test, and confirm accuracy. To do so, auditors would have to swarm over a corporation, breathing down its neck every single day, watching over its shoulder at every transaction.

*James K. Loebbecke, "The Mysterious World of the Corporate Audit," in *Tempo*, vol. 23, no. 2, 1977.

The costs of such surveillance would be prohibitive, business procedures would likely be slowed to a bureaucratic crawl, and, what's
more, there would still be margin for error. The hand is faster than
the eye: As long as there are accounting systems, there will be
brilliant schemers capable of dodging them without detection.

The problem is, most of the users of financial statements—the
investing public—have been led to believe that the auditor's signature on an annual report means the books are a totally accurate
reflection of the corporation's financial status. At the very least, they
are confident that a Big Eight stamp of approval means the company
has been investigated for fraud and that it has been found free of any
trace of wrongdoing. How shocked the "little old widow" would
be to find that auditors point to fraud as one of the factors they
provide little insurance against. Insisting that they are not police-
men, auditors state that they are, instead, management's partners in
the audit process and not their overseers. They do not set out to
catch management with its hand in the till but look to management
to cooperate with the audit team. All of The Big Eight hold that
they will not even audit a corporation that opposes being audited.
The very firms that probably need auditing most are the least likely
to come under the scrutiny of The Big Eight.

"An auditor is under no obligation to accept or retain a client
about whose integrity he has reservations; indeed such clients
should be rejected. If at any point serious doubts arise concerning
the honesty, integrity or good faith of management that cannot be
satisfactorily resolved, the auditor should consider abandoning his
attempt to audit; that is he should consider his resignation or other
appropriate response. . . .

"Auditors cannot reasonably be expected to assume responsibilities for detection or disclosure of a client's violation of law in general. Auditors are primarily accountants, trained and experienced in
activities that are basically financial. They are not lawyers, nor are
they criminal investigators, and they do not possess the training or
skills of either group. The resolution of the issue should be within
the framework of the conventional skills attributed to accountants
and auditors."*

*Cohen Commission Report.

The harmony between management and auditors is a relatively recent development. "Pioneer accountants, and PMM was among them, frequently operated in a hostile business climate. They were often obligated to contend with secretive corporate treasurers that resented having to supply the figures necessary for an independent audit. One of the firm's early engagements was the audit of the Fitchburg Railroad in Boston back in the 1920s. The Fitchburg directors were trying to verify rumors of rebates, kickbacks, and other dubious payments—yes, back then. While the audit was in progress, the chief company accountant committed suicide, and, if that wasn't enough, the day that our report was delivered, the president dropped dead. Fortunately, this attitude toward auditors has changed. Now both the management of our clients and the auditors work as a team to supply the stockholders with meaningful financial data."*

Incredible as it seems, the only investors who are well aware of the auditor's limitations and his cooperation with management are those who do not rely on his reports. Institutional investors—those money managers who buy huge blocks of stocks for pension funds, insurance companies, and the like—base their investment decisions on the reports of financial analysts, not the signature of an independent auditor. Those groups of individuals that truly understand annual reports rarely read them: They turn to much more sophisticated information.

One gets the feeling that all the people in the nation that really comprehend the auditing process and that are genuinely concerned with auditing issues (besides CPAs) could be gathered around a conference table. The auditing system purports to serve the public but is really way over its head.

The final procedure of the audit—the issuance of the auditor's opinion and report—has also become a subject of controversy. What does the opinion mean? Does it say anything substantive? The Cohen Commission was skeptical:

Evidence abounds that communication between the auditor and users of his work—especially through the auditor's standard report—is unsatisfac-

---

*Walter E. Hanson, Peat, Marwick, Mitchell & Co., *80 Years of Professional Growth*, November 16, 1977.

tory. The present report has remained essentially unchanged since 1948 and its shortcomings have often been discussed. Present research suggests that many users misunderstand the auditor's role and responsibilities, and the present standard report only adds to the confusion.

One of the key problems is that all of the work that goes into a major audit is boiled down into a brief passage that hardly reveals what the auditor did to reach his opinion.

"The auditor's standard report is almost the only formal means used to both educate and inform users of financial statements concerning the audit function. For the largest corporations in the country, an audit may involve scores of auditors and tens of thousands of hours of work for which the client may pay millions of dollars. Nevertheless, the auditor's standard report compresses that considerable expenditure of skilled effort into a relatively few words and paragraphs. The following is a typical example:

Accountant's Report

February 11, 1976

General Motors Corporation, Its Directors and Stockholders: We have examined the Consolidated Balance Sheet of General Motors Corporation and consolidated subsidiaries as of December 31, 1975 and 1974 and the related Statements of Consolidated Income and Changes in Consolidated Financial Position for the years then ended. Our examination was made in accordance with generally accepted auditing standards and accordingly included such tests of the accounting records and such other auditing procedures as we considered necessary in the circumstances. In our opinion, these financial statements present fairly the financial position of the companies at December 31, 1975 and 1974 and the results of their operations and the changes in their financial position for the years then ended, in conformity with generally accepted accounting principles consistently applied.

Haskins & Sells"*

Read most of the annual reports of the *Fortune* 500 and the opinions do sound almost identical. The words, phrases, and style change little from report to report.

*Cohen Commission Report.

The typical language is semitechnical, has a mechanical quality, and does not tell the layman what the auditor really did to arrive at the opinion.

This was not always the case. Before the passage of the 1930s securities acts, auditors used a more descriptive and informative style. The following is from the first annual report of the United States Steel Corporation:

Certificate of Chartered Accountants

New York

March 12, 1903

To the Stockholders of the United States Steel Corporation:

We have examined the books of the U.S. Steel Corporation and its Subsidiary Companies for the year ending December 31, 1902, and certify that the Balance Sheet at that date and the Relative Income Account are correctly prepared therefrom.

We have satisfied ourselves that during the year only actual additions and extensions have been charged to Property Account; that ample provision has been made for Depreciation and Extinguishment, and that the item of "Deferred Charges" represents expenditures reasonably and properly carried forward to operations of subsequent years.

We are satisfied that the valuations of the inventories of stocks on hand as certified by the responsible officials have been carefully and accurately made at appropriate cost; also that the cost of material and labor on contracts in progress have been carefully ascertained, and that the profit taken on these contracts is fair and reasonable.

Full provision has been made for bad and doubtful accounts receivable and for all ascertainable liabilities.

We have verified the cash and securities by actual inspection or by certificates from the Depositories, and are of opinion that the Stocks and Bonds are fully worth the value at which they are stated in the Balance Sheet.

And we certify that in our opinion the Balance Sheet is properly drawn up so as to show the true financial position of the Corporation and its Subsidiary Companies, and that the Relative Income Account is a fair and correct statement of the net earnings for the fiscal year ending at that date.

Price Waterhouse & Co.

Clearly, this gives more insight into the auditor's activities and better explains the hows and whys of his opinion. Since 1933, however, the profession has supported the use of a standard, less descriptive report, the form for which has been revised in 1939, 1941, and 1948. Standardization, originally adopted in order to reduce confusion that came with the wide variety of reporting formats, has had a negative effect of its own. That is that the opinions have become so similar, so familiar to readers of annual reports, that they are no longer read word for word but are merely skimmed. The auditors' reports have become mere symbols or adornments.

The Cohen Commission found that this contributes to the widespread tendency to view the auditor's report as a guaranty:

The reader comes to rely on his implicit understanding of the nature of the audit function in interpreting the meaning and significance of an auditor's report rather than on the description of the audit function that is contained in the report. If a user is generally unfamiliar with the limitations of financial information and the audit function, he may tend to view the auditor's report as a seal of approval and place unjustified reliance on it.

In any event, if a user has misconceptions about the audit function, an auditor's report that he does not read will not correct them. Auditors need to do more to assure that their reports are read, but users who tend to rely on the fact that financial statements have been audited should at least read the auditors' reports on them.

Standard reports convey two types of messages: explicit and implied. The former includes the company name, names and dates of financial statements covered, the fact that the audit is based on generally accepted auditing standards, that the data tested is but a sample, that the report is a matter of opinion, that the information is presented in accordance with generally accepted accounting principles, and that the application of accounting principles to similar circumstances has not changed from one period to another. The Cohen Report explained that the following messages must be inferred: that the financial statements are representations of management, that accounting principles deemed appropriate in the circumstances were used, and that the auditor exercised judgment in his work. The commission suggested that all the facts be stated explicitly and also said:

The present means of communicating the work of the independent auditor to users has not kept pace with developments in auditing and the financial reporting environment. The acceptance and discharge of added responsibilities should be communicated by the auditor to the users of his work. The additional messages, for example, should cover other information in the annual report, association with interim information, internal accounting controls, corporate codes of conduct, and meetings with the audit committee of the company's board of directors.

If the auditor's report is expanded to provide information on the auditor's discharge of the entire audit function in the specific circumstances of the particular client, the tendency for the report to become an unread symbol will be reduced. Once the reader's attention is obtained, substantially more information can be communicated.

Surprisingly, for a body formed by the AICPA, the Cohen Commission confirmed the existence of problems in the conduct of the audit function. Assigned to "consider whether a gap may exist between what the public expects or needs of auditors and what auditors can or should reasonably expect to accomplish," the commission found that "such a gap does exist." Not surprisingly, however, it refused to lay the blame on the auditors:

"To the extent that a gap exists between performance and expectations, it is traceable more to long-range forces than to specific performance deficiencies of auditors or the profession." The worst it would say is that "the public accounting profession has failed to react and evolve rapidly enough to keep pace with the speed of change in the American business environment." The bottom line: Auditors may be conservative but not incompetent or dishonest.

Shortly after the commission made its findings public, the Auditing Standards Executive Committee (now called the Auditing Standards Board) of the AICPA formed a task force to study possible revisions of the auditor's report. The AICPA's Audit Standards Division is the recognized rule-making body for accepted audit

procedures. Its directives are issued in the form of so-called Statements on Auditing Standards (SAS).

The task force was assigned to consider:

The elimination of the phrase "present fairly" and the reference to consistency of application of accounting principles.

The reference to financial statements as representations of
management.

A description of generally accepted accounting principles
and generally accepted auditing standards.

A minibureaucracy in its own right, the AICPA is hardly known
for prompt or decisive action. It plods along, generating a constant
stream of wordy documents and complicating even the simplest
issues. It is a formal, unimaginative organization staffed with what
appears to be many mediocre paper shufflers. The AICPA is, in the
author's opinion, a trade association that seems to spend much of its
time justifying its own existence. The Institute claims to base many
of its actions on consideration of the public interest, but it appears
to be far more concerned with soothing its most prominent members: The Big Eight.

True to form, the AICPA waited roughly three years from the
publication of the Cohen report to issue its draft for a revised auditor's report. Throughout the period, the Auditing Standards
Board's task force held a long series of meetings and conducted
public hearings as it wrestled with the issues raised by Cohen. The
result of this lengthy deliberation—which took far more time than
the Supreme Court takes to decide on matters of life and death and
the Bill of Rights—was a tame proposal seemingly designed to give
the appearance of major change and to disarm critics without forcing auditors to substantially revise their procedures. Still it was
ultimately rejected by the Auditing Standards Board. The big
hangup came on the elimination of the word *fairly.* The powers that
be refused to drop it from the auditor's report.

Today the auditors' report remains very much the mandatory tie
on a well-dressed annual report. The vast majority of financial-

statement users never read it. They simply look for the familiar "symbol" and, once found, rest assured that all is well. The Big Eight are on the job. The grand old names of the giant CPA firms mean more to many than the confusing reports that come before them.

5. MAS—At the Seat of Power

"Members of the newest, least-known of the great professions, accountants seek truth in an even more complicated corporate world. A race of men nobody knows, they split finer hairs than any lawyer. And on their diagnosis, millions upon millions of dollars may change hands."

—*Fortune*, "Certified Public Accountants"

THE GREAT NAMES OF ACCOUNTING have wheedled their way into every nook and cranny of business, government, health care, transportation, personal finance, resource management—to name but a few. In the process, they have come to exert pervasive influence in economics, foreign trade, the fate of the dollar, the price of gold, big business, Congress, the president, living standards and social values, and they have accomplished it all behind the scenes, remaining unknown to the man on the street—to the people whose lives are touched by The Big Eight. As a Senate committee found, "The Big Eight accounting firms are involved in a wide variety of activities which significantly affect practically all segments of the nation's economy, as well as society in general."

Witness: When the troubled Chrysler Corporation came to Washington, hat in hand, seeking a billion-dollar bailout, the federal government found itself in a quandary. Torn between the grand traditions of laissez-faire capitalism and the political pressure to save jobs, the decision-makers vacillated, stalling for time, and waited for a modern-day Solomon to emerge with the answers.

Most of all, they wanted some assurance that a huge loan to Chrysler would not be flushed down the drain in a matter of months. There was good reason for this fear. Chrysler's original request for $750 million was doubled to $1.5 billion as Congress was busy working on a rescue package. Was Chrysler a lost cause?

Could the corporation be saved? Would the capital request keep increasing?

Enter the Treasury Department. Its role was to evaluate Chrysler's recovery plan—to determine for Uncle Sam if the automaker's projections were based on pipe dreams or prudent assumptions. One question had to be answered: Should Congress take the plunge?

One thing was certain—the decision would have enormous impact on the economy and would establish a precedent for corporate bailouts. Faced with this staggering responsibility, the Treasury Department turned to The Big Eight for help. The assignment: to analyze Chrysler's recovery plan, to determine its soundness, and to keep Treasury officials posted on late-breaking developments as they occurred. Three Big Eighters were reviewed for the engagement (the other five had conflicts of interest: Touche Ross, for example, is Chrysler's auditor), and, in what has to be a speed record for government action, Ernst & Whinney got the nod after less than two weeks of discussions. E&W's managing partner, Ray Groves, received the first call from Assistant Secretary of the Treasury Roger Altman on September 19, 1979, and the firm was officially named to the job on Sunday, September 30.

Soon after, twenty-seven E&W specialists moved into Chrysler headquarters to begin the work. Exhibiting the depth of talent and experience only The Big Eight can muster in little more than a moment's notice, E&W dispatched specialists in financial modeling, computer programming, products planning, cost reduction, and other relevant disciplines from fourteen of its offices around the country. Quickly, with cool efficiency, the Ernst & Whinney Chrysler task force organized into six groups, each responsible for a specialized part of the engagement: historical analysis, control systems, variable margin improvements, fixed cost reductions, manufacturing and purchasing plans, and product planning.

Their efforts were directed at producing an independent and objective review of a complex, three-year recovery program for the tenth largest manufacturer in the United States and the seventeenth largest corporation in the world. The variables were almost unlimited. To narrow the problem somewhat, E&W limited its review to

Chrysler's North American automotive operations and designed a computer "model" to project the corporation's vehicle sales through the 1983 model year. In just two weeks, E&W computer experts designed the requisite computer programs and put them to work. A total of twenty-five computer runs answered most of the major "what if" questions raised by Congress, Treasury officials, and various interest groups. E&W acted with great dispatch because it had to. A written analysis was due within three weeks, ready for review by Secretary of the Treasury G. William Miller. The reason for the urgent deadline: Congressional hearings on Chrysler were scheduled to start the first week of November. The executive branch of the U.S. government did not want to present its position—to plead its case in favor of the loan—without supporting evidence from Ernst and Whinney. It wanted to hear from The Big Eight first.

The end-result was momentous. In December, Congress approved a $1.5 billion financial aid package, saving Chrysler from impending bankruptcy and giving the ailing giant another chance to make it in the marketplace. One of the biggest business decisions of all time—and The Big Eight were on the scene, influencing the outcome.

The Chrysler engagement is representative of The Big Eight's fastest growing practice area: general consulting. Officially known as Management Advisory Services (MAS) and christened with a slew of brand names by the various firms, consulting by any name is the vehicle on which The Big Eight drives its influence deep into the world around it.

Broadly defined, MAS engagements are those where The Big Eight serve not as independent auditors ostensibly protecting the public interest but instead as unabashed advisers to management. When a corporation, an institution, a government—everything from an arms manufacturer to a museum—runs into a management problem or needs help solving a problem, more often than not the call goes out to The Big Eight to devise a solution. And, as the Chrysler case illustrates, they are ready, waiting, and better equipped than any other organization to step in and provide a multitude of services across the globe on a moment's notice.

The times are right for Big Eight consulting. For the first period in history, problems are viewed not so much as matters of religion, pride, or politics, but as issues of dollars and cents. More than ever before, finance is the international language, the foundation on which so many far-reaching decisions are based. As the high priests of high finance, the big CPA firms are being called on to play a crucial role in activities far removed from corporate boardrooms. The world is their congregation.

"When the time arrives that it becomes good practice to control government expenditures rather than incur bankruptcy and economic chaos, the services of accountants and auditors are quickly sought," adds Wallace Olson, in "The Accounting Profession in the 1980s," his Cape Town address. "Financial facts must be determined. Archaic accounting and management systems must be modernized and streamlined. Audits must be performed to assure that political manipulations of funds and budgets does not continue. Perhaps most important, the efficiency and effectiveness of government programs must be measured to determine where reductions in expenditures can be made with the least amount of damage to vital services . . . Assuming that we have the courage to tackle this challenge, and that we perform well, we may also expect that an expanded role as important advisers to government will become a continuing responsibility. This can have a profound and lasting effect on the nature and stature of our profession."

When a municipality considers dropping a bus route from its master schedule, a modern city manager knows that he has more to weigh than just the inconvenience to riders and the upfront savings. Will the lack of transportation along Elm Street hurt business? Will shops be forced to shut down? Will people be thrown out of work? Will all of this reduce the tax base? Most important, will the cut in bus service actually cost the city money in the long run? Questions like this weren't raised in the past. Today they are, and in thousands of cases, The Big Eight are being called in to provide the answers.

Big Eight names are popping up in some surprising places. Consider this smorgasbord of MAS engagements:

Coopers & Lybrand, which boasts twelve hundred professionals in its Management Consulting Services (MCS) department, carried out a comprehensive study of the Tanzanian tourist industry. C&L consultants made recommendations for additional investments in hotels and for improvements in the industry's marketing and training programs.

In the United States, C&L conducted a feasibility study for a group of sixteen New York based corporations interested in establishing a single computer facility capable of handling their back-up data processing needs. The major goal of the study was to develop a network switching system allowing members to convert their entire on-line operations to the back-up facility within two hours.

Price Waterhouse assisted the United States Bureau of Indian Affairs (BIA), helping the government to improve the delivery of services to Indian people and to enhance the administrative operations of the agency. In the process, PW defined the functional requirements for the BIA's thirteen distributed area computers and telecommunications equipment.

Many of the nation's leading law firms turn to Price Waterhouse for aid in computerizing their internal operations. PW conducts requirements studies and provides counsel on equipment selection. The firm also assists attorneys in case management through document filing and retrieval systems as well as in analyses related to damage claims, pricing, and cost studies. As the legal profession seeks to manage its exploding mass of information, it is turning, like everyone else, to The Big Eight for guidance.

Cooper's Indonesian and Australian offices were engaged to design and install sophisticated internal controls and management information systems for, as well as to advise on the future use of computers by, the Indonesian railways.

Peat, Marwick developed a "profit improvement" program for banks which reduces "float" levels by speeding the collection of checks drawn on other banks. PMM's worldwide banking clients have benefited to the tune of a daily increase of roughly $2 billion in earning assets. This, thanks to Peat's improved check-handling and "float" control procedures.

PMM did the feasibility study for the midfield terminal at Atlanta's Hartsfield International Airport—the biggest in the world. Based on Peat's study, a $305 million revenue bond was issued—this too was the largest of its kind.

Peat recommended and implemented a telecommunications system for a leading New York brokerage firm with a network of offices throughout the nation. The system, designed to save the brokers $1 million a year, is adaptable to changing conditions spurred by future changes in technology.

When the New England Power Exchange (NEPEX), a group of forty-four independently owned utilities, needed an automated billing system, they turned to Peat for assistance. PMM's work is affecting not only the transfer of money, but, more importantly, the distribution of electricity.

"Our review is enabling the members to evaluate the design and performance of the billing system so that member decisions regarding the purchase or sale of power may be made with greater confidence. This will permit a more efficient response to peak load requirements in the multistate area serviced by NEPEX."*

More than a thousand foreign corporations and individuals eager to invest in America turn to Peat, Marwick's "Project U.S.A." for assistance in overall planning, market research, tax strategies, executive recruiting, compensation packages, and identifying prime acquisition candidates.

For small businesses—not traditionally associated with The Big Eight—Peat has developed a minicomputer software program called PMM/MBS. It helps bring emerging companies into the technological mainstream, preparing them for the demands of the marketplace and for future growth.

*Peat, Marwick, Mitchell 1979 Annual Report, p. 10.

Talk about clout! Peat testified before the Postal Service Commission on behalf of its client, the United Parcel Service. Serving as an expert witness before regulatory agencies is a key Big Eight activity which endears the firms to their clients and furthers their already expansive reputation in the bureaucracy. To prepare its testimony in the postal case, PMM drew on its own Litigation Support Services team. This elite corps of professionals worked with UPS executives and managers to gather detailed evidence on parcel-handling procedures, sampling studies, and projected costs. When it came time to face the commission, Peat "demonstrated that the lower rates requested by the Postal Service to make them competitive with UPS rates were based on improperly allocated costs and therefore were not justified. Moreover, we offered alternative methodologies for allocating costs to more closely reflect cost-of-service cost accounting principles."*

In what may well be the single most unlikely role for The Big Eight, Touche Ross has had a hand in prison reform. Hired by the Colorado Department of Administration, TR assisted the state in drawing up a five-year master plan for the Division of Correctional Services. Touche focused its efforts on segments of the plan dealing with organization structure, personnel and training, management information systems, offender programming, parole and community services, and custody and support services.

TR also proved that Big Eight consulting jobs are not limited to earthly concerns. The Corporation for Public Broadcasting engaged Touche to assist with its Satellite Interconnection System Project for the Public Broadcasting Service (PBS). The project was designed to transfer the interconnection system of the PBS member stations from leased terrestrial microwave facilities to a communication satellite in combination with receive-only earth terminals owned by the local member stations. TR performed feasibility studies to determine whether National Public Radio's member stations should also switch to a satellite system.

*Ibid., p. 15.

The more crucial a matter is to the nation's or the world's well-being, the more likely The Big Eight will be in the thick of it, influencing the outcome. Virtually all of the firms boast major MAS engagements in the energy field. TR, for example, was engaged by the Federal Energy Administration's Strategic Petroleum Reserve Office to develop system requirements for the nation's oil reserve program. Although mismanaged at times, the program is one of the most important in the federal government and could, in the event of an energy crisis, make the difference between war and peace, economic stability or a precipitous crash. TR was assigned to define the type of information necessary to manage and control the reserve programs and the management information systems necessary to collect and process this information. The categories of information to be monitored were all of utmost importance: the design and construction of the oil storage sites, acquiring the oil and releasing it into the storage sites, and determining how the oil would be released.

Odds are good that few miners busy breaking up coal in the darkness beneath the earth have any inkling of the fact that Touche Ross developed a Beneficiary Information and Tracking System for the United Mine Workers of America. There's hardly a miner in the land who's ever heard of MAS, Touche Ross, or The Big Eight. But that should come as no surprise. Even their shop stewards, the union presidents, and the mine owners themselves have no idea of the real scope of The Big Eight's pervasive influence.

The MAS divisions are operated by The Big Eight as distinct practice entities managed by vice-chairmen or other high-ranking executives, who in turn report to the chairmen or senior partners. MAS divisions are, for all intents and purposes, consulting firms within CPA firms.

"What the hell am I doing smack in the middle of a CPA firm? I'll admit it, that's what I ask myself at least once a month," says a Big Eight partner in charge of MAS. "I'm not a CPA, most of my people are not CPAs, we don't do audits, and most of us don't know a thing about taxes. What's more, we don't relate personally to CPAs; we're completely different animals; and we don't share professional interests. Consultants are problem solvers: We have to plunge into the unstructured and bring some order to it. CPAs feel threatened by that. The audit guys need structure to begin with or they simply can't work. They're threatened by the same things we thrive on.

"But that said, I guess we're here because consulting is a natural outgrowth of the CPA firms. All of our work does have financial implications, and we call on people throughout the firm for help in a great number of specialties.

"Clients benefit by working with us rather than the traditional consulting outfits because we do have those vast networks of experts under our roof that can be called on at any moment to bring their experience to the job. And whenever I realize that, I know what the hell I'm doing smack in the middle of a CPA firm."

Whether they adapt or not, one thing is certain: Big Eight consultants are a different breed from their auditor brothers even if, as is sometimes the case, both are CPAs. The contrast is like that between soldiers and civilians. Audit staffers, pressured as they are by rules, procedures, and the fear of litigation, tend to walk the straight line. Many, in a constant state of glazy-eyed fatigue, look to authority to light the way and to remove the burdens of accountability. Consultants, on the other hand, value their relative freedom, their ability to size up problems, design solutions, and see them through to conclusion. Basing their best work on the skills drawn from personal experience, as well as on imagination and innovation, senior consultants exude the kind of pride that is often associated with artistic achievements. As such, they find auditor's manuals to be anathema, the taskmasters of lesser minds. Still, consultants cannot have unlimited freedom.

"Consultants are creative, yes, but they do have to work within some established parameters," says Leonard Pace, head of MAS for DH&S. "All of our people on an MAS engagement work with a Task Definition Worksheet. This is a work paper that shows an individual's task objectives and the general scope of his work. It outlines the approach he'll take, the methods he'll use, and what is required to do the job. The work sheet doesn't deprive the consultants of using their own talents, because they write the worksheets and then have them reviewed by supervisors. We use the worksheets to manage the engagements, to keep them pointed in the right direction. When you have a group of bright, creative people on a job, unless there's some control, everyone can go off in wildly different directions. If that happens, we'll wind up with twenty files of information that have no common thread and that cannot be related in any meaningful way.

"Some consultants resist even the loose controls we impose on them. They insist that they are too creative for that. But, hell, we're not doing Einstein equations here. We are problem solvers. Some consultants are not good because they can never stop searching for little bits of information. They get sidetracked; they fail to identify the core issues. We have to keep them working toward that."

Big Eight management presses its consultants to stay on track for more reasons than one. Professional standards are a consideration, yes, but there is also a healthy dose of fee pressure. Some of the bigger consulting jobs are, much like major audits, let on the basis of competitive bids. The winners get the engagements by coming up with a low price tag that they must live with once the work begins. Although the firms deny it, that means cutting back on the ideal scope of the consulting process, severely limiting the staff's free-ranging analyses, and keeping the central problem in sight at all times. There's no doubt that this limits the full potential of a first-class consulting job, reducing the possibility that nondirected research into the firm will find well-camouflaged problems and will produce unexpected recommendations. The Big Eight cannot be blamed for this, because they must wrestle for business in a competitive marketplace, must be fee sensitive when the client demands it, and must squeeze a profit from this kind of engagement. At fault are the clients who treat consulting like a commodity, forcing professional firms to base fees not on the complexity of the job but instead on the need to be cheaper than the next guy. Perhaps the MAS chiefs are at fault for not admitting that this reduces the quality of consulting work, but any client with a head on its shoulders should be well aware of that. Consulting is not so different from other business services in that purchasers still get what they pay for.

For the most part, consultants bring some color to The Big Eight.

Their dress, noticeably less formal, clashes with the black and white uniform of the audit staff. Here and there one finds splashes of blue, pink, green, and yellow. Loafers mingle with wing tips, Paul Stuart suits mix up with Brooks Brothers. Although not a showplace for trendy fashion, the look on the consulting staff floor is less robotic, less like a prep school for middle-aged men. Of all the practice specialists under the roof of a Big Eight firm, consultants display the least amount of team spirit. The ties of partnership, loose as they are, do bring a sense of unity to a firm's auditors, tax men, recruiters, and the like. Only the consultants stand apart: Lone Rangers of The Big Eight.

MAS partners are different, in part because they have a wider view of the world. The components of their work are not fiscal calculations but real-life problems that extend well beyond corporate balance sheets to mine workers' benefits, strategic oil reserves, urban deterioration, satellite communications, health care. The nature of their assignments forces them to grapple with the page-one issues of politics, economics, nationalism, religion, and mores. As such, the best among them begin to see the unifying themes or common threads that run through virtually all human situations, be it in the context of an industrial plant or a city government. Skilled consultants can often bring the lessons learned from one engagement to bear on another. They see the building blocks, the common denominators.

"The hallmark of a good consultant is one who never stops asking 'why,' " says Henry Gunders, vice-chairman of MAS at Price Waterhouse. "He has a relentless sense of curiosity."

Specifically, Big Eight consulting practices offer clients the following assets:

Availability—Highly skilled experts are on tap, available around the clock for a wide range of engagements.

Specialized Knowledge—From computers, to cash controls to capital budgets, the MAS divisions are well versed in virtually every aspect of management and operations. Name the problem: Your friendly Big Eight firm will have someone on staff to solve it—or they will hire him.

Interindustry Transfer of Insight—The lessons learned from engagements at thousands of businesses can be applied to all clients, regardless of their field or industry.

"I've been in coal mines, auto plants, sawmills, retail stores, and I see one thing over and over again: Many of the problems are the same when you take them down to the basics," says Don Curtis, Touche Ross's MAS chief.

Outside Leverage—Free of the politics and bureaucratic approval procedures that are built into many large corporations, consultants (as outsiders) can often get right to the heart of festering problems and put an end to them.

Independence/Objectivity—Because consultants have not played a role in creating a company's products, structure, or operations, they are not married to the status quo and are thus more objective in deciding "what should stay and what should go."

Project Management Skills—The ability to structure a consulting assignment and manage it through to a successful conclusion.

MAS divisions vary in size and style based on each of the Big Eight senior partner's personal philosophy. Some—dyed-in-the-wool enthusiasts for this practice area—are promoting it heavily, adding staff and resources and making it a foundation for future professional growth. Peat, Marwick; Touche Ross; Coopers & Lybrand; and Arthur Andersen fall into this camp. Others—notably Arthur Young, Ernst & Whinney, Deloitte, and Price Waterhouse —are moving at a more cautious pace, not quite comfortable with the rapid shifts in emphasis away from audit and accounting services. The latter are strict constructionists, compelled to define a CPA firm as one which practices different variations of accounting and auditing services. The former are more liberal about the *CPAs'* label, preferring to establish themselves as financial-service department stores. All agree, however, that consulting equals big money, and all want to share in the pie. This ambition is not new. *Fortune* magazine put it this way in 1932:

"Certified Public Accountants (who call themselves CPAs) may descend like a swarm of locusts upon a manufacturer, explode his delusions that he is solvent. CPAs charge by the day—regardless of the amount of money involved. CPAs sometimes become millionaires—usually because they perform other services as well. . . ."

Russ Palmer, a true believer in MAS, puts it this way: "There's little we can't do in the consulting field. Who can match our competence in computers, accounting systems, feasibility studies, productivity analyses? I'll tell you: no one. We have the capability to serve industry, to serve government, to serve the public. I'll be damned if we shouldn't put that capability to good use. The only kind of consulting we don't want to do is that which requires the hiring of substantial pools of personnel not related to our basic practice area."

Palmer's zeal for MAS, much like that of his counterparts at the other aggressive firms, stems in good measure from his recognition that it represents a lush market to all The Big Eight clawing at one another for the limited number of major audit accounts.

With audit fees dropping rather precipitously, competing in this market is often like running in place. MAS, on the other hand, offers unlimited growth.

"MAS is without a doubt the most promising market now open to us," Palmer adds, visibly excited by the prospect. "The client pool is enormous, and the range of service we can provide is very substantial. Others point to small business and government work as the wave of the future. Not me. I see it as MAS."

Others are more reserved. Leonard Pace, the highly regarded vice-chairman of Deloitte Haskins & Sells, has seen his division more than double since 1975, growing from 165 professionals in the United States to more than 400 here and an excess of 1,000 worldwide. Still, he does not support unbridled expansion of the practice.

"As opposed as I am to outside controls that might force us to arbitrarily restrict MAS work, I do think that the firms should impose restrictions on ourselves to limit consulting work to those activities that are in sync with our professional status. I think it's wrong, for example, for CPA firms to do airport feasibility studies. How is that part of our business?"

Pace is a tightly controlled and thoroughly professional man deeply concerned with the stature of both his firm and his profession. In a letter to the SEC, he writes: "We believe that the maintenance of our firm's image as professional accountants is important, and, therefore, we provide only those services that our clients have come to expect of a firm in our profession. Our MAS has to do almost entirely with the organization, planning, performance, measurement, accounting, and reporting aspects of the systems for the various management functions and the development and analyses of information for management use. The performance of these services does not in any way impair the public's image of us as independent professional accountants. We do not and have not provided services such as psychological testing, public-opinion polls, plant layouts, merger and acquisition assistance for a finder's fee, or actuarial services."

A composite sketch of Big Eight MAS division looks like this: The practice generates roughly 15 percent of the firm's total revenues, employs fifteen hundred professionals worldwide, and serves thousands of businesses, institutional, and governmental clients. Staffers boast expertise in a broad range of disciplines, including general business management (M.B.A.'s), computer sciences, engineering, marketing, personnel relations, and corporate finance. Salaries start at $18,000–$25,000, rise to $50,000 in five years, and then to $100,000-plus for partners.

Unlike big audits, consulting engagements are rarely self-perpetuating. Staffers fly in to study a problem, stay long enough to design an effective solution (rarely more than three months), return the reins to client management, and then fly out again on to the next job. The results may be monitored for years after but usually on a long-distance basis. All of this shuttling back and forth from client to client takes its toll on consultants. The job demands an inordinate amount of travel, disruption of personal lives, and, in more cases than the firms like to admit, bad marriages.

"Every Sunday night I'm on a runway at Kennedy Airport, a gin and tonic in my hand, bracing to fly off to some miserable client city like Cincinnati or Lima or Birmingham," says a Big Eight consultant, his eyes deeply bloodshot. "All week it's lonely dinners in a

Sheraton, an hour with the TV, and off to bed. The closest I get to my kids is a good connection via Ma Bell. To make matters worse, my wife, who accepted this way of life for nine years without question, suddenly thinks I'm selfish and says she needs time away from the house too. That means one night tennis, one night shopping, one night taking Chinese cooking lessons. That's just great. Now the kids have no parents.

"Worse yet, when I get back home Friday evenings, yearning for a pleasant weekend at home, my wife and I feel like strangers. She's got a chip on her shoulder, we have a hard time getting into each other's rhythms; and the kids, who also resent my travel, do their best to get me pissed off. It's like they all want revenge. They act as if I'm off all week lying on a sandy beach, contemplating my navel.

"Sometimes I'd like to chuck it all and do some other kind of work. You know, nice normal hours, catch the five thirty-eight home for dinner, evenings by the hearth, and all that. But, hell, I like this crazy work, and I do it well. Also, deep down, I think I'd be bored out of my skull in about a week of routine office work."

In spite of the drawbacks, the MAS practice presents the best opportunity for young grads seeking careers with The Big Eight. The track to the top is faster than on the audit side, the early years are far more rewarding, and there is a great diversity of assignments. Young staffers can express some of their own ideas, can conduct limited experiments, and do meaningful work from the start. There is little of the numbing grunt work that is part of the dues-paying process for junior auditors.

MAS partners look for recruits who can get right into the thick of it. The emphasis is on hiring young men and women with more than a piece of parchment. At some of the firms, previous work experience is required. Touche Ross lists among its prerequisites an M.B.A. or other advanced degrees, plus prior success in private industry, preferably with a multinational corporation, a large bank, or a leading manufacturer. Analysts of all types are especially attractive to the MAS recruiters. Cost analysts, financial analysts, systems analysts—all are in great demand, for they have demonstrated the analytical bent of mind and the methodical approach to problem solving that is the hallmark of top consultants. A composite profile of the typical new MAS recruit looks like this: Twenty-eight years old, married, B.S. in computer science from MIT, M.B.A. from Cornell, work experience as systems analyst for a bank and a major auto maker, highly motivated, hard working, driven to achieve career success above all other life goals, intent on making partner and on achieving substantial earnings.

Because they are more than green college grads—because they often have significant work experience under their belts—new consulting staffers may find themselves deeply involved in interesting projects soon after joining a Big Eight MAS practice staff. The diversity of assignments is staggering. At TR alone, MAS is broken down into seven major categories:

General Management: diversification studies, merger and acquisition programs, profit improvement plans, strategic and long-range planning, management information systems, organizational restructuring, corporate and operations turnaround.

Financial Management: capital expenditures, budgeting systems, cash and credit management, cost accounting analysis, economic feasibility studies, financial planning, methods of financing, replacement cost analysis, profitability accounting.

Operations Management: inventory analysis, maintenance, operations review, production planning, transportation planning and distribution, warehousing methods.

Marketing: distribution profitability analysis, marketing controls and procedures, marketing planning, pricing, bidding and rate setting, product-line planning.

Systems Management: EDP and and non-EDP system planning and development, EDP effectiveness analysis.

Public Utility Services: expert testimony, management information, operations and management review, rate case investigation, tariff and rate development.

Human Resources Services: employee benefits, executive
compensation, management development and training, organization development, wage and salary administration.*

"Good consultants are delighted that they can participate in a
wide range of assignments," says PW's Henry Gunders. "They get
excited by every engagement. Imagine two guys walking past a field
of weeds. One of them says, 'Oh, weeds.' The other guy says, 'What
a fascinating universe this is. Let me see these interesting weeds.
Why are they growing here? Let me find out.' That's the consultant.

"When it comes to actual consulting engagements for industry,
I think the consultant does a good job when the client sees its world
differently. What do I mean by that? Here's an example: A paper
company we worked for called us in to consult because business was
so good they were having trouble meeting demands. Management
believed it needed another paper mill and called us to study the
feasibility of building one and financing it. This was to be a major
project: The mills cost tens of millions of dollars.

"But in analyzing the business, we found that equipment capacity
was not the problem. By scheduling the use of the existing plant
more efficiently, we could eliminate the need for a new mill. The
company, which prided itself on the prompt servicing of customer
orders, frequently shut down major machine runs in order to fill
rush orders.

"Our recommendation was to allow one machine to operate full
time producing the standard, most popular paper. We suggested this
as an alternative approach to stopping and starting the equipment
for each order.

"Studies showed that the new approach would save time and
would enable the constant-operation machine to satisfy a substantial
percentage of the firm's total orders. There was no need to build a
new machine after all."

PW's paper mill engagement clearly illustrates that Big Eight
MAS practitioners are not at all limited to accounting-based recommendations. Their capabilities are awesome; their staff organizations

*Touche Ross Management Consulting Booklet.

blessed with a brain trust of specialists. One might think that Big Eight consultants would be inclined to focus on the paper mill's new construction financing alternatives. Not so. PW's solution was based more on both an engineer's thinking and a CPA's. The client benefited greatly.

What's more, the engagement reveals two factors that are crucial to a successful consulting job: The client should save more money than it spends on consulting fees, and it should learn something new about its business.

The latter is especially important. The truth is that managers can be so close to their companies—so bound up in their day-to-day operations—that they fail to see the trees as well as the forest. Sometimes it takes an outsider to spot things the insiders are blind to. This is a major reason for hiring a consultant and is a key part of the consultant's sales pitch. They must perform well in this regard—and the best ones are usually up to the test.

In the paper-mill engagement, Price Waterhouse consultants had to teach client management that its business was not really selling paper but instead "profit potential per machine hour." Although this may seem like a matter of semantics, it is not. Just how management views its business—where and how it must allocate its resources—is pivotal to long-term success and profitability.

"Skilled consultants see what the business is beneath the surface," Gunders adds.

Big Eight consulting partners exhibit one of the sure signs of power: the denial that they have any. It is one of the strange quirks of the financial world that the most powerful people pretend to be mere observers, while the genuine peons play Napoleon. Ask David Rockefeller or William Paley if they have power and the answer will invariably be no.

MAS honchos issue the same denials, partly because they don't want to appear egotistical and partly because consultants must always keep a low profile. The reason for this is clear: Consultants are professional outsiders. Their job is not to join a client's organization but instead to come in as know-it-alls and to tell the insiders how to do their jobs. That has to build resentment. Imagine how a General Electric manager feels when the brass informs him that of

the three thousand people in his department, no one is capable of
solving a nagging problem—not even the manager himself. That
makes for one wounded, sulking, and vengeful executive. Chances
are good he'll be out to sabotage the consultant's work, to make the
outsiders look like incompetent fools.

"There are times when you run into solid brick walls on an
engagement," says one Big Eight consulting partner. "The client's
staff gets it in their heads that we're out to take their jobs, their
income, their status, their place in the company. The threat grabs
the real insecure ones by the throat. Sometimes for damn good
reason: A guy may have spent twenty years piecing together a little
fiefdom in the corporation—one that adds very little to the scheme
of things but continues to operate simply because in that giant
corporation no one has ever taken a close look at it. Top management may not even know that it exists. Suddenly, cost analysts are
invading, and the guy's whole life flashes before his eyes. The last
thing he'll do is cooperate with us. He'll tell his whole staff not to
say a word to us. Secrecy, he believes, will save his ass.

"Childish as this is, it can be effective. Without cooperation from
the client's people, it is hard to do our job. If we don't have access
to the right information, or, as happens from time to time, if we are
purposely fed the wrong information, we can be made to look bad.
In cases like that, we lose, the client loses, and the only winner is
the saboteur in the ranks who's got a good thing going and wants
to keep it that way.

"We were once assigned to consult for a major manufacturer that
was having labor difficulties. Factory employees were constantly
bickering with supervisors. There were fist fights, knifings, and
dozens of complaints to union officials. The situation resulted in
thousands of lost man-hours and an embarrassing amount of bad
publicity.

"When we got to the plant, management told us that one of the
supervisors had a very low incidence of complaints, that his people
never engaged in violence, and that we should develop a system
that would model all worker/supervisor relationships on this one
situation.

"Seemed like a real honor for the 'model' supervisor. We thought he'd be running at the mouth about his labor relations techniques. But lo and behold, it's stonewall time. He wouldn't utter a word to us, and his people suddenly lost their tongues as well. First, we were baffled; but then, in exchange for a small cash payment, one of the guys talked. To make a long story short, we found out that there was harmony in the group because the supervisor let each one of his men spend one full day a week sitting in the john. They could smoke, read newspapers, sleep, whatever. The supervisor got labor peace and management kudos, the men got a four-day week, and the company gave out involuntary paid vacations."

The brick wall goes up even when there are no skeletons in the closet. The notion that they are being showed up is more than enough to bring out hostile behavior on the part of many client managers. Consultants can and do get around this obstacle by going over heads, but it's an approach they take with great reluctance.

"The last thing we want is to be embroiled in internal political conflicts," the consulting partner continues. "I've gone to the mat in more than my share of those brouhahas, and let me tell you, it's the pits. The engagement turns out to be one big shouting match. Even if you turn in a good job—which is hard in that kind of environment—management gets pissed off because they've been dragged into a floor fight too. It's a no-win situation."

Another reason why consultants discount their own power is that client brass doesn't like having pretenders to the throne prowling around the premises either. A group vice-president or chief executive officer will welcome the aid of skilled consulting firms as long as that firm knows its place: as an adviser to top management, not a substitute for it; as a source of information, not a decision-maker.

The latter is the key distinction. Senior management must always retain the appearance of authority: Stockholders expect it, the board of directors demands it, and the executive's own ego craves it. Top managers cannot overtly delegate their decision-making responsibilities to outsiders. Consultants can never let on that this is the case, even in those instances where it is absolutely true. Since Big Eight consultants are seeking fees not glory, it is the better part of wisdom to stay in the background, keep a humble demeanor, wave off all notions of power, and make frequent trips to the bank. But that, of course, does not mean that the power isn't there. Just the opposite is true. MAS staffers have more power than all other Big Eight partners because their work takes them deep into the guts of a corporation, institution, or government body; and because they are dealing with so many key business, social, and political issues. The consultants' power comes not from their ability to make the final decisions for clients, but to limit the range of alternatives, to sharply define the options, and to thus greatly influence the ultimate course of action.

Just how Big Eight consultants bring their skills, power, and influence to bear on a client is evidenced by a look at a major engagement. Take Deloitte Haskins & Sells' massive project for the Office of the (U. S.) Comptroller of the Currency (OCC). Here we see not only a well-oiled MAS arm at work, but also the kind of pervasive impact it can have on the world around it.

The OCC's chief responsibility is to maintain a sound national banking system for the convenience of the public. As such, it regulates and supervises the activities of all the nation's national banks. Some of its basic objectives are:

to provide a system of federally chartered banks subject to federal laws and regulations.

to prevent undue concentration of economic power and promote competition in banking markets.

to moderate banking instability and protect the public against the worst consequences of instability.

to encourage and promote a high level of operating efficiency and innovativeness in banking.

to meet the needs of the public for conveniently available banking facilities and services.

to encourage and promote a high level of efficiency and equity in the allocation of credit to various sectors of the economy.

to promote an equitable distribution of costs and benefits among the management, stockholders, creditors, and customers of commercial banks.

Although these objectives are not solely the responsibility of the OCC, but are shared with other federal agencies, the Office of the Comptroller of the Currency is without question primary supervisor of the national banks. This role dates back to the National Bank Act of 1864, which created the OCC as the sole commercial-bank-chartering agency for the federal government and the principal regulator of the banks it charters.

For nearly three quarters of a century, the objectives of the OCC remained fairly well balanced between the need to maintain a free and competitive banking system and to insure the soundness of that system. But the shock of the depression—with banks failing by the thousands—abruptly changed things, bringing on a much tougher regulatory stance.

"Bank entry became subject to much greater discretion by regulatory agencies then ever before, although bank entry remained freer in the United States than in most other countries of the world. Competition was also dampened by controls on deposit interest rates, by curtailment of the range of activities in which banks could engage, and by the introduction of federal deposit insurance, which created a new federal agency whose major objective was bank soundness. The general regulatory atmosphere also became heavily charged with attitudes of caution and conservatism."[*]

Questions about this policy of toughness were voiced with increasing frequency in the late 1950s. With the depression psychology replaced by the glowing optimism of the postwar era, business, academic, and political leaders called for a shift away from tight controls and toward more competition. The OCC moved in this direction by encouraging applications for new charters and widening the scope of activities in which national banks could participate. In 1970, the President's Commission on Financial Structure and

[*]"Deloitte Haskins & Sells, Comptroller of the Currency: Administratior of National Banks," 1975, p. B9.

Regulation reflected the temper of the times by recommending the elimination of many commercial banking restrictions. The commission found them to be anticompetitive or anti-innovative.

But the new liberalism itself was called into question in the early 1970s. Once again, bank soundness emerged as an important concern for regulators.

"The general financial environment has become increasingly risky to financial institutions," DH&S found in a study conducted during this period, "as market interest rates and rate relationships have become increasingly volatile, while borrower credits in some sectors (especially real estate) have deteriorated. In this environment, large banks practicing liability management, with historically low capital ratios, have shown themselves to be vulnerable. At the same time the increasing competitiveness of financial markets and the potential widening of geographical market areas associated with the new branching technology have caused concern about the future viability of small banks, which have historically operated in more or less protected markets."

In short, a new decade brought with it a new economic climate, a new set of problems (some related to emerging technology), and a new attitude toward bank regulations. The OCC recognized, quite correctly (and with a surprising amount of clarity for a federal agency), that changes were likely to come fast and furious within the foreseeable future, and that to be effective it would have to change its procedures to meet evolving conditions. For the most part, this meant coming up with an efficient and flexible system for collecting and disseminating information related to its regulatory role.

When the Office of the Comptroller identified the need for outside assistance in finding ways to increase the responsiveness of its information-collection function, it called on fifty or so consulting firms (including the MAS arms of CPA firms) to submit applications for the job. About fifteen organizations (including all of The Big Eight) responded with detailed proposals; most of the others did not bother, recognizing that they did not have the capacity to handle so major a project.

"We decided to propose for the engagement from the outset,"

says Leonard Pace. "Why? First, it was a quality job, and that's what we look for. It represented the kind of activity we want our partners to be involved in. Second, it fell within our capabilities. Third, we believed we had a good chance of doing the work successfully. We always have to consider all of these factors before we bid on an engagement."

DH&S, firmly in contention in the final round of the proposal process, was asked to make a personal presentation to the comptroller of the currency. Facing the comptroller and two dozen of his senior staffers at OCC headquarters in Washington, D. C., Pace and his team pitched for the accounts in a two-hour session that featured:

An introduction of DH&S's capabilities in an awesome array of financial disciplines, including accounting, auditing, and tax.

An outline of the broad objectives of the project.

A summary of how DH&S would approach the engagement; how it would seek to accomplish the objectives.

"Generally speaking, we said the engagement would help the comptroller regulate and supervise the national banking systems more effectively and efficiently," Pace adds, talking in the careful, methodical pattern that is his style. "Specifically, that meant leading the national banking system through a period of dynamic change; increasing the capacity of the banking system to review the financial needs of all users—governments, corporations and individuals; building managerial and professional capabilities necessary to supervise the complex banking system."

Obviously impressed with DH&S's proposal, its understanding of the comptroller's problems and requirements, and its projected approach to the engagement, the OCC selection committee named Pace and his team to do the work. Deloitte partner Robert Atwood served as project manager, and the firm of Carter H. Golembe Associates (consulting economists specializing in bank regulatory matters) was hired to advise DH&S throughout the project. Two highly qualified academics from the Wharton School were also called in to assist with specialized information.

The great bulk of the work, however, was performed by an

experienced team of twenty DH&S consultants, most of whom were partners. The complexity of the banking system and the crucial nature of the issues involved demanded the use of senior consultants almost exclusively.

DH&S partners assigned to the OCC engagement fanned out across the nation, interviewing bankers and bank examiners, reviewing policies and procedures, and studying both the nuts and bolts of the banking system and the OCC's organizational structure. The primary goal was to find ways the comptroller could better monitor and supervise the banks in an era of change.

"Frankly, we'd been shaken by some major bank failures in the early 1970s," says Joe Selby, senior deputy comptroller for operations. "They made us realize how ineffective our procedures had become, how far behind the times we really were, and how important it was for us to act. The bank examination function is one of our most important responsibilities, and we just weren't doing it as well as we could have."

In searching for improvements in the examination process, Deloitte partners made an interesting observation based on their knowledge of modern auditing procedures.

"They found that we'd been taking a snapshot approach to bank examinations," Selby explains. "By this I mean our examiners would go into a bank, count the cash, verify the assets and the liabilities, and generally focus on the particulars. This approach takes a tremendous amount of manpower and an enormous amount of time and often winds up wasting a lot of both by concentrating on things that don't need an examination."

Taking a page from the modern auditing technique of basing the number and type of audit tests on a corporation's internal controls, DH&S consultants advised the OCC to look first at a bank's management policies and general procedures. Then, based on an appraisal of these central factors, determine the extent of substantive testing required.

"The consultants convinced us to switch from a bottom-up approach to a top-down approach," Selby continues. "If examiners visit a bank with solid management and effective control procedures, they can greatly reduce the amount of testing required. By first gauging the bank's management, we can tell a great deal about what is going on beneath the surface."

Taking this sampling strategy to the next dimension, DH&S recommended that the OCC establish a National Bank Surveillance System (NBSS): a computer-based data collection network used to detect adverse or unusual circumstances in the national banking system as a whole or in the individual banks. By automatically getting key data, the OCC could check vital indicators, spot negative trends in the making, and get a jump on trouble spots before they turned into crises. DH&S also proposed a computer-based management information system for the OCC; a staff reorganization to facilitate the recommended procedures; a general improvement and updating of the examination process; and a comprehensive training program for OCC examiners. The final consultant's study is book length, detailing all findings and recommendations in depth.

"Before we came in, the comptroller was doing bank examinations in a very old-fashioned way," Pace says. "We gave them a fully integrated approach to update and modernize their activities."

Selby agrees. "The consultants brought us into the twentieth century. We accepted all of their major proposals and hired them to implement them. Their work was absolutely excellent throughout. I'll go so far as to say that it was the best thing that ever happened to us. There hasn't been one major bank failure of a billion dollars or more since 1975. The entire system and the individual banks are healthier than ever."

One of the least known of The Big Eight firms—the name Deloitte Haskins & Sells probably draws blanks from more than 99 percent of the population—teaches the nation's primary bank regulators—the prestigious Office of the Comptroller of the Currency—how to regulate banks. In the process of an MAS engagement, Deloitte consultants design and implement a wide-ranging system that improves the effectiveness of the federal government, brings new sophistication to the national banking system, decreases the likelihood of bank failures, protects bank investors and depositors, and adds to the economic, social, and psychological stability of communities across the United States.

"Even the banks were forced to change their procedures and to

establish more effective controls in order to comply with the
NBSS," Selby adds. "At first, they balked, saying that we were
trying to manage them. But, eventually, they began to realize that
the new procedures worked for their benefit too. It made them
better banks.

"The benefits of the DH&S study found their way into the nation's hometowns as well because it decreases the likelihood of bank
failures. A bank failure is a traumatic experience for a community.
The consultants' work helps to prevent this from happening. Tens
of millions of depositors who have never heard of the National Bank
Surveillance System are among its beneficiaries."

Deloitte's work for the OCC was broken down into two stages:
the study and the implementation. The fee for the former was
approximately $1 million—a sum Pace insists fell far short of the
firm's costs. This was no surprise: The Big Eight often take a job
they know will lose money at first but that will hopefully produce
compensating benefits somewhere down the road. This may be in
the form of prestige or profits. Some accounts are recognized loss
leaders, sought after because working with them brings great stature
to the vendor of services. Doing this kind of work is highly desir-
able, in spite of the pitiful fees, because it helps to attract many other
clients that will fork up the big bucks.

DH&S had the best of all worlds working for it at the OCC
engagement. Prestige by the truckload and a client that soon relied
heavily on its consultants. When it came time to go to contract for
the implementation stage, Deloitte was able to successfully triple its
initial fee to $3 million.

"For the study phase of the engagement, we could bill for only
about sixty percent of the hours we spent on the job," Pace explains.
"But we were willing to accept this in order to develop a good
rapport with the client and to benefit from the excellent publicity
one gets in serving the Office of the Comptroller of the Currency.
You cannot focus on one aspect of a client relationship: You have
to look at the big picture."

It is safe to say that DH&S would have benefited mightily from
the OCC engagement even if the fees never increased. That's because the prestige factor in serving bank regulators is so important

to the CPA firms. Deloitte is very heavily involved in banking and finance, counting among its clients the likes of Manufacturers Hanover Trust; Bank of New York; Bank Ohio; Morgan Guaranty Trust of New York; Southwest Bancshares; U. S. Bancorp; First Security Corporation; Dean Witter Reynolds; First Boston Corporation; Kidder, Peabody; American Investment Company; Beneficial Corporation; General Motors Acceptance Corporation; and Household Finance Corporation. This heavyweight group is bound to be impressed with the fact that their auditors/consultants have been selected to show the light to the OCC. What's more, DH&S can use the stature gained by the OCC engagement to win over new banking clients when they are in the market for Big Eight services.

All of this gives rise to the kind of conflict of interest question that permeates Big Eight activities. Is it correct for the same firm that audits leading banks to design the bank examination system? Will the firm, in its consulting role, sidestep those issues that may displease its big audit clients? The facts, in this case, seem to say no! As noted, many banks were initially upset with the demands the NBSS placed on them. In addition, the banks' natural adversaries, their regulators in the nation's capital, found no evidence of DH&S going soft in its recommendations.

"As far as I know, conflict of interest was never an issue," Selby adds. "The consultants were totally objective."

A seemingly clearer case of conflict of interest stems from the Big Eight's role as unofficial lobbyists. The firms devote a great deal of time and attention to testifying before regulatory agencies, congressional committees, and other official panels. This quasi-consulting function is administered, for the most part, by The Big Eight's so-called national affairs offices in Washington, D. C. The common practice is to maintain two major offices in the nation's capital: one practice office to serve the business needs of local clients and the national affairs office to serve as an interface between the firm, its clients, and the rule-making bureaucracies, including the IRS.

When a fiscal matter is pending before official Washington, when a decision must be made on a complex financial matter, The Big Eight are often called in (or will eagerly volunteer) to testify at public hearings. The objective here is often to influence the outcome in a way that is favorable to audit clients. The question is: Does this not seriously erode the CPA firm's independence? Should independent auditors serve as their client's allies?

The landmark report of the Senate Subcommittee on Reports, Accounting, and Management (chaired by Sen. Lee Metcalf) on the accounting establishment had this to say:

> The traditional public image of The Big Eight accounting firms as impartial and objective experts is not founded on fact and is misleading as to their true status. As political partisans and purveyors of nonaccounting services, they become loyal agents of the clients which employ their services. As independent auditors, The Big Eight firms are unable to perform these responsibilities in a manner which commands public confidence.

Further into the report, the Metcalf committee continued:

> An example of the "free" advice given to the federal government by Big Eight firms is the testimony of representatives from Arthur Andersen & Co. and Price Waterhouse & Co. before the Special Subcommittee on Integrated Oil Operations of the Senate Committee on Interior and Insular Affairs on 21 February 1974. Their prepared testimony was presented for the purpose of describing the differences between "full costing" and "successful efforts" accounting methods as applied by oil and gas companies.
>
> Arthur Andersen & Co. and Price Waterhouse & Co. both act as independent auditors for major corporations involved in oil and gas production. As such, both firms are supposed to remain independent from the interests of their clients. Rather than declining to respond to any questions which might affect their firms' ability to remain independent, the representatives of Arthur Andersen & Co. and Price Waterhouse & Co. freely advocated the controversial views generally expressed by management of oil and gas companies.
>
> In response to questioning, both firms' representatives stated that the thirty largest integrated oil companies are competitive, that the Federal Power Commission has restricted the supply of natural gas through its pricing policies, and that oil and gas prices are being kept too low by Congress. Those views are controversial and do not fall within the expertise associated with independent auditing. Nevertheless, the representatives from Arthur Andersen & Co. and Price Waterhouse & Co. went on record advocating politically and factually controversial positions before

Congress on issues of great importance to the management of the corporate clients in the oil and gas businesses.

The Big Eight accounting firms provide extensive service to federal, state and local governments. They are able to directly influence the course of governmental policies and programs through performance of their services. Conflicts of interest occur when Big Eight firms influence governmental authorities on matters which affect their corporate clients. The Big Eight firms have been able to spread the scope of their influence across both the public and private sectors.

No doubt, the Metcalf report was given to excesses and did, at times, take on the trappings of a witch hunt. What's more, there is no conclusive evidence that Big Eight firms do alter their true findings or opinions solely to satisfy clients. But that may be immaterial. Simply supporting public issues that favor clients gives the appearance of bias, and that, in itself, is enough to undermine investor confidence in the credibility of independent audits. The concept of auditor independence is strained when auditors and clients work together to promote a variety of tax, accounting, and legislative issues.

Here again, however, The Big Eight reject the critics' argument. DH&S, in its published comments on the Metcalf study, stated its position this way. "We disagree with the assertions in the study that auditors impair their independence by taking public positions, in testifying before regulatory and other governmental bodies on issues which involve their clients' interests. As explained in the appendix to this memorandum, in many cases where representatives of our firms have provided expert assistance to regulatory bodies, consumer groups, and others, it has not been at the insistence of any audit client. Also, even when our testimony relates to matters that could be expected to have an effect on clients' interests, it must be recognized that all clients are not necessarily of the same point of view on a particular issue. Often, their views are dramatically opposed. For example, an increase in electric utility rates, which would presumably be an advantage to a utility client, would appear to be against the interest of a manufacturing client which is a substantial user of electric power. Moreover, even clients in the same industry frequently find themselves on opposite sides of the same issue.

"We believe it would be unfortunate for the federal government or any other body to prevent public accounting firms from making available the benefits of their knowledge and experience to congressional committees and to regulatory bodies in matters where accounting considerations are important. . . .

"From the selfish point of view of the public accounting firms, there is much to be said against testifying before public bodies. Among other things, it would save time and expense, and it would eliminate the risk of offending any client by advocating a position with which the client did not agree. Nevertheless, we believe that we and other large public accounting firms often can make an important contribution to the work of public bodies in situations where our skill and experience are relevant, and we would oppose any limitations on our right to do so."

The Big Eight: philanthropists or power brokers?

6. Beyond Death and Taxes

"The old saying about death and taxes doesn't apply to Big Eight clients. The never pay a nickel to Uncle Sam, and, providing they keep forking up fees, the CPAs don't let them die either."
—A loan officer with a major commercial bank.

THE BIG EIGHT'S POWER extends well beyond the world of banks and bureaucrats to that of electric guitars, base drums, and gold records. When a European rock group found itself with a hit album in the United States, it had more than groupies to contend with. One problem loomed larger than crowded concert schedules, echoing amplifiers, and fast-talking producers. Everything took a back seat to TAXES.

Rock is big business: one platinum disk generates megabucks. Artists though they may be, even the most creative songsters have learned that the white Rolls-Royce doesn't pay for itself. Someone's got to fine tune the balance sheet. In a world where classics are measured in months, and careers soar and fizzle in the course of a season, the smart money is trading in its swamis, gurus, and maharishis for another kind of magic: tax shelters.

Enter The Big Eight. Whether it's a solemn board room or a psychedelic sound stage, big-time CPAs go where the money is. Not surprisingly, they can cultivate an instant taste for acid rock, disco music, or even the outrageous antics of punk. If the song's a hit, The Big Eight can dance to any tune.

Back to the European rock group flushed with the glow and the green of a top-ten platter in the states. Determined to wrestle away from the tax man as many of the bucks as possible, the boys in the band called on Touche Ross-Netherlands to put on a show of its own. The assignment: do some fancy footwork, fiscal style. The group found itself in a bind. Like many business entities with interests spanning international borders, the musicians were caught in double taxation treaties between the United States and their homeland. They needed some plan to reduce U.S. taxes on royalty income. Touche Ross staffers went into a huddle and emerged with a scheme that dazzled the rockers.

"After an analysis of the double taxation treaties between the countries involved in the transaction, TRI's (Touche Ross International) tax consultants recommended the formation of a Netherlands Antilles company (NV), to which the distribution rights of a hit recording were contributed as capital. NV, in turn, formed a Dutch subsidiary (BV) and licensed it to sell recordings in the United States. A U.S. record distribution company purchased the distribution rights from BV in return for royalties.

"The TRI plan provided several advantages: Elimination of U.S. withholding tax on royalty payments to BV by virtue of a U.S.A.-Netherlands treaty; a favorable tax ruling to BV in Holland allowing deduction of 93 percent of its royalty income from the United States of America as royalty expense to NV in the Antilles; elimination of withholding taxes in Holland on royalty payments; and declaration of net after-tax income in Holland as a dividend to NV free of Dutch withholding tax."*

Complex as it may seem, this kind of multinational wheeling and dealing is standard operating procedure at the tax practice arms of The Big Eight. Solving every conceivable kind of personal, institutional, and business tax problem is the specialty of the house, and it's done with an inordinate amount of skill, confidence, and clout. Along with MAS, tax work constitutes a major growth area for The Big Eight. Now generating about 20 percent of the firms' total fee income, tax revenues are increasing steadily. New vistas are opening rapidly in government markets and in international corporate tax engagements. Like so many aspects of modern society, the burgeoning tax structure plays into the hands of The Big Eight.

"Why will highly skilled professional tax practitioners be needed

---

*Touche Ross International, *Our Worldwide Approach to Taxation,* 1979.

in the future as in the past?" asks William Raby, the distinguished national director of tax services for Touche Ross, in a University of Massachusetts lecture on the future of CPAs in tax practice. "One reason is the complexity of our tax laws. Every time we have simplified the tax law, it has become enormously more complicated. Every time we reform the tax law, it becomes more inequitable in some ways—thus setting the stage for further reform and complication. Every time we make it more complicated, we obsolete a whole generation of people who knew something about the tax law before. The tax person of five years ago cannot analyze tax situations today with any confidence because the rules of the game are different. . . .

"A key reason the CPA has such a dominant position in tax work is, therefore, its sheer complexity, and a related reason is the speed of change. As a profession, CPAs are very bright people. We learn rapidly and we are used to adjusting. Thus, to maintain our position in tax practice, we are going to have to continue attracting and retaining people who are good at dealing with words and numbers.

"There is not only the complexity of the present law, but the probability that the United States is going to have more complex laws to replace what are presently simple laws."

Adds Wallace Olson: "As society becomes more complex, accounting takes on greater importance. Because increasing complexity is virtually a certainty, our profession is faced with a challenge and opportunity whose dimensions are so immense as to be staggering."

CPAs know that the nation's governmental bureaucracy—its layers and layers of tangled laws and regulations—puts money in their pockets and assures a steady flow of fees. Big Eight partners have split personalities: One side joins clients in bemoaning the evils of government; the other bubbles with delight at news of massive tax legislation that fills ten volumes and takes a team of experts to understand.

"There were two things that made it (the profession) grow: (1) the immense expansion of American industry that knit its vast machinery together in gigantic mergers, requiring the most intricate accounting; (2) the federal income tax, according to the rules of which individuals and corporations had to learn to play, for the protection of their profits, an ever more and more complicated game. The accounting of small industrial units in a simple society is simple also; the immense modern complex of parent and subsidiary companies, of vast stock flotations, of no-par stocks, of reorganizations of loans requires accounting by accurate, subtle, and imaginative minds. The machinery of American business has grown so fast that old definitions of capital, of earnings, of assets, surplus, and profits, in all their infinite subdivisions and ramifications, have become invalid and questionable overnight. The giant has outgrown the ability to talk intelligently about himself; it is the accountant's job to discover and define and speak the words that will describe him. . . ."*

One quipster adds this remark about one of the major laws of recent years, the Employee Retirement Income Security Act (ERISA): "This legislation was nobly planned to give Americans more retirement security through tighter controls on retirement plans. But, shit, did you ever read that thing? No layman, no banker, no corporate pension manager can fully understand it. I knew from the start that the biggest beneficiaries of the law would be the professionals who'd be called on to translate it—for fees, of course. We renamed it the 'Accountants, Lawyers, and Actuaries Retirement Income Security Act.' "

No other professional organizations are as well positioned as The Big Eight to decipher the tax laws, find the loopholes, discover the angles, and push their cases through the IRS, HEW, and equivalent bodies in and out of the United States. The sheer size of The Big Eight tax practices is awesome: They can eat competitors for breakfast. Touche Ross' tax department, for example, is staffed with CPAs, attorneys, and M.B.A.'s—a total of eleven hundred professionals in eighty offices.

The calibre of The Big Eight tax partners is of the highest level. Bill Raby's resume is revealing: a CPA and Ph.D., Dr. Raby is a member of the U.S. Tax Court Bar; member of the Executive Committee, Federal Tax Division, AICPA; chairman of the Subcommit-

---

*"Certified Public Accountants," *op. cit.*

tee on Tax Determination, Planning Task Force; and the IRS Advisory Committee on Rules of Professional Conduct. He is also the author of numerous books, including *The Income Tax and Business Decisions,* and is a contributor to the *Journal of Accountancy,* the *Journal of Taxation, Taxation for Accountants,* the *Accounting Review, Taxes,* and other professional publications.

An energetic and hospitable man, Raby plainly enjoys talking about the inner workings of a Big Eight tax practice and is quite frank about its objectives.

"We sell dollars for discount," Raby declares. "What I mean is that when all is said and done—when all the air is cleared of the legal gobbledygook—clients want to know that they saved more money in taxes than they paid to us in fees. I think that's a reasonable expectation. At Touche Ross, 'Selling Dollars for Discount' is our tax practice marketing slogan."

The intense pressure on fee levels that is shaving profit margins in the audit practice is not a significant factor in tax work. Tax planning is an elective management tool that can produce a windfall of extra dollars to fatten the bottom line—dollars otherwise slated for the federal treasury. The very fact that enlightened tax counsel can be a money-maker in its own right encourages clients to measure fees only in terms of the savings they produce in taxes.

This attitude helped Col. Robert H. Montgomery (once considered the leading figure in American accounting) build Lybrand, Ross Bros. & Montgomery into a giant CPA firm. Montgomery was "known and respected in Washington as a man who can turn government tax claims for $500,000 into refunds of $4 million."*

Even clients that balk at the first sight of a whopping Big Eight tax department invoice often come around in due time.

"I once billed a client $75,000 for a job that took only a small amount of time but required super work," Raby recalls. "It involved a case that had to be settled—a tax controversy. We handled the matter and in the process saved the client three times the amount of the fee.

"Still, the client sent us a check for only $37,500, half the amount

---

*"Certified Public Accountants," *op. cit.*

billed. I told him we wouldn't sue for the balance but I wouldn't represent him again. If he wanted the best tax advice in the world, he'd have to send me another $37,500.

"Two years later I got the check, and we resumed our relationship."

The Big Eight tax practices have evolved from a very close association with the audit arms to a position of much greater independence. Once engaged almost exclusively in solving tax problems that cropped up in the course of an audit, the tax divisions now earn the bulk of their fees from separate engagements, many of which are for nonaudit clients or for the audit clients of other Big Eight firms.

Tax work is prized by The Big Eight because there is a tremendous growth potential in the market and because tax engagements don't play games with a CPA firm's self-identity. Unlike MAS assignments—in which the accounting firms can find themselves planning airports and promoting tourism—tax engagements are closely related to the accountant's traditional role. There's no need to rub elbows with architects, pilots, or market researchers. Although nothing the Big Eight does these days is free of controversy, tax engagements produce less flack than any other major practice function.

Big Eight tax staffers serve clients as planners and problem solvers. Most of the firms bring "mixed practice units" to bear on specific cases. Experts from a cross section of financial disciplines—accounting, consulting, and law—work together to hammer out an integrated tax plan. Top practice teams are blessed with knowledge and imagination, with technicians and schemers.

The problems tackled here are not the garden variety office-at-home or medical-deduction issues that occupy the talents of thousands of lilliputian tax firms across the United States. Far from it. A local tax practitioner with little international experience would get an Excedrin headache just hearing some of the problems that routinely come through the doors of The Big Eight tax offices. Another Touche Ross mind-boggler provides a good example: An Australian manufacturer planned to construct a new facility in Malaysia to supply established markets which were threatened by rising costs at home. Since the project qualified as a so-called pioneer industry in Malaysia, it was exempt from that nation's taxes for a period of several years.

But the endeavor produced an interconnected problem which TR's tax partners in Australia were called in to solve. The problem was three-pronged:

> Because income was exempt from Malaysian taxes, it did not qualify for exemption under Australian tax law. If the Malaysian plant was found to be a branch of the Australian company, the income was fully taxable in Australia.
>
> There would be compulsory distribution to shareholders of dividends declared to the Australian parent company. The shareholders would then be taxed, or the company would pay 50 percent undistributed profits tax.
>
> An interposed company in Hong Kong was not permitted, as the Crown Colony is on the "sanctions" list for Australian exchange control procedures.

"We proposed that the Malaysian operation be set up as a company," says TR in its description of the case. "A holding company was established in Brunei to own shares in Malaysia. A Hong Kong branch of the Brunei company was formed to do reinvoicing on the sale of components from Australia to Malaysia. Losses were created in Australia on the sale of these components via Hong Kong, which would then be offset against other Australian taxable income.

"Dividends were declared back to Australia from Brunei to compensate for loss of cash flow to Hong Kong. These dividends were not taxable in Australia. Dividends were paid from Malaysia to the Hong Kong branch of the Brunei company.

"Cash flow to Australia was arranged by a back-to-back loan from a Hong Kong bank to satisfy the cash requirements of Australian shareholders. As a result, taxes in Malaysia, Brunei, Hong Kong, and Australia were negligible, and deductible losses were created in Australia."

With so many tax problems rooted in legal issues, there is no wonder that The Big Eight tax departments have a full complement of lawyers on staff. What is remarkable, however, is that these highly skilled attorneys insist that they do not practice law. By this they mean that they do not offer clients legal advice apart from tax issues, and that they do not litigate. By and large, Big Eight tax attorneys limit courtroom appearances to the Tax Court. Whether it is accurate to say that because of these limitations The Big Eight tax attorneys don't practice law is open to question. Certainly their understanding, interpretation, and manipulation of the tax laws serves a key role in the formulation of client strategies. To many, that is practicing law.

Like their major competitors, the prestigious corporate law firms in New York, Houston, and Los Angeles, Big Eight tax divisions recognize that it is more profitable to advise than to litigate. Far more can be accomplished for a client in a few hours of intensive brainstorming at the office than in weeks of hanging around a courtroom suffering through the legal system's interminable delays. When a case requires traditional legal representation, The Big Eight tax partners generally farm it out to law firms specializing in this work.

Tax partners are, in many cases, the elite professionals within The Big Eight. Many have impressive academic credentials, perform highly sophisticated work, and win an abundance of client praise. What's more, tax partners appear to view themselves as superior: One gets the impression of a learned group of gentlemen, terribly confident in their abilities and convinced that they alone can make sense of the complex tax laws that leave mere mortals dumbfounded. It doesn't hurt their ego any that they are called on to prepare the income-tax returns of all the other partners in The Big Eight. In prestigious organizations staffed with some of the best financial minds in the world, only tax partners are deemed sufficiently capable of handling their partners' personal affairs.

"Our tax people fill out the tax returns for most of our partners, most of whom are very bright guys but who are no longer able to cope effectively with what needs to be done," Raby stated in a speech given when he was tax chief for Laventhol & Horwath, a well-respected mid-size CPA firm.

Big Eight tax departments attract two different types of professionals. The vast majority are Young Turks, recently out of school and eager to make a mark in the world as top tax practitioners with hot-shot law firms or major corporations. To this breed, The Big Eight tax office is a revolving door; one enters for a year or two and then exits on the way to bigger and better things. The stint at Deloitte Haskins & Sells, Arthur Andersen, Touche Ross, or the rest is viewed as part of the educational process—a salaried finishing school and a solid-gold credit on the résumé. Most don't stop long enough to get comfortable—they're in too mad a rush for money and position to wait the ten years usually required to become a Big Eight tax partner.

The truth is that in spite of its reputation as a key to the mint, a Big Eight partnership (and this applies to all practice areas) is not the way to get wealthy. Young tax attorneys, for example, enter the firms at $30,000, climb up to $50,000 in five years, and then after more than a decade pull down $130,000 as partners. Not chicken feed, to be sure, but less than their rock-group clients make in a one-night stand and, more to the point, less than half of what a partner in a top law firm pockets in a good year. With visions of a quarter million dollars annually dancing before their eyes, the fast-track crowd isn't about to toil away for what it views as just decent earnings. To stay with The Big Eight and make the kind of bucks these ambitious joggers have in mind, they'd have to rise to vice-chairmen or better. That's a long, long shot.

Tax pros who do come to The Big Eight for the long haul are like their counterparts in audit and MAS in that they are the kind of men and women who enjoy working in large organizations, who thrive on the team spirit, and who like having specialists in house to share information and opinions with.

"We're not the Lone Ranger type riding off into the sunset," Raby says.

Adds another Big Eight senior tax partner, "The atmosphere here is somewhat collegiate. Those of us who make careers here enjoy the emphasis on scholarship, on continuing education, and on working with colleagues to devise joint solutions to difficult problems. There's a feeling of camaraderie with our partners all across the globe. It's genuinely thrilling and satisfying to be able to get on the phone with partners in Tokyo, Britain, and Africa. Sure, many of the guys here could make more dough somewhere else, but they like the team aspect of Big Eight work and are more than willing to accept the trade-offs."

Because so many of the tax-department recruits have no intention of staying on, there is far less tension in the air here than on the audit side. Relatively few are out to make partner. As such, staffers can work together without peering over each other's shoulders and without trying desperately to look good at another's expense. There is a refreshing lack of internal politics.

"It was like getting released from a mad house when I pulled off my transfer from audit to tax," says a former Big Eighter now with a small CPA firm. "At audit, the guys talked about making partner nonstop—at lunch, at the urinal, at the happy hour after work. It was pathetic, driven, insane.

"When I got to the tax department, I was amazed to see that people spent their lunch hour talking about issues; about interesting cases they were working on. The atmosphere was exhilarating. I couldn't believe I was still in the same firm: It felt like a different world. But I left anyway because I couldn't wait for the long career build."

Not to say that The Big Eight tax departments are bucolic settings. There are pressures here, intense pressures, but they emanate more from the nature of the practice rather than the petty jealousies and competitions that arise in the race to make partner.

The migraines in tax land can be traced to two major factors: work loads and client expectations. It is standard operating procedure for CPA firms to inundate their staffs with work—to force-feed each professional with enough projects to keep him walled in behind a pile of client files sixteen hours a day. Collective wisdom has it that this work overkill is the best way for CPA firms to make big money. It is a simple formula followed throughout The Big Eight: Push the staff to the limits and bill the clients accordingly. Rack up those billable hours. Work. Work. Work. This pressure to produce takes a heavy toll on the tax partners. They have smaller staffs than their audit colleagues, they cannot rely as much on computers, and there is less grunt work to be farmed out to new recruits. Tax work tends to be partner intensive—requiring the big guns' active involvement rather than a supervisory presence.

Even experienced pros, most of whom are well adjusted and relaxed off hours, say that life is helter-skelter in the office—a mad rush in ten different directions. The greatest pressure on the tax staff, however, comes from the fear of being caught ill-prepared.

"You live in a sort of controlled state of terror that a client will call and ask a question that you not only don't know the answer to but don't even know what the hell the guy is talking about," says a Big Eight tax partner. "With such a huge body of tax information in existence, and many of the rules changing on a daily basis, there's always a lot even the best of us don't know. That's accepted here at the firm: tax partners don't have to play at being superhuman. But, and this is a big 'but,' some clients aren't so enlightened. They're paying the bills, and they expect us to have all the answers. If we look foolish just once, they lose all respect for us. I've seen it happen over and over again. Clients like to have this fantasy about their tax advisers being miracle workers. It's a matter of pride to talk about your ingenious tax guy—real cocktail-party banter. But it's the nature of the business that you can fall from grace faster than it takes to drink a vodka tonic. All it takes is one error, and the client's off to shop for another tax genius.

"So you read as much as you can, and you spend half your life at tax seminars, and you pray like hell that you don't get that one call that leaves you mumbling like a fool."

Adds Bill Raby: "A great artist has the ability to see things differently. The same goes for a great tax attorney. He has to be able to see things others don't, he must alert clients to opportunities they miss.

"It goes so far as to be able to salvage benefits from a court case a client loses. In spite of the loss, there may be opportunities for another client. You have to have that artist's vision: Where will the opportunity fit in to help another client?"

Most of The Big Eight tax practices are woven through their far-flung network of offices and operations. Tax experts are stationed at all key posts in the organization in order to service those clients seeking tax advice and to assist in those audits and MAS engagements requiring tax expertise. Just how one Big Eight tax division is structured can be seen by a close look at Arthur Young's well-respected setup. A national director of tax, reporting directly to the firm's managing partner, runs AY's tax arm. Along with regional tax directors and a high-level tax advisory committee, the national director develops policies and procedures for firm-wide application. Considering the enormous size of The Big Eight firms, it is essential that each develops its own uniform standards for all practice functions. That's the only way to assure that the names of Arthur Young, Arthur Andersen, Price Waterhouse, and the rest stand for the same calibre of work in Denver as in New York, in London as in Singapore.

At AY, each of the firm's offices has a separate tax department supervised by an office director of taxes. This front-line executive is responsible for enforcing firm standards on the local tax practice, for sweet-talking local clients, for generating new business, and for turning on the pressure to meet deadlines and increase billings. Regional directors coordinate the work of the various offices involved in an engagement and allocate the number of staffers at each location. Office tax directors report administratively to the managing partner of the local office and functionally to the regional tax chiefs. The entire domestic tax organization gets support services from the National Tax Department, which has offices in New York and Washington, D.C.

For worldwide engagements, experts in international taxation are stationed in most of the major practice offices. In addition, the firm's International Tax Department boasts a group of specialists experienced in those tax matters involving two or more countries, as well as related currency regulations and government controls. This elite unit sorts out the thorny issues, including reviews of proposed international transactions—such as acquisitions, reorganizations, and liquidations of foreign interests. When a major U.S. food marketer, for example, courts a cash-rich biscuit company in France, it may call on the AY International Tax Department to spell out the tax implications of an acquisition and to advise on the best way to structure the transaction. Arthur Young's international team also does counseling on tax credits, source and allocation of income, return requirements, and taxation of individuals. Like most of its competitors, AY is an aggressive marketer of tax services for expatriate employees. With so many corporations now multinational in scope, there is a huge market for providing personal tax services to corporate employees based outside of their homelands. The services, arranged and paid for by the employers, can involve thousands of individuals for a single client company.

"The United States, unlike most major industrial companies, taxes its citizens on their worldwide income wherever earned. As the tax aspects of overseas assignments grow more complex, an increasing number of multinational employers provide tax assistance for their employees working abroad. This segment of our practice has grown to such an extent that during 1980 we established a separate unit in New York City to serve a number of these clients located in the metropolitan area. A staff of more than 100 provides a comprehensive tax planning and tax return preparation program for U.S. citizens overseas and for aliens working in the United States. We now have fifteen practice officers that provide these services year-round to employees of multinational clients."*

Big Eighters like to make expatriate services part of their tax practice mix because it is one of the functions the tax partners can computerize. Arthur Young's computer program, brand name AY-Expatriate, serves multinationals with employees working abroad. A flick of the data processor's switch helps clients plan overseas assignments, evaluate tax-law changes, structure reimbursement policies, and analyze tax-planning techniques. Once programs of this sort are designed, they can be pure gold for The Big Eight. Just plug in the client's name and particulars, and out comes the necessary data. The service generates substantial fees from each new client, with very little in the way of incremental cost. Hence the big push to promote and market these programs to a long list of corporate prospects.

In the domestic arena, AY's tax department (again like its competitors) features a wide range of client services:

*Price Waterhouse 1980 Annual Report.

"Pre-year-end review of operating results for tax-saving opportunities.

Evaluation of present client policies, practices, and procedures to ensure that tax accruals, reserves, and payments are in conformity with current regulations and are computed so as to take maximum advantage of available opportunities for tax reduction.

Evaluation of the tax effects of important business decisions.

Determination of the current position of the IRS in specific areas through private ruling requests or requirements for technical advice from the field.

Assistance in state taxation, including representation of clients before state tax authorities.

Representation of clients before the IRS.

Distribution of client memorandums on significant tax developments. These frequently include information not available in published tax services. Information of specific importance to a particular client is conveyed directly to that client, as a matter of routine, by the tax partners or manager responsible."*

The latter part of the list features what can best be called Big Eight "clout" services. Here the firms, through their national offices in Washington, D.C., make their clients privileged subjects of the U.S. tax system. Although this is roundly denied by the IRS, it appears that the firms can and do reach into the Internal Revenue Service's inner sanctum to win special treatment for big business and wealthy individuals. There is no evidence of illegal or unethical activities but simply a classic demonstration of how to win friends and influence people.

A perfect example of The Big Eight's clout is evidenced in the use of "private rulings." Put simply, this is the process by which taxpayers can learn, in advance, the tax implications of a proposed

*Arthur Young, *Serving Our Multinational Clients.*

business or personal financial transaction. If a group of investors plans to form a limited partnership to purchase a herd of cattle and to use X amount of breeding costs as tax deductions, they may request a private ruling to check if their deductions are legitimate. Some group members may not want to invest until they have an answer.

"The rulings are like insurance policies," says Henry Ferrero, partner in charge of the National Affairs Tax Group for DH&S. "They give the firm or individual a formal, written opinion that the taxpayer can rely on. The IRS will not override it."

The problem for the unescorted is that private rulings can get bogged down in a bureaucratic quagmire, taking up to a year or more to come sputtering out of the IRS National Office. What's more, the answer may wind up being negative. If that is the case, there's no chance to negotiate immediately with the examiner. Revised applications, once they can be prepared, have to queue up on another processing line. It's enough to make the most patient of mortals scotch investment plans or take a flyer without the government's blessing. But that's a roll of the dice that can produce enormous and unexpected tax bills years down the road.

The Big Eight help their clients to sidestep the delays and risks by ramroding private rulings through the IRS and by staying on top of each case to its conclusion. Making things work quickly and efficiently in Washington, however, takes a secret weapon, and The Big Eight have a beauty: They routinely hire former IRS insiders, put them on the payroll for up to twice their government salaries, and then set them loose shepherding client rulings through the Internal Revenue Service's National Office. The strategy is clever: Those men and women most familiar with the ruling process are transferred from the government to the client's side. Not only are these specialists familiar with the private ruling machinery, but they also have a network of old school ties at the IRS.

The heavy concentration of former IRS insiders at some of The Big Eight national tax offices is apparent by a look at the DH&S setup. Of the four partners and three managers on staff in the firm's national tax group (as of summer 1980), five had previously worked for the IRS and one for the Treasury Department.

"Many of the IRS guys we hire are frustrated by government work because they can't progress to their potential," Ferrero adds. "The most they can make is about $50,000 a year at the IRS. We can't double their salaries right away, but we will give them immediate raises of $25,000 to $30,000 and the chance to make more than $100,000 in years to come. Some of these people are hired on as partners to start.

"We select the best and brightest people in the IRS. When they come to us, they do retain their contacts in the service. Most have put in eight to ten years before joining a CPA firm. They know the ropes; they can get better treatment for our clients because they know who to call on the inside and how things work there. It's all very proper and on the up and up, however. Just good use of experienced people. We'd never let a partner in our firm do anything illegal or unethical."

Just how The Big Eight make legal use of their well-connected tax partners is revealed in this typical case: A local practice office's corporate client wants to acquire another company but is concerned with the tax implications. To determine if the IRS sees eye to eye with management, the corporation structures the transaction on paper and sends this over to its CPAs. Tax specialists at the practice office draft a private ruling request based on the deal and relay it to the firm's national tax office.

Experts there review the ruling as prepared by the practice office to determine if improvements or changes are necessary. The ruling is then hand-delivered to the IRS examiners group focusing on corporate acquisitions. Typically, the examiners will call the CPAs within fifteen days, confirm that they are in possession of the ruling request, and tell who is reviewing it. Once the supervising IRS specialist is identified, the Big Eighter keeps close tabs on him, calling frequently to check on the ruling's progress. The examiner may have questions or requests for additional information, all of which is supplied promptly by the CPAs or their clients.

"Sometimes the examiner will say he can't rule the way we had hoped he would because of a technical problem with our reasoning," says a Big Eight tax partner. "Well, that's an obstacle we can surmount with a conference or a memo clarifying our position. All taxpayers are entitled to this, but most simply aren't aware of it. "We do more than just present the client's position and then sit back. We stay close to the case. We pressure the IRS examiners. We argue the issue, negotiate, and try to iron out the differences. If all goes well, it takes us about three months to get a ruling. We can't get the client's request moved ahead of others on the waiting list, but we can drive it through much faster once it's up for consideration. That's because we find ourselves appearing before the same IRS examiners time and again. Our people are very well acquainted with many of the people there. That really helps us to get things done quickly."

The IRS, for its part, refuses to comment officially on The Big Eight. After repeated efforts to get some response to Big Eight revelations of its IRS-related activities, the author received this letter:

Dear Mr. Stevens:
This responds to your recent letter to Commissioner Kurtz asking why no one at the IRS will comment on The Big Eight accounting firms.

All IRS employees are covered by a code of conduct. A section for this code, Section 228.5 of the "Handbook of Employee Responsibilities and Conduct," states: "Employees may not recommend or suggest, specifically or by implication, to a taxpayer, any attorneys or accountants in connection with any official business which involves or may involve the Internal Revenue Service." Section 228.4 of the Handbook further states that "adverse or antagonistic criticism of the work of accountants or attorneys employed by taxpayers must be avoided at all times."

Therefore, to make favorable or unfavorable comments would be improper and in violation of the rules to which all IRS employees are subject.
Sincerely,
A. James Golato
Assistant to the Commissioner
(Public Affairs)

The rules concerning chumminess between The Big Eight's national tax staffers and IRS examiners can be viewed as comic attempts to rule out impropriety. One firm forbids its staffers to treat examiners to lunch but has no prohibitions against taking them to dinner, providing the partner rather than the firm pays the tab.

The Big Eight makes its partners favorite sons of the tax system in more ways than one. As recognized experts in tax law—and as advisers to the nation's leading corporations—Big Eight firms are frequently called on by government agencies to help in the shaping of tax rules and laws. When the House Ways and Means Committee considered a bill before Congress that would prevent states from taxing corporations on a "unitary basis," DH&S testified in favor of the legislation. Put simply, the bill was designed to prevent states from hitting corporations with disproportionate taxes based on the companies' overall operations. Naturally, big business favored passage of the bill and had powerful allies on the scene in Congress.

"We testified in favor of the proposed legislation," Ferrero adds. "Not because a client asked us to, but because we think unitary taxation is wrong. But we do have clients who complain about this tax. It's an unfair tax and an administrative nightmare.

"We don't get paid for testifying. We do it as a service to the country—to provide our expertise."

Praised be The Big Eight!

Tax practice illustrates how well The Big Eight can provide a complex and sophisticated service—and how they can do it better than just about anyone else. Few professional organizations are big or rich enough to staff up with all manner of experts, to put "think tank" groups to work dissecting minute tax issues, and to pick off top IRS staffers, hire them, pay them a bundle, and put them to work for clients rather than the government. This awesome firepower makes The Big Eight the darlings of corporate America and assures their place on the accounts payable rolls of the *Fortune* 500.

But it works against the firms in an increasingly important practice area: providing service to small business. The problem is that, to many of the nation's small companies, anything big is not to be trusted.

But so what. Why do The Big Eight care what diddling merchants, struggling manufacturers, and bush-league distributors think about them anyway? Why concern themselves with fledgling ventures—many of which can barely pay their bills—when they have a lock and key on the billion dollar multinationals? The answer is rooted purely in marketing considerations: The Big Eight desperately need small business clients in order to expand and prosper in the 1980s and beyond. Certainly, the audit market is saturated. Here, The Big Eight simply trade clients: lose one, win one; lose another, gain another. Each turnover involves a $100,000-plus proposal—most of which wind up in the shredder. Very expensive litter.

The small-business market is crucial to The Big Eight because it is enormous, and because it is ripe for a wide range of services. In short, it is a vehicle for future growth. With the likes of Peat, Marwick and Coopers soon to be in the billion-dollar-a-year category, even modest 10 percent revenue increases will demand $100 million in new business annually. Snaring five colossal audit accounts in a single year (a highly unlikely feat) will yield only about 15 percent of that figure. Although substantial growth can be generated by the consulting and tax practices, many believe that the greatest long-term potential is in bringing in tens of thousands of small-business accounts.

"The opportunities in this practice area are open-ended—nothing less than that," says Al Bernikow, a partner in the Touche Ross's small-business arm, called the Private Companies Advisory Service. "That's because in the small-business community there's a terrible lack of financial expertise. Entrepreneurs usually are not financial people. There is total financial disarray at many of the small firms we're called in to serve.

"They wind up contacting us once they start making good money. That's when it hits them that they have to pay big taxes. Suddenly, the call goes out for help. Sometimes we can't be of much help in the first year, but we can plan for the future and reduce the tax bite later on. We know how to generate legitimate tax losses. Because entrepreneurs want this, and because they are forced by lenders to get their fiscal house in order, there'll always be a tremendous amount of work for us in the small-business market. We're first starting now to tap those opportunities in a big way."

The Big Eight small-business practice is a world within a world.

Everything here is in marked contrast to the more established divisions, especially tax and audit. Most striking is the fact that the small-business-practice partners bear a closer resemblance to their clients than to their Big Eight colleagues. They tend to be an earthy lot, given to the use of slang and to the shirt-sleeve style that the traditionalists at the firms abhor. The polish, the formality, the Brooks Brothers-business-school reserve that characterizes many audit departments is not found here. Instead there are cigar-chompers, knuckle-crackers, poker-players. It's a different crowd; a different way of viewing the world.

The differences are due, in part, to both the nature of the practice and the calibre of partners it attracts. First, serving small business is totally dissimilar to serving the Fords or Exxons of the world. Entrepreneurs have no time or patience for the sluggish, double-checking, do-it-by-committee approach of the giant corporations. When an owner calls his CPA—and he may do so at 2:00 A.M.—he wants immediate advice or perhaps a personal visit in the middle of the night. When corporate America is fast asleep, small business is wide awake thinking of ways to survive. Accountants have to be up with them.

Many of the trappings of the multinational audit practice are absolute no-no's on the small-business side. Busy tire dealers don't take to leisurely lunches at nouvelle cuisine restaurants. If they lunch with the CPA, it will be over a bowl of chili or a burger in the office. Also, the treasured corporate practice of having a secretary call a client's secretary, having both push the hold buttons until the bosses are ready, is simply not tolerated in small business. You want to make a call, you pick up the receiver and dial. No secretaries, no hold buttons, no delays, no formalities, no etiquette.

"Try to get fancy with seat-of-the-pants entrepreneurs and you'll get a dial tone for your efforts," says a Big Eight small-business-practice staffer. "They don't put up with anything that is not direct and essential—and I respect them for that. Serving a small client is ninety percent work and ten percent bullshit. In other areas of accounting practice, it's just the reverse." Many small-business practitioners come to The Big Eight through acquisitions. Small CPA firms blessed with healthy practices are widely sought after by

The Big Eight. By acquiring these local firms, the giants can gain solid footholds in new markets overnight. What's more, they can add thousands of small businesses to the client roster with one fell swoop. Along with the new accounts, however, comes the existing staff, which is absorbed into The Big Eight small-business practice. As products of a vastly different background, however, the new additions mix with their colleagues like oil and water.

"I've worked on both sides of the fence, and there's no doubt in my mind that the differences between Big Eight CPAs and small-firm practitioners is great," says one sole practitioner formerly with Deloitte Haskins & Sells.

"I've had offers from the big firms to buy me out, but I've declined even though the prospective deals were attractive from a financial standpoint. My actions are based on a firm desire to stay in business for myself. I work hard now, hell yes, but it's enjoyable and gratifying work. You're in it for yourself, close to your clients and practicing without all the silly formalities. Some of us like it this way; others prefer The Big Eight style."

Small business differs from other Big Eight services in substance as well as style. The former is comprehensive in scope, including everything from filing tax returns, designing cash control procedures, and drawing up estate plans. The CPA in charge of a small-business account does a little bit of everything: He is the only true generalist in The Big Eight.

"In small-business practice, we have to have medical degrees, psychiatric degrees, and legal degrees," jokes Bernikow. "We have to hold the client's hand, worry about his heart, control his fears.

"Some of the engagements we work on are really wild. One small client wanted to grow rapidly by purchasing another company twice the size of his. One problem: The owner of the target firm hated our client and would hang up on him if he called to propose a deal. Our engagement was to come between the two partners, negotiate for the purchase, and structure the acquisition. One provision of the deal was that the principal of the company being purchased didn't have to deal directly with our client. He was willing to negotiate only on that basis."

Adds Jeff Sands, a manager with Peat, Marwick's Small Business

Advisory Services: "We're the only ones who have to be confidants as well as accountants. It's a very close, hands-on relationship. Small-business owners tell you their problems and expect you to be thinking of solutions as they speak. They demand expertise in raising capital, tax-planning, business structure options, lease vs. buy decisions—just about every aspect of business operations. You have to have a lot of experience in a wide range of functions, and you have to keep the lessons learned on the front burner. When an entrepreneur wants an answer, he wants it fast. We call in experts from throughout the firm for specialized work, but I have to have some familiarity with it all. Small-business owners expect that!"

The scope of PMM's small-business practice is wide indeed, including the following major services:

Planning for new ventures, organizational structures, growth strategies, and routes to going public.

Financial analyses of working-capital needs, cash management, credit and collection procedures, and return on investment performance.

Preparation of operating budgets and capital-expenditure budgets.

Accounting and management information systems analysis, new systems analysis, systems implementation, work simplification techniques, procedures manuals, inventory control, and the design of minicomputer business systems.

Minimizing taxes through alternative business organizations, such as joint ventures, partnerships, associations and trusts; self-employment retirement plans; real-estate ventures and gifts of income-producing assets.

Counseling on adoption or change of accounting year, annual and one-time elections, installment sales, inventory evaluation methods, and depreciation guidelines.

Estate planning through transfer of interests in business, personal balance sheets, gifts, life insurance, and buy-sell agreements.

Tax return preparation, review of prior returns, and representation before tax authorities.

Specialized projects, including pension and profit-sharing plans, stock options, ESOPs [Employee Stock Ownership Plans], executive searches, organization studies, client training programs, minicomputer feasibility studies, hardware and software selection, and computer system analyses and design.*

This range of financial services is bewildering to small-business owners. Most have never heard of half the functions and have no intention of contracting for them. But that's no surprise to the Big Eighters. Their carefully cultivated marketing strategy calls for a slow build. The idea is to sink the CPAs' teeth into small companies via the most basic services—tax returns, loan plans, and the like. Then, with a foot firmly in the door, they seek to expand from this base, showing the client where he must have additional services and how they can pay off. Once the entrepreneur starts thinking and acting like a manager, as well as a wheeler-dealer, he is likely to purchase a full complement of Big Eight services.

When the marketing plan works, it benefits both the client and the CPA firm. There is no doubt that The Big Eight have much to offer small firms, and that many fledgling ventures fail precisely because they lack financial counseling. Many owners don't really know if their businesses are healthy or comatose. Quite frequently, problems that fester beneath the surface emerge in one awful moment, quickly smothering the life out of the company. Sound financial controls can go a long way toward preventing these sudden strokes. Those small businesses wise enough to add more and more accounting controls—and who turn to the CPAs for open-ended advice—stand a much better chance of prospering over the long term.

The accounting firms benefit from this too because they are hitching their wagons to rising stars—much like investing in growth stocks that take off. As the company explodes from its meager beginnings, it seeks more and more services along the way. A dot on the client map can turn into a big-bucks account, graduating

*Peat, Marwick, Mitchell & Co., Small Business Advisory Services.

from the small-business practice and into tax, MAS, and audit.

"I started serving the United Foods Corporation when it was a spanking new grain-storage business with just a few employees," says Bernard Z. Lee, managing partner of Seidman & Seidman, the tenth largest CPA firm* and one that specializes in serving small and mid-size companies. "That was in 1958, and our fee was $50 per month to do the firm's books and tax returns. Gradually, the company diversified and evolved into one of the largest producers of frozen foods.

It is now listed on the American Stock Exchange, does several hundred million a year in sales, and is still a client."

B.Z., as he is widely known in the profession, is an engaging and hospitable Texan, based in Houston even though his firm's headquarters are in New York. A former independent practitioner who came to Seidman & Seidman through a merger, B.Z. likes staying close to his clients. And he enjoys deflating The Big Eight's love affair with small businesses.

"They're too big to really care about the little guys," he snaps. "In the small-business area, you have to be everything to your clients—adviser, hand-holder, sounding board—and the giants aren't going to give that much. They're not geared for it. They're also too big: Who needs an elephant gun to kill a mosquito?

"The small-business practice takes great dedication. Why, I still worry and lose sleep over the clients I've lost in all my years of public practice. I toss and turn and try to figure out why I lost them. You can't get this kind of concern from The Big Eight."

Of course, Big Eighters deny this vehemently. They point to dramatic examples of their small-business ties.

"Talk about taking on small clients, how about an American Legion employee who brokers lumber, part-time, from his basement," says Russ Viewheg, a Touche Ross small-business partner. Like others on the small-business staffs throughout The Big Eight, Viewheg is animated about his work, proud of its comprehensive nature and of the key role he plays in shaping successful ventures. There's a sense of pride here—one that comes from meaningful involvement in a client's business.

---

*One hundred sixty partners, $50 million in annual revenues.

"My lumber client came to me when he had just enough brokerage business to leave the Legion and devote himself to his own venture full-time. He didn't know much about management, but he knew enough to call in an expert to guide him from the start. I took the job because it was an interesting challenge, and because I believed I could help him make a go of it. It's great to roll up your sleeves and get in on the ground floor. There's a lot to do but it's rewarding if the business succeeds.

"When you come into a seat-of-the-pants operation, you see a hundred fires burning and you have to decide which ones to put out first. In the lumber guy's case, I went directly to the accounts receivable. They were pleading to be straightened out. All the man had was a notebook; no formal financial records of any kind."

Next, Viewheg set up a bookkeeping system and trained the client's secretary to maintain it. CPAs frequently find that clients use all manner of makeshift books. Because this can lead to major problems with the IRS, accountants move quickly to install a meaningful bookkeeping system. They view it as a cornerstone of sound management.

"We had a small-business client who used to keep a big notebook containing the names of all his customers," Viewheg adds. "For those who were delinquent, he'd put a paper clip on the account's page. He was very pleased with this system and couldn't be persuaded to adopt a more formal procedure. Well, a simple accident did more to change his mind than the pleadings of a dozen CPAs. One day the prized notebook fell off his desk and the paper clips fell out. Just like that he lost all track of his receivables. That's when he asked us to set up a bookkeeping system. It's probably the only time we were called in because a book fell off a desk."

Big Eighters refuse to serve as bookkeepers per se. Insisting, and rightly so, that there is no good reason to pay top professional fees for clerical services, they seek to train clients' staffers to do the books. Small firms hiring CPAs solely for bookkeeping services are simply not acceptable to The Big Eight. They are picked up by those small practitioners hungry for business of any kind.

"With the bookkeeping system in place, my lumber broker soon had things under control," Viewheg recalls. "The company showed real promise but needed capital to expand. So the next thing I did was to help set up good bank relationships. This involved calling on contacts in the banking community and preparing the kinds of statements and reports lenders demand."

With loans soon coming through, the fledgling business took its first big step forward and acquired a lumber yard. With this, the entrepreneur moved out of his basement shop, bought a respectable business facility, and purchased a sizeable inventory. The timing was right: Sales exploded, and a second yard was acquired soon after.

The company grew to the point where a full-time financial executive was needed on staff. Viewheg alerted the client to this and helped in the search for a competent controller. As the business continued to expand, the former American Legion employee found himself to be a man of means with substantial assets and ominous tax problems to match.

For Big Eight CPAs, this is the ideal case history: a ground-floor start with the one-in-a-thousand small firms that make it big and demand a wide array of professional services. Viewheg's work for the lumber concern included structuring the yard purchases, doing inventory controls systems, estate-tax plans, audits, corporate tax plans, management consulting, and the design and implementation of profit-sharing and incentive plans.

"I have taken this from a shoestring business to an audit account," Viewheg says, literally glowing with pride. "The company now does about $160 million a year and has about five hundred employees. That's dramatic growth by any measure. The owner's a terrific businessman; we helped him by providing professional services at every stage of the company's evolution. He's still a client, and we're still giving him the same kind of personal attention he received in the early days."

In spite of these and other impressive case histories, there is still question as to whether The Big Eight and small business can find true happiness together. In the rush to tap this enormous market, Big Eighters have not considered all the implications of working with "the little guys." Just collecting fees from small firms can be like pulling teeth.

Creative solutions are required. "Sometimes our billings come in

big lumps," says Neil Driscoll, partner in charge of the small-business practice at DH&S' Boston office. "Small firms can find this
hard to swallow. Cash flow is extremely important to them, so they
panic when they see how much they owe. Some keep promising to
pay and never do. We billed one client $13,000 before we realized
he was a deadhead.

"To avoid this, and to make life easier for our small clients as well,
we design payment programs geared to their operations. One broadcast client of ours, for example, bought two new stations and asked
us to structure the deals. There was a lot of work involved, and we
billed a considerable amount for it. In fact, they had bills from us
up the kazoo. The owner said he couldn't pay that kind of money.
We said sure he could, but maybe not at once. Our solution was for
him to put us on the payroll and pare the bills off gradually but
consistently. The client now sends us a check for $500 per month
and everyone's happy with the arrangement. We make it clear to
small firms that if they have trouble paying the fees, little bits and
pieces are as good as one big check."

For high-powered professional firms accustomed to the straightforward billing procedures of the *Fortune* 500, this wrestling and
wrangling over every dollar can be too much to take. Big Eighters
are not skilled at the fine art of telephone shouting matches; they are
not used to defending minor invoices to skeptical and demanding
clients. Too bad! When it comes to small business, that's the price
you pay. Ask any entrepreneur: It goes with the turf.

Fees for small-business services are computed on the same basis
as those for Mobil Oil. Partners', managers', and staff accountants'
hourly rates remain the same regardless of the client. While $150 per
hour for a tax partner's services may not shake up a General Motors
executive (who may, himself, earn the equivalent of $200 an hour),
it can sit wrong with a restauranteur working sixteen hours a day
to make $50,000 a year. Even if the client agrees to the rates in
advance, seeing all those big-buck invoices piling up causes hyper-
tension. Quite frequently, fears of a rip-off set in, and that alone can
damage even the most productive professional relationship.

"Sometimes we can't service a small business because the owner
went to a local Joe accountant who quoted him a fee that he then

wants us to match," says Bernikow. "This kind of client belongs with local Joe. He has it set in his mind that professional fees should not be more than x dollars, and that's all he wants to hear. We can't deal with that kind of person."

Big Eighters insist that their fees, when viewed in the proper context, are competitive, that most of the work can be performed by young staffers, that this lowers the average hourly rate to $50 rather than $150, and that the quality of the work is high enough to warrant a slight premium over the rates of local practitioners. What's more, they sing the familiar chorus about the benefits of a worldwide organization, in-house expertise, and an enormous data bank.

Still, the entrepreneurs' basic instinct is on target: The Big Eight are, in the vast majority of cases, too big and too expensive for small business. It's a case of overkill on rates, experience, and resources. Ninety percent or more of The Big Eight's services are over the heads of small companies. A lot of excess horsepower.

The argument about the staff vs. partners billing is full of holes. There's no doubt that the greenest recruits put in most of the labor on small-business engagements, and the billing reflects this, but what does that prove? Simply that by turning to The Big Eight, a small business can pay $40 to $60 per hour for the services of a twenty-two-year-old kid fresh out of Hofstra University (and still learning on the job), rather than an equivalent fee for a skilled, local professional thoroughly experienced in small-business affairs and personally rooted in the community.

Although The Big Eight are trying to outdo one another in passionate pledges of devotion to the small-business community, this seems to be mostly hot air. There is ample window dressing—separate small-business divisions, partners specializing in emerging ventures, involvement with entrepreneurial issues and organizations —but not much in the way of substance. The truth is that The Big Eight's heart belongs to the corporate behemoths; the realization that there's some money to be made elsewhere can't change that.

There is something missing in The Big Eight's small-business practices. The glamourous aura that swirls around the firms hardly rubs off on the partners and staffers serving small clients. Top

accounting students shy away from this work: Few will kill themselves to graduate with honors and to land a spot at a prestige CPA
firm just to tell friends and family that they're counting quarters for
Bob's Bake Shop. The cream-of-the-college crop wants to write
home to mom about the prestige engagements—Texaco, Procter &
Gamble, or CBS audits. The same goes for most Big Eight partners
transferred to small business from other practice areas: There's a
mood of men in exile—of professionals who've sinned and have
been banished from the mainstream.

Much of the blame for this can be traced to the top executive suite.
Although managing partners are leading the drive to service small
business, most still define themselves and their firms as auditors and
advisers to the giants.

All tout the glories of long-term engagements with big glamour
accounts. This is The Big Eight's real source of pride. There's no
doubt that the heavyweight partners are those in charge of *Fortune*
100 engagements; their small-business counterparts are viewed as
strictly bush-league.

In spite of all the noise to the contrary, small firms are definitely
second-class citizens to The Big Eight. Their needs are way down
on the list of priorities. In a typical case, a group of investors asked
a Big Eight firm to structure an organization for joint purchases of
real estate, stocks, and gems. The investors sought the clout and
diversity of pooled funds, while still retaining individual rights and
personal tax advantages. The assignment was to design a financial
structure for that purpose.

Responsive at the outset, the CPAs welcomed the engagement
and pledged to tailor services to the group's needs and budget limitations. The client looked good on paper: a small account, but one
with growth potential and with sophisticated principals consciously
seeking quality work. But when it came to delivering for the client,
the Big Eighters proved lackadaisical, disinterested, preoccupied
with more pressing matters. Partners failed to show up at client
meetings, making eleventh-hour excuses about flat tires and the like.
Worse yet, the firm played musical chairs with the client, shifting
responsibility for the assignment to a revolving cast of partners.
Each partner named to the job seemed eager to pawn it off on a

colleague. Those identified as experts in group investments proved, on questioning, to be lightweights, clearly unfamiliar with the issues at hand. A terribly disappointing view of the mighty Big Eight in action. The greatness doesn't translate well to small businesses.

But why do some small business owners flock to The Big Eight? Between them, The Big Eight serve more than a hundred thousand small clients. The reason for this is simple: There are two kinds of entrepreneurs. Those that instinctively distrust big organizations, who see through the hype and know that signing up with The Big Eight is the best way to get lost in the shuffle. This group also knows that you can't talk to a Big Eighter as you can to a CPA down the street. More than anything else, shopkeepers, service-station owners, distributors and plumbers want accountants who can help them beat Uncle Sam for a few tax dollars. It's The Gospel According to Small-Business Owners that you can't make money if you're honest with the Fed. The only way to survive, they say, is to sneak a healthy cache into the vault or under a floorboard.

"I use the one-out-of-four method," says the proprietor of a successful gourmet food shop. "One out of four sales go directly to my pocket. No stops at the cash register, thank you. Of course, I wind up with a good piece of loose change. My accountant—a guy I went to high school with—knows this. We talk about it openly and plan ways to spend the money. He's had some damn good ideas. That's why I like him and pay him well. Anyone can do a tax return. I need someone I can trust.

"Can you imagine talking about loose change with the stuffed-shirt crowd at the fancy accounting firms. Forget it. They're too damn proper for my taste. The last thing I want is an accountant who goes by the book. Might as well mail all your income to the IRS. Why pay a middleman to do it for you?"

Still, a tiny minority of entrepreneurs do get their money's worth with The Big Eight. The high fees and halfhearted attention are acceptable to those who can benefit from the private-ruling mechanism, need a prestige audit signature to impress lenders, or who are involved in so-called target industries that get the full measure of The Big Eight's resources and capabilities.

The latter is an interesting phenomenon and offers the only hope for a lasting marriage between small business and The Big Eight. A case in point concerns the activities of DH&S' Boston office in the cable-television field. After years of fiddling around with small business in The Big Eight's typical halfhearted fashion, DH&S got religion in 1978.

"For the first time we made a real commitment in terms of personnel," says Neil Driscoll. "The regional partners promised not to steal our small-business staffers for emergency assignments on major audits. This had been a nagging problem in the past: When there were two jobs to be done and only one man to do them, small business got the short end of the stick. Well, you just can't service the self-employed with revolving personnel. Entrepreneurs expect to work with familiar faces—with CPAs who know their firms inside out. If strangers keep marching through the door, they lose all faith in the service.

"In 1978, we took one partner, three managers, four senior accountants, and two paraprofessionals and shaped them into a small-business group. The regional partner promised to respect the group's integrity as small-business specialists, and he did just that. The commitment is a tough one to make. The nature of the small-business practice is such that staffers may, at times, be underutilized. Clients with seasonal activities, for example, may be in their slow period. Well, you can't shift around a small-business staffer just because he's not working to capacity one week.

He must be free to rush to a client's side the minute business picks up again or a crisis strikes. That's the only way a small business practice can perform well: It needs reserve capacity. That's exactly what we now have."

Hyperbole aside, DH&S has picked up an impressive roster of cable-television clients by focusing on this market, developing customized programs for it, and computerizing many of the services involved. When The Big Eight commits itself to a target market in this way—when it is willing to make long-term investments in specialized client programs—it can deliver superior services to small business, price them competitively, and earn a healthy profit in the process. The secret is the design of computer programs capable of performing sophisticated services for hundreds or thousands of small companies in a particular industry. Once the program is on stream, there is little incremental work. The client's numbers are simply plugged in, and the data comes tumbling out. Loan statements, cash-flow analyses, income statements, budget projections—all can be prepared this way. Small companies can enjoy the benefits of Big Eight association without the prohibitive fees. Computers, rather than partners or green staffers, do most of the work.

When DH&S launched its Boston small-business unit, one cable TV firm adorned the local client list. But Boston is fertile ground for the emerging cable industry, and by coincidence another cable client soon came on board. Like others in the field, the two firms served by DH&S had tremendous capital requirements and, as such, required comprehensive forecasts and projections to satisfy bankers and investors. Alert to the long-range market opportunities, Driscoll changed these services from manual to computerized processes using DH&S's own Falcon Forecast System. This time-sharing setup permits clients to put together forecasting and budgeting packages quickly and efficiently on computer terminals. All of The Big Eight have similar facilities: They are used to service a wide range of clients.

"The cable industry is highly leveraged," Driscoll explains. "Budgeting and forecasting on a sophisticated basis is therefore extremely important. Before a cable company starts making any money, it must raise capital, install the system, and sign up customers. They have to sell like hell to reach a break-even point as soon as possible. Bankers want reliable data on just when that break-even point will occur. The more confidence they have in the projections, the more likely they are to approve a loan. Our work in the field has proven to be accurate, and so we have a super track record with the bankers. The money comes easier when our name is on the documentation."

As word of Deloitte's proficiency spread, more cable outfits signed on as clients.

"This encouraged us to move ahead," Driscoll adds. "We started working on specific programs for the cable TV industry on taxes, computer models to gauge the return on cable franchises, and models for state applications for cable licenses. Our abilities grew, and before long we had eighteen cable television clients.

"We think we are just beginning to tap this market. Our people attend the National Cable TV Convention. They man a booth there, using the opportunity to acquaint entrepreneurs, investors, and bankers with our full range of services for the cable TV industry. Within two weeks after one convention in Dallas, ten of our offices nationwide got leads for new cable business. The Boston office now coordinates a national, firm-wide effort to attract and service cable clients."

DHS cable accounts are now plugged into a highly specialized computer program called Cable Plan. A refinement of the early Falcon program, this mechanical wunderkind is geared solely for the cable industry. Among its many functions, it can:

Answer "what if" questions to list the financial impact of various operating alternatives, such as rate increases, construction costs, new programming, and various debt/equity structures.

Perform analyses on future profitability, including assessments of expanding existing cable systems, moving to adjacent areas, offering and pricing new services, or renegotiating debt/equity structures.

Evaluate financing requirements and develop business plans for presentation to bankers, institutional lenders, venture capitalists, and other investors.

With programs like Cable Plan in place, small companies in a target market become lucrative clients rather than nuisance accounts. Both sides profit. But cable-television ventures are unusual small businesses in that they need highly sophisticated services in the very first days of operation. Whether The Big Eight can develop similar formats for bike shops, dry cleaning stores, and art dealers is questionable. What's more, one-to-one relationships are more important than dazzling computer runs to these neighborhood operations.

The deep-seated fear haunting many local CPA firms that The Big Eight machine is thundering toward their turf may be a phobia. All signs indicate that there's not much to worry about.

With small business, The Big Eight have met their match. Here, less is truly more.

7. Big (Eight) Men on Campus

"At scores of schools around the country, getting into accounting courses is tougher than seeing *Star Wars* on a Saturday night."
— *Forbes* magazine.

WALK ON ANY CAMPUS in the nation. Mingle with the students. Loaf around the cafeteria, hang out at beer joints, sit in the back of a class. You'll hear talk of sex and drugs, beer, Selective Service, war and peace, politics, grades, parents, Reagan, and The Big Eight. Yes, The Big Eight. Here, their enormous size is worshipped.

The Big Eight are awesome powers on campus because they are the single biggest group of recruiters, they are highly sought-after employers, and they lay claim to some of the best and the brightest from Stanford to Duke, from Hofstra to Michigan. Few recruiters can match The Big Eight for pure sex appeal among the nation's collegians. They are viewed as glamourous and powerful firms offering an inside track to successful business careers. What's more, they promise both substantial starting salaries and the opportunity to work on prestigious engagments with the blue-chip powers of the *Fortune* 500. Heady prospects for ambitious grads with visions of Horatio Alger.

That CPA firms are viewed as glamour boys on American campuses comes as a big surprise to those who remember when accountants were considered slightly more attractive than morticians. But those days are over. The image of the CPA as a boring nebbish— a combination Don Knotts and Wally Cox—has been replaced by that of a distinguished professional practicing in the thick of the action, rubbing elbows with the movers and the shakers, and providing respected counsel on a host of key business decisions. To many students, accounting is a sure ticket to the top.

This glamourous view of CPA careers is closely related to the new role accountants play in the corporate scheme of things. Once relegated to the back room—quiet bookkeepers who talked when they were spoken to—CPAs have in recent years found themselves in the corner office. Their new status reflects a more fundamental change in American business. As the old entrepreneural spirit of the giant corporations—the emphasis on technology, innovation, and bold marketing strokes—has given way to the worship of highly formalized management systems, the accountant's role has grown ever more central. When industrial lions dominated the business landscape—men of incredible vision and confidence—accountants were called in to put things in order after the CEO had acted. The William Paleys, the Walt Disneys, the Edwin Lands never waited for a printout to see if they should launch a network, a fantasy world, or a technological wonder. Great minds, they believed, make things happen; someone can always be found to count the beans.

This spirit has vanished from the hallowed halls of General Motors, Gulf Oil, and Ford. Now, the bright minds of *Fortune* 500-land have to come before the accountants before they get a dollar of funding. The newest candidates for the Business Hall of Fame aren't innovators or empire builders but turnaround specialists (many are CPAs) skilled at lopping off subsidiaries, firing employees by the thousands, and dismantling giant corporations rather than creating them. It's a new world.

Ralph Saul, former president of the American Stock Exchange, has "commented on the shift from industrial capitalism to financial capitalism, with a change from concentration on producing goods and services to an increasing concern with earnings per share, price-/earnings ratios, and financial results, almost independent of the process of production and consumption of industrial products and services."*

The emphasis on tight, disciplined management has brought the CPAs out from under the rocks and into the executive suites. In a

*Abraham Briloff, *Unaccountable Accounting* (New York: Harper & Row, 1972), p. 10.

good many of the *Fortune* 500, climbing the financial ladder is the best way to enter the president's office. A growing number of firms are run by CPAs. According to *Forbes*, 20 percent of the eight hundred highest paid CEOs have financial backgrounds. Finance is the modern business religion.

"Well below rock stars and sex symbols in earning power but well above the typical corporation president stand the nation's top professionals—doctors and lawyers—thousands of whom earn upwards of $100,000 a year. These wealthy professionals are in many ways the economic aristocrats of our affluent society. . . . Now add to the elite professional groups the certified public accountants. Their business is growing by leaps and bounds, and their earning power now equals that of lawyers and is approaching that of physicians.

"What is happening is clear enough in Adam Smith terms. The demand for accounting services is expanding faster than the supply. . . .

"None of this has been lost on the more alert of today's college students. Listen to Dr. Anelise N. Mosich, chairman of the accounting department of the University of Southern California:

" 'Suddenly students see accounting as glamourous, sexy. Many of our best students who would have gone to law school a couple of years ago are now going into public accounting.' "*

Fortunately for the hopefuls, schools across the nation are beefing up their accounting departments, claiming classrooms from more exotic courses, and hiring as many accounting professors as they can get their hands on. But even these efforts are proving inadequate. The demands of the accounting profession are enormous, outstripping academia's ability to provide qualified recruits to fill the burgeoning manpower needs. As a result, the big firms are forced to compromise, accepting a lower common denominator of student then they would prefer if there were a surplus of bright grads.

The great pressure on accounting students is not the struggle to land a job, but the competition to win a slot in The Big Eight.

*Lawrence Minard and Brian McGlynn, "The U.S.'s Newest Glamourous Job," in *Forbes*, September 1, 1977.

Considering the massive needs of the profession, virtually every accounting grad is assured of gaining employment with one of the thousands of CPA firms or on the financial staff of a corporation. But that is widely viewed as second best. The near-universal goal is to score the 3.0 or better grade-point average required for entry into The Big Eight. This myopic focus on the giant accounting firms is understandable: The big boys offer the best starting salaries ($16,000 to $20,000 for undergraduates; $20,000 to $25,000 for those with masters degrees), have the blue-chip accounts, and hold out the promise for both big bucks and prestige to those who make it as Big Eight partners.

"All but 5 of the 118 students in our CPA prep program who got offers from The Big Eight accepted them," says Rick O'Rourke, former placement director for Pace University. "Almost everyone who gets a Big Eight offer takes it, because it is very prestigious to start a career with these firms. Some use The Big Eight as a stepping stone; others use it to become a partner. If you go to a corporation first, it is very hard to go to The Big Eight afterwards. But if you go to The Big Eight first, you can then go to a corporation later. You have all the options."

Adds one Big Eight partner in charge of recruiting: "Even those accounting students who don't want to make public accounting a career seek positions with us upon graduation. Some want to be analysts, consultants, corporate financial executives—you name it. What they have in common is a strong desire to get that Big Eight name on their résumés. To work for Peat, Marwick; Coopers; or Price Waterhouse right out of school is a real door-opener. It gives the person credentials that can be of enormous value throughout his career."

The Big Eight is ambivalent about revolving-door staffers. Partners find it particularly galling that some of the best recruits are the first to leave. Brilliant business students, especially M.B.A.'s from top schools, can climb to lofty salary levels without the decade-long wait The Big Eight imposes on them. Their options are wide: with an Ivy League parchment and a Big Eight stint on their resume, they are welcomed with open arms on Wall Street, in boardrooms, in every corner of the financial community. That they freely reject the almighty accounting giants, that they soak up thousands of dollars of training time, and that they enter The Big Eight with the full intention of using their employer for personal gain rubs many partners the wrong way.

Price Waterhouse partners, for example, got all worked up when they discovered that some of their most sought-after recruits were taking the firm for a ride. But Price had no one to blame but itself. In order to lure more people from the Ivy Leagues, PW launched a program to make accountants out of liberal arts majors, first ramming them through an intensive accounting program at Cornell. Wise to a good opportunity, many students used the paid education as a chance to get started on a master's program with PW footing the bill. Upon completing the accounting program, many bid adieu to Price and stayed on campus for their M.B.A.'s.

"In my day, we viewed it as an honor to be selected by a prestigious CPA firm—a real honor," says an aging partner at Deloitte Haskins & Sells. "If we got more than one offer, we deliberated the choices very carefully. Not only for our own good, but for the good of the firm too. It was simply out of the question to accept an offer unless we planned to honor it with the utmost of our skills and abilities.

"But, hell, these young men today don't have the word *honor* in their vocabularies. I swear they don't. I'll spend months sharing the wisdom and experience of my years in this profession with them, and damned if they'll leave with hardly a good-bye when a better offer comes along. They'll spit in your face. It is a sad commentary."

That Big Eight traditionalists view the revolving door with disdain doesn't mean there isn't something in it for the CPA firms. The truth is that The Big Eight are so enormous and their work loads so great that they need a constant flow of humanity, some of which doesn't want to stick around for a gold watch. The system is designed for people to be hired, to serve five to seven years, and then to leave for corporate jobs upon learning that they will never make partner. This nonpartnership material—thought of as deadwood—must be pushed out the door to make room for new waves of young grads.

Robert Half, founder of a highly successful, franchised personnel-recruiting business bearing his name and an astute observer of The Big Eight says: "There is a method to the mass hiring of students. Five years later they transfer the staffers to the clients and then go back for a fresh batch of young people. This does three things: keeps the staff age and salaries down; enables The Big Eight to go back to campus for more youngsters; and fills the clients with the firm's alumni. When they do the latter, it's almost impossible to lose the client: The company is loaded with the CPA firm's former employees.

"Even a partner who falls out of favor with his firm doesn't worry, 'cause he'll just be placed with a client. That's why there is so much security in The Big Eight. They take care of their people, and by planting them with clients, help to assure that they will keep the accounts."

When you boil it down to the nitty-gritty, The Big Eight make their bread-and-butter fees by winning giant engagements, doling out the lion's share of the work to young staffers, and billing clients several times what the grunts earn. The recruiting function must be to find small armies of young men and women to keep the ball rolling. It is a never-ending process, and one that promises to grow increasingly complex. As The Big Eight's scope of practice continues to expand, more and more specialists will be required on staff.

"To meet the demand for a broader range of services and improved financial reporting, both of which will involve dealing with subjects that tend to be highly subjective, the profession will find it necessary to draw representatives of other disciplines into its ranks," Wallace Olson notes in his Cape Town speech. "This suggests that specialization will grow within the profession, since the greater number and more complex bodies of knowledge required will make it even more difficult for a single individual to maintain competence in all areas of accounting.

"The formal accreditation and recognition of specialists within the profession will not come about without a great deal of controversy. The competitive effects of distinguishing between qualified accountants on the basis of specialization will make it difficult to depart from the present position that a qualified accountant is competent to provide the whole range of services.

"Also, the profession's organizations will find it difficult to restructure themselves to accommodate specialist groups drawn from other disciplines. But if the profession is to expand its horizons to meet the predicted demands for service, it will have to come to terms with the notion of a multidiscipline base. The umbrella may have to become the [accounting professions'] broader role of providing expertise on the utilization of and accounting for resources. If so, the preparation and auditing of financial statements will become only one of several different functions, albeit a very basic and important one.

"A transition to a multidiscipline-based profession with formal recognition of specialization would have a far-reaching impact on the entrance and education requirements. . . .

"Pre-entry education for a broader-based profession would entail an expansion in the subjects covered in the curriculum. A likely result would be the emergence of separate schools or programs of professional accounting geared to teach the bodies of knowledge covered in the profession's entrance examinations."

The implications are clear: The recruiting net will have to snare a wider range of college grads. This will open the doors to a greater variety of students and will expand an already enormous hiring program.

Together, The Big Eight screen about 160,000 applicants annually and choose about 10,000. The recruiting activities are carried out at about five hundred colleges and universities. Most every school with an accredited accounting program gets on The Big Eight's recruiting list at one time or another. Marginal schools with small or substandard accounting classes may convince The Big Eight to come around for a look see but will be dropped from the schedule if the visits do not produce successful hires.

"Each year, we review the schools on our list and decide which to retain and which to drop," says William R. Gifford, national recruitment partner for Price Waterhouse. "Sometimes we learn of a school that's off the beaten path. If we find that it's qualified, we'll arrange for a visit. Sometimes a school's program improves. The faculty and curriculum are upgraded. When that happens, we will recruit there."

There is no doubt that The Big Eight visit many more schools than they would like to. The recruiting itinerary is a mixed one, with a significant number of second-and-third-rate schools commanding attention along with the likes of Duke, Yale, Stanford, Michigan, Columbia, Cornell, Brown, Princeton, Chicago, and Harvard. The Big Eight are forced to recruit at Iona, Hofstra, and Miami as well because they simply cannot attract enough grads from the top schools alone to fill their burgeoning quotas.

Although recruiters keep it mostly hush-hush, many admit to a strong preference for the Ivy Leagues. One calls it "demeaning" for the hallowed names in public accounting to be sniffing around proletarian schools. Even though most of the current partners are not themselves Ivy League grads, there is a deep-seated feeling that the best in accounting should command the best in academia.

Only the prestige law firms can hold out for the superachievers. With their comparatively tiny staffing requirements, the likes of Vinson & Elkins, Cravath Swaine & Moore, Paul Weiss Rifkind Wharton & Garrison—can pick and choose from the extraordinary students at the elite schools. A big law firm will fill twenty-five places; a big CPA firm fifty times that.

The Big Eight content themselves with selecting the cream of the crop at the mediocre schools. Generally speaking, candidates need a B average to get a foot in the door; those with B+ or better are most likely to come away with an offer. Certainly, a Harvard senior with a 2.5 will get an interview; his counterpart at a no-name school may not. If both manage to impress the recruiters and get offers, the Harvard man will command a higher salary. Starting wages vary by school, with grads of the better colleges pulling down an extra $1,000 to $3,000 per year to start.

Typically, the interview process is a three-stage affair that begins in the fall of the senior year.

"Comes that final September and the pressure sets in on the students hot and heavy," says Rick O'Rourke. "This is the big payoff time for them—everything is at stake. They're a bundle of

nerves during the interviewing months. I have to hold them together; calm them down."

Phase one starts right after the summer vacation. In the prescreening process, students submit resumes to The Big Eight firms they
most want to work for. Most cover their bases, submitting applications to all eight. This is a wise strategy: Because personality quirks
play a key role in the hiring process, even the most qualified students
run the risk of being rejected by their first-choice firms. The savvy
candidates have lots of backups.

The first cut is made in October. Those students winning an
on-campus interview on the basis of their résumés are notified in
writing by The Big Eight; the rejects get thumbs down at this point.
Making it this far is by no means a guarantee of employment. The
prescreening process is the easiest cut to survive. Mindful of their
huge manpower needs, The Big Eight are willing to meet with any
and all candidates who even remotely meet the minimum standards.
The hope is that a student that looks lackluster on paper may be an
outright winner in person; one with a glowing personality that can
be turned loose winning new clients. Big Eight representatives hit
the campuses in late October. The recruiters are either personnel
professionals on staff at the Big Eight and assigned exclusively to
recruiting, or partners who take a few hours away from practice
activities to meet with potential recruits. In many cases, the partners
are better at interviewing than the personnel guys: They are, after
all, in the best position to paint an accurate picture of life inside the
firms.

"The Big Eight people, be they personnel pros or partners, usually come in pairs," O'Rourke says. "One is a recruiter and the other
a warm-up man. The latter is usually an alumnus of the college, now
with the accounting firm. His job is to sit outside the interview room
with the dozens of students waiting to see the recruiters. He makes
small talk with them—comforts them—tells them what it's like to
work with the firm."

Warm-up men are only moderately effective. The tension that
charges through the waiting room cannot be dissipated by folksy
chatter. Students gearing up for Big Eight interviews hardly hear
what the warm-up man says. Within minutes, they know they'll

have to march into a small office and put the efforts of four years
on the line. The worst part is that they don't know how to act, how
to present themselves, or what to say. Employment interviews, by
their very nature, distort natural behavior, causing tremendous anxiety and insecurity. Students are told repeatedly that in spite of their
scholastic accomplishments, the single best way to get a job offer is
to hit it off with the recruiter. Success depends, to a great extent,
on pleasing a perfect stranger. Does the recruiter respect aggressiveness? Does he like wit or does he prefer straight-faced sobriety? Does
he view unbridled ambition as an asset or a threat? The candidate
must grope for signals, feel out the recruiter, size up the person on
the other side of the desk, and then adjust his presentation accordingly—all of this in a matter of minutes and in an atmosphere of
great stress.

The interview process is unnerving because it discourages
honesty and forces the candidate to measure every word—to try to
be what he thinks the recruiter expects of him. Every question
demands a snap decision that can make the difference between a Big
Eight career or rejection.

Interviewing Techniques—a booklet published by Pace University
(New York)—lists these questions most frequently asked by college
recruiters:

Do you feel that you have received a good general training?

What candidate in his right mind would say no to that? Would
the applicant at any college get a star for honesty by saying: "This
is a terrible school and I know my training has been inferior. I hope
you people at Touche Ross can make up for this with your internal
training program"? The applicant may get points, but not a job.
Interview questions beg for dishonest answers.

Do you have a girlfriend/boyfriend? Is it serious?

How do you answer this one? Flip a coin? Say no and you may
be judged cold and antisocial. Say yes and you could be deemed too
preoccupied with romance to focus on a new job. It's a personal
question the recruiter has no business asking, but he does, and the
candidate must decide in an instant how to field it.

Will you fight to get ahead?

How's this for a loaded question? There's no safe bet on this one.

Go in one direction and you look like a backstabber; take the opposite tack and you're a wallflower.

*Are you primarily interested in making money? Or do you feel that
service to your fellow man is a satisfactory accomplishment?*

Again, who can risk honesty here? It's safe to say that less than
one one-hundredth of 1 percent of the nation's accounting majors
are out to join the profession for the rare motives that brought
Albert Schweitzer to Africa. But dare they tell the truth? Imagine
a typical play-it-by-the book uptight recruiter hearing this very
honest response: "I feel competitive with my fellow man rather than
sympathetic to him. No, I'm not going into accounting because of
any noble reasons. The truth is, I like Italian sports cars, beach
houses, and well-cut English suits. I think I have a good chance to
afford these things by becoming a partner in your firm. I'm out for
the dough—as much as I can make, as fast as I can make it."

In spite of the fact that the entire interview process encourages
dishonesty—and in some cases demands it—the number one reason
recruiters give for rejecting applicants is that "they are caught
lying." Other major reasons for rejections include:

has arrogant attitude

has limp-fish handshake

has low moral standards

presents extreme appearance

All of these complaints are subjective, except for the handshake
factor, which is simply a moronic reason to reject anyone for anything. Is a pin-striped shirt an example of extreme appearance? To
a senior partner stuffed into nothing but white shirts for thirty-five
years, the answer may be yes. The fact is that students are judged
arbitrarily, in ways they cannot anticipate and, worse yet, cannot
control. When careers hang in the balance, that's a nerve-racking
prospect.

"Don't blame yourself for every failure," the Pace booklet continues. "Regardless of the strengths and qualifications you could bring
to the job, the employer and/or interviewer may not like you, and

people usually do not hire people they don't like. Employers share some of the same irrational prejudices as the rest of the population. If he doesn't like tall women or native New Yorkers, you may not be able to overcome his initial bias and survive an interview. . . .

"The five, ten, twenty, or more days you spend job-hunting may be filled with more frustration, degradation, and uncertainty than you ever bargained for; but, if you work at it, your chances of finding a reasonably interesting job are excellent."

There's no doubt that qualified students submitting résumés to at least half of The Big Eight stand a good chance of gaining an on-campus interview and coming through at least one unscathed. Those that make it this far advance to phase three of the hiring process—an in-depth interview at The Big Eight's business office.

This is a rather chummy affair—a lot of handshaking and one-to-one conversations with the partners on their home turf. Employers like it because it gives a broad cross section of the staff an opportunity to size up the prospective recruit. Sort of like kicking the tires and taking the demo out for a test drive. Although few candidates enjoy the experience, most find it a way to gain valuable insight into the firms and their principals.

"Hokey—that's the best way to describe the on-location interview," says a recent Cornell grad. "All these middle-aged partners come on to you like long-lost friends, slapping you on the back and proposing toasts to your business career. They tell you how wonderful accounting is, how wonderful their firm is, and how wonderful it would be to work together. Wonderful, wonderful—you hear the word over and over again. It's surreal—like you're on the "Lawrence Welk Show.""

"And those luncheons—talk about terminal boredom. The partners love to take you to lunch and spend half the interview downing martinis. In a space of two weeks, I interviewed at Coopers, Andersen, Touche, and Peat. It seemed as if I was drunk or nursing a hangover everyday. I'm no lush, but they put the pressure on, and you've got to do as the Romans do.

"It's really incredible to see the transformation in some of these guys after a few snorts at the bar. The on-location interviews usually start first thing in the morning and conclude after lunch, about 3:00

P.M. Well, before the drinking starts some partners are models of the straitlaced corporate personality: stiff, uptight, all business. With each lunchtime drink, however, the mask peels away layer by layer. Suddenly they're using foul language, telling racy stories, acting pretty much like college freshmen hanging around a campus beer joint. Nothing terrible about the behavior—just that for some it's a radical change from the office personality.

"One guy in particular comes to mind. He was an academic, just working with one of The Big Eight as a consultant on a special project. Well, this guy's the epitome of the Ivy League business professor: vested and cuffed navy wool suit, gold pocket watch drapped across his chest, hair parted in the middle and combed back, horn-rimmed glasses. He comes on like an icebox—cold, disciplined, pompous. That's until the firewater goes to his brain. He downs about three Chivas Regals in quick succession, and the eyeballs start to glaze. Soon he's getting very loud, cursing out President Reagan as a fucking actor, going on and on listing his grievances while putting away more scotches. Needless to say, even the partners were embarrassed. Thankfully, the booze caught up with the old fool, he stumbled into the men's room and collapsed in a stall. None of the partners came to his aid: They asked a waiter to call an ambulance."

Certainly, this grad's experience is atypical. Few on-location interviews result in heavy drinking or crude public displays.

But there is a general consensus that partners do loosen up over luncheon drinks, acting more like fraternity brothers rushing new pledges than distinguished members of a conservative profession. The change in mood and personality over the course of the interview day forces job candidates to play two distinct roles: that of the serious student of the profession, seeking both knowledge and a lowly starting place in the grand world of the Big Eight, as well as a social butterfly, skilled at the arts of small talk and barroom bravado.

"You feel as if you are on display all day," says an M.B.A., now a junior consultant with a Big Eight MAS division. "The partners really focus on you; they seem to consider every word you say. That may be pure paranoia, but I don't think so. You can tell when someone's checking you out. You get that feeling in spades at the on-location interview. When you meet the firm's interviewer on campus it's just ten minutes and out. But at this point you are on stage for hours—they expect you to perform.

"There's a lot of tension because you're afraid of making a mistake. Like saying the wrong thing or asking the wrong question. Who the hell knows what kind of pet peeves these partners have?

"One asked me if I thought there were too few or too many women in this profession. What the hell do you do with that hot potato? Immediately, my mind races: Is he a liberal or a chauvinist? There's no way to tell. And hell knows everyone feels strongly on this issue. No one sits on the fence. Say the wrong thing and this guy's going to write me off. Luckily, I'd been coached by my Uncle Saul, a Big Eight tax partner himself, on how to handle myself. I did just as he advised: talked around the question without giving an answer. That's the golden rule for a successful interview: Be a diplomat, don't give a clear opinion on anything."

Try as both sides will to evoke an image, their true personalities shine through clearly enough for the employer and the grad to determine if they want to work together. That's the real purpose of the on-location interview: The opportunity to make a gut-level evaluation of the other party. Beyond the résumés, grade-point printouts, scholastic references, recruiting brochures, house organs, client lists, there is a need to see if people like each other enough to share an office. From all accounts, this is the critical phase of the recruiting process. Grads simply will not accept job offers if they don't like a firm's personal chemistry.

"The major reason we have lost candidates to other firms is because they were not impressed with the people they meet at our offices," says Salvatore Luiso, national director of personnel for Coopers & Lybrand and a former dean of students at Hofstra University (a big CPA mill). "Those who accept our offers do so because they are impressed with the people they meet. This is the single most important factor in their acceptance decisions. We know because we send a questionnaire to all people who accept or reject our offers.

"We also keep track of our partners' performances in getting students to accept offers. We get to know who is best at this. Some partners can go out and make twenty offers and get no acceptances. We try not to use that person for this kind of work."

Sometimes other factors come into play. One powerful force is the student grapevine. When Peat first took on the New York City audit, many grads shied away from the firm, fearful of being buried in an enormous lackluster audit (much the way many top law school grads tiptoe around Cravath Swaine & Moore, worried about falling into the endless IBM case and never being heard from again). One Peat partner claims that recruiters from other Big Eight firms stirred up this fear in students, convincing them that a Peat, Marwick job was like a ticket to New York's sewer system. To counter this, Peat is said to have rotated staffers assigned to the New York audit, giving them prestige assignments to complement the city work. All in all, the firm's recruiting efforts were not seriously hampered, and some grads actually sought out the city job. Objective sources agreed that the city engagement made for a good learning experience.

Big Eight personnel directors consider a ratio of one-third accepted offers to be a satisfactory recruiting performance but all shoot for 50 percent or more. Andersen, Price, Deloitte, and Coopers are said to fare best nationally, with Peat and Touche strong in some key urban markets.

"Price Waterhouse comes on campus with its nose up in the air," says one college placement officer. "It considers itself 'the' firm and expects students to be thrilled to death if it wants them. It's arrogant, yes, but I must admit that a good many grads seem to feel about Price Waterhouse the same way the firm feels about itself. For many, Price is the first choice."

In the competition for top grads, the firms fall over each other trying to put on a pretty face. All produce lavish recruiting brochures filled with full-color photographs of smiling young staffers traveling the world, inspecting corporate facilities, attending private conferences with the chairman or senior partners. Certainly the firms have the right to engage in some hype. They are, after all, selling themselves on the open market. Still, there's a point of diminishing returns. This must be checked to prevent wholesale exaggeration. In the rush to chalk up high acceptance scores, partners and recruiters are tempted to promise pie in the sky. This may well lead to an increase in new hires, but an unacceptable number of the new recruits will leave as soon as they arrive. The gap between actual working conditions and the partners' promises are too great to bridge. It leads to disappointment, anger, and resentment.

"Some of our interviewers paint too rosy a picture of the work here," Luiso adds. (His problem in this regard is shared by all of The Big Eight.) "They tell students there's no overtime, no hard work —that's counterproductive. I sat down with one partner whose interviewing tactics were videotaped. He seemed more like a used-car salesman than an accounting recruiter. He promised students too much. This is not nirvana here.

"What happens is that pride gets involved. When we make a Coopers & Lybrand offer, we want the person to accept it."

In many ways the recruiting process has become increasingly methodical. There is less and less spontaneous discovery and more and more gamesmanship. Both employer and employee suffer as a result.

The videotaping of mock interviews, for example, conducted by partners, by Big Eight personnel directors, and for students by college placement officers, prompts recruiters and grads alike to act in prescribed ways. The emphasis is on camouflaging personality quirks, regional accents, hand or facial gestures, aggressive traits and the like. Recruiters are instructed to look for, and applicants are told to be, clean-cut, cooperative, confident, courteous, and respectful ladies and gentlemen.

With recruiters intent on rejecting any signs of unorthodoxy, it must be said that the interview process effectively screens out some of the most extraordinary students in the land. Are brilliant, scholarly mathematicians likely to exhibit the smooth charms of advertising-account executives? Certainly not! The Big Eight lose out by standardizing the recruiting formula and by accepting the vanilla-ice-cream standards developed by unimaginative personnel executives.

Coopers & Lybrand's Luiso is out to change this. "We try not to overformalize hiring. We try to make room for those who have not always walked the straight and narrow. It's important to find people with different kinds of skills. Our partnership is not a trombone section, it's an orchestra. We must get people to fill all sections of that orchestra."

Not all the firms are of like mind. "I had a student with a near-perfect grade average," O'Rourke adds. "But I worried about his job prospects because he did not do well on interviews—too introverted. But with role playing I helped him show he was 'human'— that he had other interests outside of school, and that he didn't consider himself a genius."

Cases like this have convinced students that they must bone up on the latest job-hunting techniques before venturing into the marketplace. Grads can no longer believe that they can simply show up for the interview, look into the camera, and hope for the best. Applicants know they must play the angles; learn in advance what recruiters expect and learn how to provide just that. Most turn to popular "how to" books for tips on landing a job. The problem is, this leads to robotic behavior.

"We used to be able to tell something about a student from his résumé, but no more," Luiso adds. "So many copy the form suggested in the books, that it's hard to tell one from another. The individuality has been removed."

One of the most blindly obeyed job-hunting commandments is to limit résumés to a single page. Why? Simply because a personnel executive exhibiting that profession's love of silly rules, deemed it so. As a result, superachievers with a list of accomplishments a yard long feel compelled to squeeze it all on a single page. A Harvard grad with a wealth of scholastic and athletic awards presents his curriculum vitae in the same space as an Adelphi laggard who's never done much more than go to class and eat lunch. No one bothers to think: Will Price Waterhouse refuse to consider a Yale valedictorian with a three-page résumé? Of course not, but the one-page rule is etched in granite, and the students obey.

For successful applicants, the years of schooling and months of high-pressure interviews have their reward in the form of a Big Eight offer letter.

"It's shake-in-your-pants-time when you see the envelope with the Arthur Young; Coopers & Lybrand; Peat, Marwick, Mitchell, or other Big Eight name on it," says a Michigan M.B.A. who accepted a Big Eight offer, only to leave five months later for a management post with an automaker. "The envelope looks so impressive: heavy cotton rag, richly embossed, and all that. It's the big time, you know it, and you're scared shitless to open the envelope, because you may find they won't let you join the club. I mean I walked around the house for ten minutes just trying to get up the courage to read the damn thing.

"The letter is all business—short, and if you're accepted, very, very sweet. It's no more than two or three paragraphs: Just enough to extend an offer to join the firm and to confirm the starting salary. But, hell, it feels absolutely delicious. The feeling is one of great relief and exhilaration. You're in—hallelujah, you're in. At the moment, that's all that matters in the world. It's a rush—one of life's tremendous highs."

But for most it is a fleeting high. The promise of recruiters, the daydream of brilliant careers, the visions of money and power, the expectation of prestige engagements, the thoughts of making partner all reach a crescendo as the new recruit wraps up the senior year, dons cap and gown, and makes the shattering transition from campus to the real world. Two weeks on the job is more than enough for the headiest euphoria to collapse into disillusionment. Most learn quickly enough that Big Eight entry-level jobs are not tickets to glamour and intrigue at the pinnacle of corporate power. They are, instead, commitments to continue learning, to serve as apprentices, to put in long and arduous hours performing basically menial work.

"The first day on the job they gave me an expensive attaché case as a gift," the M.B.A. adds. "I was delighted with it. The real leather smelled terrific, my initials were embossed on top. First-class all the way. I felt like a million bucks.

"But that all changed in a few weeks. It was then that I discovered the real reason for the case: something for them to shove the homework in. The way I looked at it, they weren't paying me much either. For $20,000 I worked sixteen hours a day, and that was like having two eight-hour-a-day jobs for $10,000 each. I had so much work that the brass hinges on my briefcase would bulge like Marty Feldman's eyes. Work on the bus, work on the train, work till my head hit the pillow.

"What made matters worse was the nature of the work. I wouldn't have minded the hours if I was involved in fascinating engagements. But, no way. As a green auditor you are an absolute grunt. It's so damn regimented—like the military. One of my buddies had to take off a few days cause his dad was dying of cancer. Well, the supervisor got pissed at that! Can you believe it?

"You always have to follow rigid directions. There's no room to put your own stamp on anything. I found it beneath me—as did a substantial number of coworkers. About twenty-five percent of us—the graduates who came to work at the office in the summer of 1979—left within a year; most of the others were unhappy but were willing to slug it out, to wait for the work to get more interesting, and to keep hanging in there for the chance to make partner."

Blame for this extends beyond The Big Eight. Some of the disillusionment and the lack of preparation for the real-world demands of a career in public accounting can be traced to the universities and to the full-time accounting professors. The Cohen Report stated:

"Many new accountants find that their education did not adequately prepare them for the responsibilities they face after graduating. Every year, public accounting firms spend amounts greater than the budgets of business schools training newly hired accountants, almost all of whom have just received accounting degrees. For reasons based on fact or myth, a schism has developed between practicing and academic accountants. . . .

Formal education does not now adequately prepare students to meet the demands and risks of professional practice. Immediately after school, new staff accountants must be assigned to work that requires a professional attitude and professional diligence and that carries significant responsibilities. However, formal education furnishes students with little exposure to the types of strains and pressures that they will be immediately subjected to in practice, and at present it usually does not instill in them an appreciation of the legal and ethical obligations assumed by independent auditors.

Perhaps the new grads' difficulty in adjusting to life in The Big Eight can be traced to the commission's findings that:

. . . an increasing number of teachers of accounting proceed directly through the educational process to teaching positions, without a period of employment in public accounting in which practical experience could be obtained: Although they may be quite capable of passing the uniform CPA examination, those in states with experience requirements for the CPA are effectively procluded from obtaining the certificate. . . . The net result is that an increasing proportion of accounting-faculty members are not CPAs and, therefore, are not eligible for membership in professional accounting organizations such as state CPA societies and the AICPA. Consequently, those faculty members do not have regular contact with the public accounting profession—they are not aware of its needs and concerns. . . .

Certainly this could be one of the major factors behind this observation by a CPA questioned in a Cohen Commission survey: "To begin with, staffmen seem to know less and less when graduating from college. Used to be a new man at least knew the difference between a positive and negative confirmation and knew how to prepare a bank reconciliation and proof of cash. Now they have to be spoonfed the entire job, and they fail to respond to a request to follow a budget. After having to cut our fees on a couple of jobs, the juniors panic, and even though they still don't have enough experience to make necessary decisions, they shortcut on work to start 'looking better' come time to bill the job."

Undoubtedly, the quality of the work does improve for those grads who survive until the third year of employment at a Big Eight firm. At this point, the junior staffers gain some supervisory responsibilities and limited decision-making authority. As the individual graduates to manager and ultimately partner, all of the grunt work is passed off to new rounds of lowly staffers. For those in key positions, the work of a Big Eight practice—be it tax, audit, consulting, or other—is both challenging and rewarding. The hard part is suffering through the early years.

The ones who don't make it probably don't want it badly enough —and never did.

"I see lots of grads head for The Big Eight without examining what they're getting into and what they really want out of life," says an accounting professor. "They're attracted by the glitter, but don't realize that a lot of pressure, politics, and hard work goes along with it. Many of these people are better off with small CPA firms, but they reject those offers out of hand. Many have to actually report to work at The Big Eight before they realize that it's not their cup of tea. I try to impress students with the fact that small accounting firms have some distinct career advantages—for one thing you're thrown right into meaningful work—but I know that I'm usually talking to deaf ears. Students don't want to hear it. It's only when they're slaving away on a massive audit that they remember what I said. Suddenly it all clicks."

It must be said that every profession has its internship period. Those mired in the hectic schedules and relatively low pay are wont to bitch about their plight. Medical residents complain about hospital conditions, and young lawyers wonder why they're always in the library. It's the way of all lucrative professions to make the newest members pay their dues. Once admitted to the club, even the wildest rebels seek to perpetuate the system. In this way, Big Eight partners are much like attending surgeons and princes of the court.

Where The Big Eight is at fault, however, is in painting a glorified picture of the new staffer's routine.

Peat, Marwick's recruiting booklet, *Your First Year Assignments,* gives this impression of an entry-level auditor's work schedule:

Staff Training
Attended Audit Level I training in local office during first week. Completed Audit Level II training with new staff members from other offices.

Medium-Sized Manufacturing Company
Assisted in the interim examination. Worked closely with the in-charge senior evaluating client's accounting system.

Electronics Manufacturer
Participated in physical inventory observation at a plant. The inventory consisted of more than 100,000 separate items.

Ethical Drug Manufacturer
Helped management consultants gather data for the design and installation of a computer system. Reviewed billing and purchase procedures.

Staff Training
Attended local office seminar on new FASB releases.

Machine Tool Manufacturer
Assignment included reviewing and evaluating internal control, tai-

loring the audit program based on our evaluation of this multinational client's system, and performing interim audit procedures.

Shoe Manufacturer

Participated in an audit engagement for a new client considering an initial public offering of securities.

Continuing an Audit

Returned to the medium-sized manufacturing company and to the electronics manufacturer for completion of their audits. For the first time, helped prepare financial statements and assisted in drafting letter to management on recommendations for improvement in internal control.

Commercial Banks

Participated in surprise cash and securities counts on three commercial banks. We had been requested by the Examining Committees of the Boards of Directors to assist them in their annual surprise examinations.

Career-Planning Discussion

Met with a partner to discuss overall progress with the Firm and to begin to formulate a plan of assignments and professional development in line with my objectives.

Tax Department

Accepted assignment under the Tax Optionee Program. TOP provided exposure training and experience in taxes to help me decide between a career in taxes or accounting and auditing.

Coopers & Lybrand publishes this diary "relating the actual experiences" of a first-year staff accountant at its San Francisco office:

July 13—My first day at work! I completed employment forms, became acquainted with Firm policies and procedures, and met with the assignment manager to discuss my upcoming assignments.

July 16–27—Attended the Firm's core course—Staff Course I—on a college campus in Southern California.

July 30–August 17—My first assignment, a stereo component manufacturer. I worked with a Staff A in analysis of accounts receivable and fixed assets, and on development of the client's investment tax credit.

August 13—Attended a planning session for a large timber and natural resources corporation audit. Engagement goals were outlined, potential problems identified, and our audit approach reviewed and discussed.

August 20–24—Assigned to assist a senior in the examination of a labor union's six-month financial statements.

August 27–September 7—Began work on the timber and natural resources corporation audit. I reviewed and tested procedures for payable and cash reconciliation systems. My work revealed that our year-end validation could be reduced because of effective internal control systems.

September 10–October 2—Assisted in "return on investment" simulations and analyzed policyholder dividends for an insurance company client.

October 3–5—Helped with examination of a joint venture termination agreement. As a result of the investigation, our client recovered substantial cost overcharges made by the other party.

October 8–12—In preparation for the year-end audit of a construction company, I completed a sales-system analysis.

October 15–November 2—Analyzed dividend distribution and compliance with SEC regulations for a mutual fund.

November 4—Was asked by the partners to assist in hosting the annual international partners' meeting held this year in San Francisco. I helped with the hospitality room and answered visitors' questions.

November 5–9—At the headquarters of a retail clothing chain, a senior and I performed tests of a new computerized accounts receivable system using AUDITPAK.

November 12–23—Worked on the audit of a national charity's local chapter. As this was a brand-new client, it provided an opportunity to present complete documentation, such as a set of systems flowcharts detailing their revenue/billing cycle.

November 26–December 31—Returned for year-end audit of the retail clothing chain and performed validation tests on various balance sheet accounts. I also utilized our Firm-developed computer program and time-sharing terminal for computing footnote lease disclosure data.

December 10–21—In auditing a small client, the senior and I discovered what looked like unethical business practices in regard to a bank loan agreement. We called this to the attention of the partner and manager in charge, who, after conferring with the client and the bank, decided to dissociate the Firm from the engagement.

December 26–28—Took some of my accumulated overtime in days off. (Went skiing!)

January 2–25—Returned to the timber and natural resources corporation.

I assisted in validating 12/31 account balances and conducted a procedural review of their computerized inventory-control system.

January 28–February 8—For the audit of a small nonprofit home health agency, I did almost all of the field work myself, with a senior reviewing my completed workpapers.

February 11–25—Returned for year-end audit at the construction company, where I performed validation tests of balance sheet accounts.

February 26–March 1—Performed physical inventory for a security service firm through "on-site" visits to the Bay Area branches of this New York office client.

March 4–29—Returned to the audit of a mutual fund. I reviewed and tested the security buy and sell procedures and helped in validation of the investment portfolio and preparation of the annual report.

April 1–5—Asked for and received a week's assignment to the tax department to gain experience in individual income tax preparation.

April 8–12—Took one week of my vacation.

April 15—Talked with several college students, answered their questions about the Firm, and chronicled my work assignments to date.

April 16–26—Was assigned, with complete responsibility, to audit and prepare tax returns for two pension funds of an automobile association.

April 25—Attended our office's annual staff golf and tennis outing.

April 29—My promotion to Staff A, effective May 1, was announced.

April 29–May 17—Returned to the automobile association to answer review notes on my previous work, to do a profit and loss fluctuation review, and to prepare their corporate tax return for review by the tax specialist.

May 3–7—Took time off to study for the upcoming CPA exam.

May 8–10—Sat for the CPA exam.

May 20–31—Audited the financial statements of an automobile insurance company's profit-sharing trust fund and drafted the entire financial report including footnotes.

June 3–28—Spent four weeks in Los Angeles, where I, as part of a five-man team, examined the revenue cycle of a large public utility and reviewed consolidated statements and reports to stockholders, the Federal Power Commission and the SEC. Our findings were discussed with the client in an "exit" conference.

July 1–5—Took my second week of vacation.

July 8–12—Assigned to interim audit of an electronics company. In performing procedural review of the cost system at my location, I toured the manufacturing operation and computer center to see the interrelationship of operations and paperwork flow.

July 15—Attended an "in-house" class and discussion group on APB15—a session bound to prove valuable in future financial-statement preparations.

July 16–August 15—With the assistance of a Staff B, I performed the audit of a small private college. As a result of our work, the client discovered that it was in breach of certain covenants of the original endowment. A court order allowing the actions was applied for and granted.

Equally attractive scenarios are spelled out for the first-year tax staffers (corporate-merger rulings, estate planning, speech writing), management consultants (work with county government, hospitals, hotel chains, urban mass transit), and small-business division recruits (engagements with a television station, a real-estate company, and seminars in minicomputers). Full-color action photographs picture staffers on location at the steps of the Treasury Department, inside a bank vault, at the entrance of a museum, and in a client's office.

All of The Big Eight firms evoke a Hollywood image of the staffer's first year.

"We don't believe that the work for new hires at Price Waterhouse is grunt work," says Bill Gifford. "We rely on the newest staffers to be alert and professional. Some of the worst scandals have occurred at the level where junior accountants would be able to find the information.

"Our new people get the excitement of public accounting right away. One day they are at a cosmetics company, the next at an electronics plant, then it's a food company. They get a behind-the-scenes look at business."

Few recruits will agree with this assessment. Yes, they get around, shifted as they are from one engagement to another—whenever an extra body is needed. And, yes, they get a behind-the-scenes view, but it's mostly that of a back office.

8. "You Need Eyes in the Back of Your Head."

"To those who say accountants are fulfilling their role responsibly, I say,
What is their role? They are making the debits equal the credits—yes. But
is that enough? No."
—Abraham Briloff—Professor of accounting at New York's Baruch
College and The Big Eight's most tenacious critic.

RECRUITING—FOR ALL ITS HEADACHES—is the least of The Big
Eight's problems. The firms' practice is a minefield. Every stroke of
the pen, every client engagement carries explosive issues that bring
the threat of professional liability, damaged reputations, and governmental restraints. Always, there is the spectre of economic and
psychological loss. Big Eighters live with the unsettling knowledge
that their privileged way of life—their high earnings and vaulted
prestige—is under attack and is in constant jeopardy. They look to
the future with anticipation and fear.

It's ironic that a profession viewed by many to be quiet and
conservative is actually the most controversial in the land. The Big
Eight are deluged with complex and thorny issues that impact the
broad scope of their practices. Hard as they try to free themselves,
the firms seem only to fan the flames, generating new issues and new
problems in the process. They are buffeted by social, political, and
economic forces, some of which seek to destroy this power, others
to balance it, and still others to give it unbridled freedom. In some
cases, they are victims of a society that both worships and despises
power—a "60-Minutes" mentality that seeks to root out any hint of
impropriety in high places and publicly embarrass it. In other instances, they are victims of their own greed, obstinance, and un-
professionalism.

"Someone's always sniping at us," says one angry tax partner.
"You hear the barbs on television, at cocktail parties, in your own

family. You never know when a critic is going to attack. I swear, a guy needs eyes in the back of his head."

Adds Wallace Olson, "Technological developments have had a significant impact on our lives in a number of ways. One of these has been the emergence of the broadcast journalists who have engaged in almost constant investigative reporting and in some cases muckracking exposés. As a result, governments, politicians, corporations, and virtually all of society's institutions have come under intensive scrutiny and attack. Full disclosure and operating in a fishbowl environment have become the norm of the day.

"This erosion in privacy has revealed a variety of imperfections that has stimulated the idealists to express loud demands for reforms of all kinds with little regard for whether the cures will be worse than the newly discovered ills. The steady drumfire of faultfinding has taken its toll in the form of a pervasive loss of confidence in our institutions. We have become to a considerable degree a world of cynics, distrustful of those in power and of most of what we do not individually control."*

The Big Eight emerged as a major target of social reformers during the muckraking days of the late 1960s. An introspective nation embroiled in an unpopular war vented anger and frustration against its "establishment" figures from university presidents to business executives. As powerful creatures of the establishment—and as members of one of the country's few unregulated businesses—The Big Eight came under the close scrutiny of congressional investigators. Led to the accounting profession by spectacular audit failures and financial debacles of the period, the Senate Subcommittee on Reports, Accounting, and Management of the Committee on Government Affairs put The Big Eight under the microscope:

Historically, Congress and the public have regarded accounting as an arcane subject better left to accountants themselves," the committee noted. "Continual revelations of wrongdoing by publicly owned corporations have caused a new awareness of the importance of accounting practices in permitting such abuses to occur. Unexpected failures of major corporations have led to requests for substantial assistance to such companies from

*Speech before the Sixth National Conference of Chartered Accountants S.A., Cape Town, South Africa.

taxpayers. Accounting practices ultimately involve social issues that affect the nation's economic welfare.

Because of their broad social and economic significance, accounting issues must be addressed by Congress and the public in a manner which insures that the public interest is protected. If past abuses are to be prevented in the future, it is important that the accounting establishment, which has permitted many abuses to occur, be understood. *Accounting issues are too important to be left to accountants alone.*

The committee went on to say that:

Serious questions have been raised concerning the independence and competence of 'The Big Eight' accounting firms and other independent auditors. Those questions have arisen because of accounting and auditing problems involved in the Penn Central collapse, the Equity Funding fraud, improper and illegal activities by Gulf Oil Corporation and Northrop Corporation, and the many other abuses by corporations which have come to public attention in recent years. The common complaint in such cases has been 'Where was the independent auditor?'. . . . Public confidence in independent auditors, which is essential to the federal securities laws, has been seriously eroded.

The committee's labors resulted in the famous Metcalf Report (named after the committee's chairman, Sen. Lee Metcalf, now deceased), which brought to the surface a wide range of issues, some of which were as old as the profession; others which reflected The Big Eight's enormous growth both in organizational size and scope of practice.

"Had we understood the depth of the gap between our and the public's perceptions of our responsibilities, we would have realized that we were sitting on a keg of dynamite. That keg was ignited in the late 1960s and early 1970s by an unprecedented series of corporate failures and frauds. As event followed event, and Watergate and revelations of corporate bribery and questionable payments added fuel to the fire, the low-profile, responsible, and competent profession we all thought we were was dragged into the spotlight and subjected to public and governmental scrutiny more intense than we had ever before received."*

---

*Speech by Gilbert Simonetti, partner and Washington liason of Price Waterhouse, at University of Kentucky, November 14, 1979.

The Metcalf Report differed from most governmental tomes in that it was a meaty, fact-filled, and conscientious piece of research, presenting an in-depth profile of The Big Eight. That the report is seemingly biased against the accounting firms does not detract from its value as an informative study which crystallizes many of the issues swirling around The Big Eight. One must simply discount its excesses and focus on the fundamentals.

That the Metcalf Report is a despised document throughout The Big Eight should come as no surprise. It had this to say about the firms:

> The Big Eight are often called "public accounting firms" or "independent public accounting firms." This study finds little evidence that they serve the public or that they are independent in fact from the interests of their corporate clients. For that reason, this study refers to 'The Big Eight' as simply accounting firms.

Although the Metcalf committee took The Big Eight to task for a long list of controversial practices, the brunt of its attack was leveled at the firm's alleged lack of independence. It is widely agreed in and out of the accounting profession that audits serve a legitimate purpose and conform with the securities laws only if the auditors remain completely independent. Metcalf laughed at The Big Eight's claims of independence, insisting that they are paid servants of their clients rather than objective third parties. This position was based mostly on the fact that the giant accounting firms have extended themselves far beyond auditing and provide clients with a feast of lucrative services:

> The Big Eight firms have seriously impaired their independence by becoming involved in the business affairs of their corporate clients and by advocating their clients' interests on controversial issues," the Metcalf Report continued. "It appears that The Big Eight firms are more concerned with serving the interests of corporate managements who select them and authorize their fees than with protecting the interests of the public for whose benefit Congress established the position of independent auditor.
>
> The management advisory services provided by Big Eight firms are intended to aid corporate managements in operating their businesses and

necessarily involve Big Eight firms in the business affairs of their clients. Such involvement creates a professional and financial interest by the independent auditor in a client's affairs which is inconsistent with the auditor's responsibility to remain independent in fact and in appearance.

When a Big Eight firm recruits executives for a corporate client, shareholders and the public may wonder if the firm is retained as the client's independent auditor primarily because of the relationship existing between the firm and the influential executives it recruited. Similarly, the public may reasonably question the ability of a Big Eight firm to act as independent auditor for a corporate client which has also retained the firm to provide marketing analysis, financial management services, actuarial services, or other management advisory services. In such cases, an independent auditor not only becomes involved in the business affairs of its clients, but may be placed in the position of auditing its own work.

That aggressive, profit-minded firms like The Big Eight can remain independent and objective with audit clients who also enrich them with multimillion-dollar fees for tax, MAS, and the like is a hard notion to swallow. The instincts of a well-paid professional are, after all, to bend over backwards to satisfy clients, to be responsive to their needs, and to keep them happy and loyal customers. Is The Big Eight auditor likely to blow the whistle on a plum account in the name of independence, knowing full well that this action may sever the client relationship? Are the firms so steeped in principles that they will hold their ground while a treasured client walks across the street to a competitor, taking $5 million or more in annual fees with it?

Critics of the profession—including the Metcalf committee staffers—shout a loud no to this. They insist that there is a clear conflict of interests when accounting firms perform nonaudit services for audit clients; that the clients' interests become more important to auditors then the need to protect the public from questionable financial reporting. Most advocates of this opinion clearly want to proscribe accounting firms from providing nonaudit services to audit clients.

Even the Executive Committee of the AICPA SEC Practice Section called for eliminating services which are not accounting or auditing in nature (This was quashed by the Institute's Public Oversight Board).* The Metcalf Report went much further, asking for a total proscription of MAS activities:

> The major responsibility of independent auditors is to perform their services while maintaining strict independence from the clients, both in fact and appearance. Public confidence in the accuracy and usefulness of corporate financial information depends upon a firm belief that such information has been checked and certified by qualified auditors who are truly independent. Confidence in the independence of auditors requires that they have no direct or indirect interests in the affairs of their clients.

Statements of this kind cause convulsions in The Big Eight suites. The mere mention of practice restraints brings palpitations, clenched fists, rising tempers. In fact, there's no better way to disrupt the genteel quiet of an accounting office than to casually broach the subject of curbing MAS, tax work or the like.

An otherwise mild-mannered CPA is bound to mount the soapbox, launching a half-hour tirade against "dangerous critics, socialists, do-gooders, overpaid bureaucrats, and half-cocked reformers." Feelings run so high because there are billions of dollars at stake. Stripped of their non-audit divisions, The Big Eight would instantly shrink to roughly 60 percent of their current size and would lose a fortune in fees. For Big Eighters, this bleak scenario is alarming—and they are not about to sit by and let it happen. Not without a fight, anyway.

All of the firms—and their trade group, the American Institute of Certified Public Accountants—have armed themselves to the teeth with defensive propaganda designed to destroy the critics' arguments and to justify the wide scope of services. They are not at all shy about expressing themselves. In booklets, pamphlets, flyers, newsletters, position papers, speeches, seminars, conferences, and interviews The Big Eight seek to win favor for their positions and to ward off any threat of external regulation.

The CPAs' big gun in this war of words is one very sound

---

*The POB—charged with the responsibility of overseeing the SEC Practice Section—was established to add credibility to the profession's program of self-regulation.

argument that even the most determined critics have a hard time diffusing. They point out that even the purest auditor/client relationship requires the payment of a fee in exchange for services. The sum involved often reaches into the millions of dollars. If a CPA firm is trusted to remain independent in the conduct of a multimillion-dollar audit, why should this trust be denied simply because an additional service is provided? Is a professional firm recognized to be honest and forthright for a $3 million engagement likely to turn into a bunch of crooks for an extra $1 million in fees—or an extra $5 million for that matter? Highly unlikely!

"There isn't a single case critics can point to where providing non-auditing services led to a bad audit or hiding facts," says Coopers & Lybrand's strong-willed chairman Norman Auerbach.

Adds Wallace Olson, "Some of the criticism of consulting services by accountants comes from critics who are in competition with us. This criticism must be taken with a grain of salt. There are professional consulting firms who don't want accountants to take away their business.

"I also think that the objective critics like the SEC make irrational arguments. The fundamental question is not the nature of services provided, but whether the auditor is objective. As long as an auditor is outside the company and remains independent, he is effective. I don't buy the argument that the auditor becomes more of an insider just because he provides more services. If he is objective, he is so in the audit and all other services; if he's not objective, he won't be objective no matter what he does. As long as the auditor remains an outsider—is not an employee or someone with financial interest in the client—he is in good standing."

Olson's argument is echoed throughout the accounting establishment: Gauge the firm's commitment to independence, not the diversity of its work. Giant CPA firms say they can dish up a full menu of client services without jeopardizing audit integrity because there is a genuine and deep-seated commitment to independence at The Big Eight.

There is truth to this. The traumatic events of the past decade have had a sobering effect. All the firms realize that they have far more to lose in professional reputations, legal liability, and government control by going soft on fat-cat clients in order to keep a large fee. The problem is that this is evident only to Big Eighters themselves or to those who have studied the firms closely. Try to convince the man on the street, the average stockholder, or, for that matter, the SEC staffer that hungry professional firms won't sell out for the almighty dollar. Few will believe a word of it. The system that is supposed to work for their protection—and at their pleasure —seems like just another rip-off. The rich get richer, and all that.

Recognizing that the best defense is a good offense, The Big Eight have mounted an aggressive propaganda campaign to convince critics that expanding their scope of practice improves rather than hinders audits. Chairmen, senior partners, and assorted mimics like to speak of "countervailing benefits"—the ways man, beast, and the heaven above benefit from diverse accounting activities.

"If you do more services for a company—like actuarial and consulting work—you are more involved and better able to audit them," Auerbach says. "The more we know about a company, the better auditors we are. A richer scope of practice actually improves our performance. Many of the bad cases have come from auditors who did not understand the businesses they were auditing."

John Burton, former SEC chief accountant and a widely respected figure in the profession, wrote this in a letter presented to the AICPA's Public Oversight Board (POB) during its review of the scope-of-practice issue.

"When I was a staff accountant, one of my clients asked our firm to develop a system for translating foreign currency statements in U.S. dollar statements for consolidation purposes. I and a consultant worked on the job and developed an understanding in depth of the translation process which would not have occurred otherwise, and in a subsequent audit I was able to point to certain implications of particular changes in exchange rates on the client's statements which required careful audit consideration.

"In a second case, I as a professor was consulting with an accounting firm in the area of management services research. One of my areas of interest was credit policy, and the firm was given an engagement to study the credit policy of one of its large mail-order clients who wished to develop an improved system of credit control. I worked on the engagement with a consultant from the firm's management services staff and an audit manager. We assisted in the development of a credit policy and a system of credit control, and in so doing achieved an understanding of the variables affecting credit loss for that firm that could never have been achieved through normal auditing techniques. This understanding was of great importance to the audit staff in evaluating the adequacy of the client's allowance for uncollectible accounts. In the year prior to the consulting engagement, the client's allowance was materially understated in the financial statements, and its income was overstated, even though procedures were performed. In the year following the engagement, the audit staff, assisted by work papers from the consulting engagement, were able to appraise the adequacy of the allowance with far greater accuracy."*

So goes the argument for "countervailing benefits": An auditing firm with MAS involvement is said to have deeper knowledge of the client and is therefore a better auditor.

The list of benefits said to emanate from the auditor's conduct of MAS service does not end here. The accounting establishment, most notably The Big Eight and the AICPA, is highly skilled in developing sophisticated arguments for conducting self-serving practices in the name of the public good.

"While the rendering of management advisory services has been attacked from many directions, it has also been praised by credible sources," states the POB report, *Scope of Services.*

"First, from a client's viewpoint an accounting firm that has conducted an extensive and competent audit is a logical choice when that client needs management advice. Assuming that the accounting firm has the competence to render the services needed, its audit clients will naturally want to take advantage of its knowledge, experience, organization, and personnel. Each job may begin more quickly and proceed more efficiently than if the client had to engage a different firm. . . .

"Another benefit of MAS appears to be the quality of young

*Public Oversight Board Report (AICPA), *Scope of Services by CPA Firms,* March 1979, pp. 17–18.

professionals who are attracted to accounting firms because of the opportunity to practice MAS. Time and again, the Board heard testimony that the best and brightest students emerging from business schools are most interested in firms that will afford the opportunity to work in the MAS area. . . .

"There are other advantages to allowing accountants to provide MAS to audit clients in addition to attracting bright students and enhancing audit quality. One is that an auditor who also has some responsibility for advising its client on internal financial controls can facilitate an audit by improving the underlying structure of what is audited. Auditors are naturally aware of deficiencies in information systems. If they can work with a client to improve a system, the result is twofold. First, future audits should be less costly because they will be more easily accomplished. Second, improved controls will in turn make financial statements more accurate and reliable because the system on which they are based is equally so. Thus a great benefit can be seen in allowing an accounting firm to communicate to a client weaknesses and defects in an audit and also to make specific recommendations for improvements through its MAS services."*

That the inherent conflicts of audit/MAS engagements should be ignored to enable The Big Eight to successfully recruit the best students is absurd. Securities laws were not passed to make public accounting firms attractive employers.

The argument that auditors are in the best position to improve financial controls makes a more legitimate point—but this too is a complex issue. There is no doubt that having a single firm conduct an audit as well as consult on controls saves time and money. But this produces a major conflict of interest: that of the auditor auditing his own work. Who can deny that a CPA firm is likely to find merit in its own control systems and to accept them at face value. The checks and balances of an independent, third-party review are missing. Does audit quality suffer? Certainly there is reason for intelligent observers to think that might be the case.

This is precisely where the accounting establishment shows its

*Ibid., p. 19.

ugliest side. Rather than recognizing that there are grounds for legitimate differences of opinion, Big Eighters label all critics as wild-eyed radicals or hopelessly ignorant buffoons. Abe Briloff, the profession's best-known gadfly, is pictured as a revolutionary. To hear it from Big Eight senior partners, you'd think the aging, mild-mannered CPA is a guerilla warrior. Briloff's insistence that "there should be no separate MAS services by accounting firms because the coach of the team cannot then go put on a nice clean uniform and become the umpire," incites the Big Eight to discredit the man as well as his arguments. Go against the accounting establishment, and you learn that it can hit below the belt.

"Briloff is extreme—he's an extremist," says a former official of the AICPA. "He seems to believe that all you have to do is set standards and everything gets cleared up. He believes that there is a 'right' way, that there are 'undeniable truths.'

"Briloff's major impact has been to erode the confidence in financial reporting. He has taken away some of the faith from accounting standards."

Hearing his boss break the ice, an AICPA staffer continued the attack. "Briloff's an old record. No, a broken record. His message emerged in the late sixties and it's remained the same since. He's still saying the same things, but it's no longer new. The press doesn't talk to him anymore."

After years of single-handed battle against The Big Eight, Briloff is used to the low blows. He handles them deftly. His problem is that he expects too much from the profession—he presses for a quasi-religious code. "If they say I play the old tunes, then morality, truth, and virtue are out of style, because these are the tunes I play. The tunes are as old as the Old Testament."

Those critics not branded as extremists by The Big Eight are dismissed as idiots. One hears over and over again that the scope of service controversy continues simply because "lesser minds" cannot grasp the issues involved—that only the "well-informed" see the benefits of providing multiple services to a single client. Big Eight executives come on strong here, referring to average investors as a lower form of life. It's the old "great-white-father" syndrome: if only the natives would understand. Clearly, the accounting estab-

lishment exhibits the kind of behavior it attributes to Briloff. That
is, proclaiming that it alone has all the answers.

The Cohen Commission, for its part, presented a more reasonable
assessment of the problem. Although the commission did not warn
against the delivery of MAS services, it did admit that rational
people can be uncomfortable with it:

> Except in the Westec case, the Commission's research has not found
> instances in which an auditor's independence appears to have been com-
> promised by providing other services. Nevertheless, consideration must be
> given to the belief of a significant minority that some of the other services
> do impair the auditor's independence. Auditors and issuers of financial
> statements should consider the trade-offs involved in obtaining audit and
> other services from the same public accounting firm.

Odds are that the scope-of-services issue—and for that matter
most of the controversies swirling around the professor—will fade
away in the 1980s. The passionate reformers of the past decade are
now investment bankers, corporate attorneys, and music executives.
With the election of the Reagan administration and a conservative
Congress, strong probusiness forces have taken up positions of
power throughout the nation's capital. The liberals have been sent
packing.

"As recently as a year ago, it seemed that the accounting profession would continue to face strong criticism for an indefinite time,"
writes PW's Joe Connor in the firm's 1980 annual report. Connor
is known to be an astute observer of the profession. "Congress and
the bureaucracy seemed to be dead set on imposing arbitrary and
unwarranted constraints on corporate governance, financial reporting, and professional accounting service. As we enter the new decade, however, there are many signs that a sense of balance may soon
be restored. . . .

"There seems to be a change of mood among our critics, the
dawning of a realization that the profession is striving to meet
reasonable expectations. Hopefully, we can now turn our full ener-
gies to the issues that are of genuine concern: inflation, capital
formation, government accountability, and the expansion of our
capabilities to serve the needs of our clients and the public."

Another key factor is on The Big Eight's side. As America's giant corporations, public institutions, and governmental bodies prepare for the enormous challenges of the twenty-first century, they will be searching for expert counsel in a broad range of disciplines. Even routine decisions will demand sophisticated data on multinational taxes, return on investments, cost/benefit analyses, budget controls, market elasticity, revenue projections, and much more.

The Big Eight are blessed with teams of specialists capable of churning out the answers.

"We're in a unique position to expand our practices," says Ray Groves, chairman of Ernst & Whinney. "That's because our firms have awesome pools of talent, unmatched by any organization. We'll be doing more and more of the work we do because no one else can take up the slack."

This unrivaled ability to deliver a rich diversity of professional services is a great source of power and wealth for The Big Eight. As a result, no argument on earth can dissuade Big Eight management from performing tax and MAS work for audit clients. Man for man, The Big Eight leaders refuse to budge on this central issue, insisting that there is no inherent conflict of interest as long as the firms are committed to independence.

Some will admit, however, to an "appearance" of conflict and concede that this appearance alone demands some remedial action. The accounting establishment prefers to deal with the profession's fundamental issues as "appearance" problems. This allows great flexibility. Actions can be taken in the name of appearance without accepting the critics' basic arguments.

"There we were sitting in a Waldorf Astoria conference room well after midnight," says a private consultant and former Big Eight auditor. "I'm tired as hell, there's about a foot of snow piling up around the city, and I still have to drive to the suburbs. You'd think they'd call the meeting early, but, no way. We're brainstorming a position paper that our Washington office is going to present to the SEC. The assignment is clear: We have to word the thing to show that we're willing to police ourselves in the conduct of management advisory services, but we don't want to come off sounding like there is a conflict of interest.

"One of the partners volunteers that we admit that there has been some conflicts, but they'll never happen at our firm, because we have tough controls. Well, shit, the vice-chairman tears into him in front of the entire group—calls him an asshole, a naive son of a bitch, and on and on. The poor slob hasn't opened his mouth at a meeting since.

"About 3:00 A.M. we come up with an approved paper. The party line is that there's no such thing as conflict of interest—not a single proven case of it. The critics are all wet. But because some dummies may think there's a problem, we'll take some steps to diminish the appearance of conflict. The notion is that we are such superprofessionals, so concerned with the public good, that we'll bend over backwards to do the right thing.

"Hogwash. The appearance issue was simply an excuse. It allowed us to make some motions at dealing with a problem without admitting that there was one. It was a clever ploy."

To show that they are good boy scouts truly concerned with the appearance issue, all of The Big Eight limit the scope of their practice activities by refusing to perform one or another minor services, like plant design or market research. The rationale is that these functions are not closely related to the accountant's traditional function; they should therefore be discontinued in order to preserve the image of professionalism and to eliminate the appearance of conflict.

"Although the issue of scope of service has been raised with regard to independence, it is our view that the issue is more closely related to professional image," says a statement by Deloitte Haskins & Sells in response to the SEC's Accounting Services Release (ASR) 264, which sounded an alarm on possible limitations on MAS work.

"It should be evident that there are certain services that are totally unrelated to the practice of public accounting and pose no threat to independence but which may be inconsistent with the maintenance of appropriate professional image. Although the matter of professional image is important, it should not be confused with independence. . . .

"We believe that the maintenance of our firm's image as profes-

sional accountants is important, and therefore we provide only those
services that our clients have come to expect of a firm in our profession. Our MAS has to do almost entirely with the organization,
planning, performance measurement, accounting, and reporting aspects of the system for the various management functions and the
development and analyses of information for management use. The
performance of these services does not in any way impair the public's image of us as independent professional accountants. We do not
and have not provided services such as psychological testing, public-
opinion polls, plant layout, merger and acquisition assistance for a
finder's fee, or actuarial services."

Clearly, The Big Eight believe that to voluntarily curtail minor
services will be viewed as a fair compromise, and that its big guns
—tax and MAS—will be protected. The greatest threat comes from
the SEC. As the overseer of the accounting profession, the SEC may
issue rules (ASRs) severely limiting the scope of services. All of The
Big Eight live in fear of this action.

Although the SEC has for years been pointing fingers at the
potential for audit/MAS conflicts—and has been hinting at some
sort of restrictive actions—it keeps coming to the brink and then
backing off. ASR 264 (issued in 1979), which brought the threat of
tough action to new heights, was issued to "sensitize the profession
and its clients to the potential effects on the independence of accountants of performance of nonaudit services for audit clients". In
doing so, ASR 264 directed CPAs and clients to consider the relative
size of MAS and audit fees:

> While hard-and-fast lines cannot be drawn, any firm which finds that a
> substantial portion of its aggregate revenues arises from nonaudit engage-
> ments should seriously evaluate the resulting impact on its image as a
> professional accounting firm and from the standpoint of the potential for
> impairment of its independence. Similarly, where the firm's revenues from
> a given audit client are heavily weighted towards MAS, the impact on both
> the fact and appearance of independence merits thoughtful review.

ASR 264 also cautioned the CPAs to avoid supplanting client
management's role, to be cautious of accepting engagements that
involve an audit of their own work (such as a review of internal

controls installed by the auditor's MAS arm), and that client audit committees should gauge the relative merits of the firm's auditor providing nonaudit services. As is its practice, the commission concluded the release with a threat of further action should ASR 264 prove to be inadequate.

> The Commission recognizes that the question of independent auditor MAS activity is both difficult and controversial. If future events indicate that further action is necessary, the Commission stands ready to reconsider this issue in order to assure the confidence of investors in the financial reporting of publicly held companies.

This threat of further action annoys and frightens The Big Eight. Although the SEC has proven to be pretty much of a paper tiger in its role as accounting overseer, there is always the possibility that it will back up its whinings and warnings with some decisive measures. The firms must continue to walk the minefield.

The SEC's cocked trigger is its power to suspend a firm from practicing before it.

For any of The Big Eight—loaded as they are with publicly owned clients—this would be crippling. Under Rule 2E of the SEC's Rules of Practice and Investigation, the commission can hold administrative hearings, making individual CPA firms answer to complaints of improper practices under the federal securities laws.

"Rule 2E says we can suspend an accountant from practicing before the commission," says Linda Griggs, general counsel for the Chief Accountants Office of the SEC. "The accountants could no longer attest to reports that have to be filed with the SEC. But Rule 2E is controversial in that the courts have not been clear about our ability to suspend an entire firm from practice before the commission. Some observers say we can; others disagree. The issue has never come before the Supreme Court."

Still, one general counsel of a Big Eight firm puts it this way: "Rule 2E is the atomic bomb and the SEC has it. They've never activated the weapon, but they could—they could drop it at anytime."

To make things worse, ASR 264 has prompted clients to reconsider their MAS/audit assignments with an eye toward preventing any hint of conflict or lack of independence. By simply throwing up the aggregate fee precaution without saying how much is too much, the SEC has caused some audit committees to shy away from awarding its auditors with nonaudit engagements. The Big Eight have complained bitterly about this "chilling effect," insisting that it has tainted MAS work without ruling against it.

The SEC responded in its 1980 annual report to Congress on The Accounting Profession and the Commission's Oversight Role:

> The Commission's intent in issuing ASR 264 was, of course, not to promote the indiscriminate termination of MAS engagements or any other nonaudit services. Rather, its purpose was to encourage a careful assessment by management, audit committees, boards of directors, and accountants of the potential impact on auditor's independence resulting from nonaudit services engagements. . . .
>
> In this regard, many in the accounting profession believe that independence should be evaluated in terms of individual engagements only, and that the evaluation of the independence of a relationship should not be colored by the magnitude of the accounting firm's firm-wide involvement with MAS activities. While the Commission agrees that independence is primarily dependent on the nature of the accountant's relationship with individual audit clients, it disagrees with the notion that the profession may disregard the magnitude of MAS activities on a firm-wide basis. Undue emphasis on MAS could ultimately have an unfavorable effect on the quality of audit work performed. Similarly, the apparent tendency of some accounting firms—particularly larger firms—to compete on the basis of total revenues, and the array of MAS activities offered, is troubling. The Commission is concerned that the ultimate result of such a philosophy could be a subtle shift in emphasis—perhaps real, perhaps apparent—away from the auditor's primary function. It is this eventuality, and possible consequences on audit quality, or on user confidence in the reliability of the auditor's report and the credibility of financial reporting, that the Commission sought to warn against in ASR 264.

As usual, the SEC left The Big Eight hanging in the balance, leaving no doubt that Big Brother would be hovering about, keeping an eye on things:

> Although the Commission believes that ASR Nos. 250 and 264 provide a meaningful framework for the determination of the appropriate scope of

services to be performed by independent accountants, it has not ended its examination of the scope-of-services issue. Rather, it views the issuance of ASR Nos. 250 and 264 as part of a continuing examination of the relationships between registrants and their independent accountants. After further monitoring of practice, the Commission will be in a better position to determine if any further action is necessary in this area.

Big Eighters accuse the SEC of indecisiveness, meddling, and ignorance of the issues. Certainly, there is some truth here. The commission just muddles along, issuing rules, fanning controversies, rarely taking a firm stand on anything. Proudly beating its chest, it menaces the profession with the threat of action, only to back off with little more than a scold or a slap on the wrist. Worst of all, from The Big Eight's standpoint, is that its fuzzy guidelines leave CPAs and their clients more confused than informed.

Ask ten CPAs how to handle the audit/MAS problem and you get ten somewhat different answers. There is, however, considerable support throughout the accounting establishment for a proposal outlined by John Burton in the April 1980 *Journal of Accountancy*. Based on his experiences with the SEC during a troubled period for corporate audits, Burton believes that difficulties arise from too little involvement in a client's activities rather than too much. He considers the scope-of-services problem to be one of appearance, resting primarily with those laymen unfamiliar with accounting concepts:

The basic question to be resolved in dealing with an appearance criterion is whether appearance should be examined on the basis of that which would be perceived by an informed person with a knowledge of the facts or by a person with no understanding of the audit process or the nature of relationships that conventionally exist. Most reported surveys of perceptions of independence indicated that the greater the degree of knowledge about the profession and auditing, the less concern there is about threats to independence emerging from the scope of services performed. On the other hand, those without information or background of this sort are inclined to perceive a problem.

If the pursuit of the appearance of independence is to continue and is to be expressed in terms of the suspicions of uninformed persons, there seems to be no way in which the current structure of auditing and the accounting profession can be sustained. No uninformed and suspicious citizen who views the world through skeptical eyes could be expected to be convinced of an auditor's independence when the auditor is paid for his services by the client.

Burton's argument is basic and unassailable: Skeptics will distrust the paid auditor/client relationship regardless of the scope of services provided. To satisfy this type of critic, the entire system would have to be changed.

Burton outlines the following steps to deal with the appearance problem much less drastically:

Better educate the layman to the objectives and limitations of a corporate audit.

Adopt a strong self-policing mechanism to assure audit quality. Establish a viable disciplinary process to identify and penalize those who do not meet the standards.

Further integrate audit and nonaudit services to emphasize the totality of audit services.

Gradually replace the term *independence* in professional literature with words such as *professional, unbiased,* and *objective.* It is felt that this will reduce confusion about the auditor's role.

Disclose all aspects of the auditor/client relationship, including actual services provided and fees for each.

Expose all parts of the CPA firm to peer review.

Burton's "new framework" is a sound approach to the scope-of-services issue—providing one believes that the current system of paid, independent audits should be maintained. In spite of its many drawbacks, the system seems to be the best way to bring some credibility to financial reporting. The number of services provided is truly not the key issue: It is the payment of a fee to a supposedly "independent" party that is troubling. The Big Eight do, however, appear to be committed to preserving independence regardless of the sums involved. The good that their diverse skills can bring to American corporations and governments should be allowed to continue until there is substantial evidence that providing nonaudit services to audit clients is corrupting.

The threat of government regulation of the accounting profession should frighten the man on the street and the corporate executive as much as it does Big Eight partners. Surely the nation needs no further proof that the bureaucratic influence is a stultifying one— a negative force that drains energy, imagination, and innovation. The plodding activities of the SEC make this clear. For all their self-serving and questionable practices, The Big Eight are decisive, no-nonsense, profitable businesses that bring efficiency and fiscal savvy to a nation and a world that needs as much of that as it can get.

The Big Eight's closest brush with government regulation came in 1978 with the introduction of H.R. 13175, the so-called Moss Bill.* The measure called for the enactment of a National Organization of Securities and Exchange Commission Accountancy. CPA firms would be required to register with the new body and to furnish it with audit reports relating to financial statements filed with the SEC. The bill, officially titled the "Public Accounting Regulatory Act," also authorized the proposed Accountancy Commission to conduct a continuing program of review and investigation of audits performed by independent public accounting firms and to take disciplinary action against the firms and their principals, including economic sanctions, fines, and suspension of or repulsion from registration.

The prospect of having to register with a central body—and of being subject to its close surveillance—scared the pants off The Big Eight. Partners objected vehemently to a number of its key provisions:

Only one member of the new agency's five-man board could be from a major accounting firm. Big Eighters are not comfortable with this lack of representation. Most of the profession's own self-regulatory bodies are weighted with members drawn from the big CPA firms. The Cohen Commission, for example, was widely touted as an

---

*Named after John E. Moss, former chairman of the House Commerce Committee's Subcommittee on Oversight and Investigations.

"independent study group" assigned to "develop conclusions and recommendations regarding the appropriate responsibilities of independent auditors." But how "independent" was the commission? It was established by the board of directors of the AICPA, Big Eight firms provided partners to fill commission staff positions and to serve as staff director, and the AICPA paid the bills for travel, meeting facilities, printing, mailing, and the like. This is the kind of "independence" the Big Eight can live with. Congress had something else in mind.

The Accountancy Commission would review the work of individual accounting firms every three years, checking for "acts or omissions by such accounting firms or principals in such firms which are contrary to the interests of the investor public." Regulations would also zero in on specific audits, closely examining the firms' policies and procedures on a case-by-case basis. The bottom line: The review of the accounting firms' activities would be conducted entirely by outsiders.

CPA firms' legal liability would be greatly increased, making them accountable for negligence even without evidence of fraud or intentional misconduct. Taking a very wide brush to the liability question, the bill read that "any independent accounting firm shall be liable for any damages sustained by any private party as a result of such party's reliance on an audit report by such firm with respect to a financial statement, report, or other document filed with the Commission under any federal securities law, if such accounting firm was negligent in the preparation of such audit report." This would open The Big Eight to successful billion-dollar class-action suits for minor audit mistakes. Every wheeler-dealer who lost money on the market would try to pin it on the auditors; with this kind of loose legislation on the books, most plaintiffs would likely succeed.

"Uncle Sam can make a thousand and one giant mistakes—like sending a generation of young men to a mindless death in Southeast Asia—and is supposed to be excused for it," snarls a Big Eight audit partner. "But if CPA firms innocently forget to dot an *i* or cross a *t*, we're crucified. Can you imagine that kind of gall! I sure as hell can't."

The Moss Bill never passed the House, but its spirit still lives— still haunts The Big Eight. Copies of the bill can still be found throughout the firms, the AICPA, and the halls of Congress. With politics being as unpredictable as it is, the firms worry that a sudden shift in the winds could breathe new life into the bill. H.R. 13175 is down but not out. As long as serious matters go unresolved, a new accounting regulatory body remains a threat.

In calling for the Accountancy Commission, the Moss Bill stated that "the accounting profession has not established and appears unable to establish a satisfactory self-regulatory arrangement." Sensing that the creation of such an "arrangement" would diffuse criticism and would thus reduce the likelihood of outside intervention, the profession embarked on an elaborate, albeit questionable, program of self-regulation. This has become the heavy artillery of its defense against government regulation. It is intended to prove that accountants are sensitive to the public interest and are serious about policing themselves.

Until 1978, the AICPA and the accounting profession in general had no vehicle for dealing with CPA firms as entities. Only individual CPAs could join the Institute; only individuals were subject to its sanctions and requirements. In response to the legislative and regulatory ferment of the mid-1970s, the Institute launched a new division designed to bring CPA firms into the fold. Two sections were established: one for small accounting firms serving mostly private companies and another, the SEC Practice Section, for the giants serving huge public corporations. Members of this SEC section, including all of The Big Eight, must submit to reviews of their audit quality controls at least once every three years. The reviews are conducted by other public accounting firms.

Some of the other requirements of the SEC Practice Section—which do have legitimate value in terms of self-regulation—include:

A provision that the auditor report to the corporate audit committee* or the board of directors any disagreements with management concerning auditing or accounting matters which if not resolved would have resulted in a qualified opinion.

---

*Another reform of the 1970s. Audit committees are panels similar to boards of directors but concerned exclusively with auditor relationships. They are designed to insulate management from the auditors.

A requirement to provide the audit committee or the board directors with an annual report on consulting services rendered and the fees for these services.

A system to rotate the partners in charge of an audit at least every five years; and to have a partner other than the one in charge of an audit review the audit work before issuing the annual audit report.

The "peer review" process is at the heart of the profession's self-regulatory program and is representative of the program's overall substance and style. In spite of the lofty language promoting it as "a major first step forward by the profession,"* peer review is little more than a slick way of keeping objective sources away from the profession's internal affairs.

"The oversight of professional practice should remain within the profession, and the concept of individual firms having responsibility for the quality of their own practice should be retained," the Cohen Commission reported. "A voluntary program consisting of the following three elements would provide effective oversight:

Independent peer review of accounting firms.

Detailed reports of the results of peer review made available to concerned parties.

Appointment by individual accounting firms of independent oversight groups, analogous to corporate audit committees, to supervise the peer review process.

These recommendations can be achieved without creating new structures either within the profession or by government agencies. . . . Peer reviews of large, complex firms are probably better performed by another CPA firm that has the experience and the ability to conduct a large and complex audit. . . ."

With The Big Eight firms facing essentially the same problems, sharing roughly the same goals and perceiving the same villains, can

---

*Deloitte Haskins & Sells' comments on accounting establishment.

they be critics of each other's performance? Many say no. In spite of their competitive differences. The Big Eight still recognize that Congress, the SEC, and the public at large are their real enemies. When it comes to dealing with controversial issues, their tendency is to draw the wagons in a circle rather than shoot at each other.

"I have yet to see the peer-review program effectively implemented in the accounting profession," says Briloff. "I think it boils down to you scratch my back, and I'll scratch yours.

"Peer review has its equivalent in the medical profession—such as surgical-review committees that review procedures. But how effective has it been in any profession? If you use it to identify, expel, and otherwise discipline the wrongdoers, then it's good. But if peer review is just a *Good Housekeeping* seal of approval that the brethren give one another, then it's not effective.

"It's not that I'm the hanging judge—it's not that I'm sadistic—but I want those who are in power, mainly The Big Eight firms, to know that if they are unprofessional, they will be punished. I have not yet seen this."

Peer reviews could put *Good Housekeeping* to shame. As far as The Big Eight are concerned, the program carries little promise of changing their processes or procedures.

"The firms do not have to make the changes suggested in peer-review reports unless the report says the firm's quality-control procedure is not adequate," says an AICPA official. "A major firm has never had a modified report. I would not expect them to get one.

"You cannot expect peer reviews to find that Big Eight firms are really deficient. These firms have been in business for many years reviewing the statements of major corporations. You can never expect to find them terribly deficient."

Not a single Big Eight firm has ever been forced by the peer-review process to adopt a quality-control measure that it objected to. Although the AICPA has such power, the odds of it being exercised are not very real. For all its posturing as a forceful organization committed to upholding professional standards, the Institute appears to be a loyal protagonist of The Big Eight. The atmosphere at the AICPA's New York headquarters—just blocks away from most of the giant firms—is that of a propaganda arm for its biggest members. Many staffers seem more eager to protect The Big Eight than to make them fully accountable to peer review.

Besides the natural inclination to keep their dirty laundry in the family, two other factors make peer review less than "a giant step forward." First, the firms can select their own reviewers. Big Eight chairmen can tap the sister firms with which they have the best relationships and who are most likely to render a sympathetic accounting. Even a strong supporter of peer review, Russ Palmer, gives credence to this when he says, "the others don't choose us to do peer review, because they know we'll be aggressive and tough. The only rules of the game we play by are superprofessionalism."

Second, the profession has fought hard to deny the SEC access to peer-review papers. It is on these documents, which are similar to audit work sheets, that the nitty-gritty of peer-review data is reported. By steadfastly refusing to let the commission see these papers, the profession has made it clear that it wants to package the information in neat summaries all tied up with red ribbons. Although some concessions have been made in this regard, the SEC does not yet enjoy complete and open access.

The view from the other side of the fence is quite different. Big Eight executives insist that review of the work papers must be limited to protect client's confidentiality, and that this minor matter in no way diminishes the success of peer review.

"A tough, gutsy, no-nonsense process—that's the way we see peer review," Palmer adds. "This is no damn game, no show. We lay ourselves open to another CPA firm—bare ourselves to them. Tell me another business that does the same.

"At Touche Ross, we want the most honest, straightforward review we can get. We select our reviewers on that basis alone. When you're as concerned with professional quality as we are, you look at peer review as a learning process—a form of quality control. You're only cheating yourself by trying to get an easy going-over. We picked Price Waterhouse to do our review, and we're quite proud of the results."

PW's letter to Touche Ross concerning its peer-review findings is revealing. The opening passages serve as a disclaimer for the entire process, confirming that it is not comprehensive nor necessarily

reliable. What's more, recommendations are gentlemanly sugges-
tions limited mostly to rather nebulous matters. Anyone expecting
a hard-hitting examination of one CPA firm by another might well
be disappointed.

To the Partners of   October 10, 1979
    Touche Ross & Co.

We have reviewed the system of quality control for the accounting
and auditing practice of Touche Ross & Co. in effect for the year
ended March 31, 1979, and have issued our report thereon dated October 10, 1979. This letter should be read in conjunction with that report.

Our review was for the purpose of reporting upon your system of
quality control and your compliance with it and with the membership
requirements of the SEC Practice Section of the AICPA Division for
CPA Firms (the Section). Our review was performed in accordance
with the standards promulgated by the peer review committee of the
Section; however, our review would not necessarily disclose all weaknesses in the system or lack of compliance with it or with the membership requirements of the Section because our review was based on
selective tests.

There are inherent limitations that should be recognized in considering the potential effectiveness of any system of quality control. In
the performance of most control procedures, departures can result
from misunderstanding of instructions, mistakes of judgment, care-
lessness, and other personal factors. Projection of any evaluation of
a system of quality control to future periods is subject to the risk that
the procedures may become inadequate because of changes in conditions or that the degree of compliance with the procedures may
deteriorate.

During the course of our review, we noted the following areas
which we believe could be improved to further strengthen your
system of quality control:

Improve documentation of key issues considered and audit work performed

It is the firm's policy to require for every audit engagement a
complete record of audit procedures performed and the facts and
rationale for key judgments and conclusions. We believe documentation in the engagement record could be improved in the following
areas:

—The facts, discussion of the issues considered, consultations, if any, with designated local office consultants and reviewers, and related reasoning for the conclusions reached on significant accounting, auditing and reporting matters.

—Procedures performed when using work of outside specialists and internal auditors.

—Effect of EDP control reviews on audit scope.

—Procedures followed in limited reviews of interim financial information.

—Communications between offices participating in a multi-office engagement.

We recommend that the importance of appropriate documentation procedures be reemphasized to the professional staff.

Codify consultation policies

The firm's technical inquiry policy requires consultation with the Executive Office Accounting and Auditing Technical Staff in specific instances, as well as in cases where additional consultation outside the local office consultation process is considered necessary. We believe compliance with the firm's consultation policies could be improved by codifying in one firm publication the instances where such additional consulting is appropriate or required.

Improve compliance with firm policies on use of the work and reports of other auditors

The firm's written policies on the use of the work and reports of other auditors are reasonable and consistent with authoritative guidance. Firm policy requires timely approval of the National Director of Accounting and Auditing before accepting certain engagements involving other auditors and approval of the Executive Office Accounting and Auditing Technical Staff for exceptions from performing specified audit procedures concerned with the work of other auditors. Based on our review we recommend that the firm review its compliance with firm policy particularly in the areas of (1) acceptance of principal auditor responsibility, (2) reference in the firm's report to the work of other auditors, (3) the performance of appropriate procedures for supervising the work of other auditors, and (4) documentation of other auditor independence.

Improve compliance with firm policy on client representation letters

The firm's policy requires that representation letters obtained from clients conform with a model letter supplied as a part of the firm's reference material and that deletions, except in certain cases, from specified standard paragraphs be cleared with the Executive Office Accounting and Auditing Technical Staff. Firm guidance and professional literature also require consideration of additional representation paragraphs beyond those included in the model letter when unusual accounting or reporting requirements exist. Our review disclosed instances where letters of representation did not conform with firm policy. We recommend that the firm emphasize the importance of obtaining management's representations on all significant matters reflected in the financial statements and clarify the circumstances where deviations from the model letter are to be approved by the Executive Office Accounting and Auditing Technical Staff.

Emphasize importance of timely preparation of staff performance reports

Firm policy requires timely preparation of a formal written staff evaluation report for each staff member assigned to an engagement of appropriate length and complexity. We recommend that the firm emphasize to the appropriate responsible personnel the importance to the firm's overall quality procedures of timely evaluation of staff performance on qualifying engagements.

*   *   *   *   *

The foregoing matters were considered in determining our opinion set forth in our report dated October 10, 1979, and this letter does not change that report.

PRICE WATERHOUSE & CO.

In a profession where appearances are vital, for The Big Eight to pass judgment on their own operations is absurd. All of the firms now have internal quality-control teams that tour the offices worldwide, checking that everything is up to snuff. Because the findings are kept strictly confidential, these patrols produce more meaningful recommendations than peer reviews. But as long as the SEC demands that a show be staged, the firms will get up to dance. They'll continue paying each other sizeable sums (about $1 million per peer review) to do little more than what is already going on quietly behind the scenes.

There's no doubt The Big Eight are buffeted by social and political currents. As auditors and advisers to the high and mighty, they are caught up in the great flow of human events. So pervasive is their influence, that they must adjust to hundreds of changes and developments in the world around them.

Take the persistent (and potentially disastrous) problem of inflation. Like all businesses, families, and institutions, The Big Eight must revise their own budgets and billing rates to compensate for rising costs. But this is only the tip of the iceberg. As inflation ravages the very foundation of capitalism, a growing chorus of leaders is demanding that CPAs help to protect the economic system by engaging in so-called inflation accounting.

"Clearly something must be done to account for the effects of inflation on corporate earnings," says Robert Sprouse, vice-chairman of the Financial Accounting Standards Board. A pleasant, pipe-smoking former college professor, Sprouse seems very much at home at the board's quiet, campuslike offices in Stamford, Connecticut.

"Put simply, the problem is one of distinguishing real profits from numbers that are just swollen by inflation. A corporation may appear to have tremendous profits, when in fact inflation is a big factor in the bottom-line figure. Real earnings have not increased much at all.

"These illusory profits are problemsome because they can anger the public and lead to cries for congressional action. Congress may act to push back profits which are not great to begin with. What's more, inflated earnings force companies to pay more taxes, even though those earnings are artificial. Finally, these exaggerated earnings figures prompt corporations to pay out higher dividends.

"Taken together, these problems deprive the corporation of the money it needs to replace the assets it is using up in the course of its business. It does not have enough profits left for reinvestment and is therefore deprived of the fuel for growth. The company stagnates."

Bob Cushman, chairman of the Norton Company, put the problem in perspective when he explained in a *Business Week* story that although the corporation reached the $1 billion sales level in 1979, 79 percent of the growth since 1971 is attributable to inflation, and that if Norton just stands still, it will be a $2 billion company in five years. What's more, despite a solid financial performance, the shareholders are receiving only a small return in constant dollars.

Antibusiness forces who find it hard to fret over the plight of giant corporations or to shed a tear for the beleaguered *Fortune* 500, must bear in mind that the impact of inflation extends well beyond the boardroom, tearing at the very fabric of our political and social structures. The consequences are far-reaching, leading to unemployment, a marked decline in living standards, and social unrest.

"If the problem is left unchecked, our economic system will actually cannibalize itself," Sprouse adds. "Our studies show that some corporations actually pay out more in dividends than they earn. They cannot renew themselves. This reduces the productivity of U.S. industry and further fuels inflation. It's a vicious cycle.

"Unless there is creditable financial information adjusted for inflation, we cannot manage either individual companies or the overall economy. That's because we can't really gauge where we are going. The financial reports do not present an accurate picture of where we are."

Recognizing a problem is only half the battle; when The Big Eight are involved, determining who should solve it always seems to be a war of its own. In this case, the skirmish is between the SEC, which feels compelled to put its two cents into every accounting question while rarely adding much, and the FASB.

To understand the controversy, we must trace the roots of the FASB. This purportedly independent body establishes Generally Accepted Accounting Principles (GAAP)—those accounting procedures that are considered appropriate, ethical, and fair for CPAs to use in the course of their work. Without these standards, CPAs would be free to invent their own techniques—to portray financial transactions in any way that would make the client look best. Although critics contend that there is still a dearth of "creative accounting," the existence of GAAP puts more restraints on the

CPAs freedom to "doctor the books." Auditors' reports must indicate whether or not the client's reports conform to GAAP. The problem is that there is still no single set of accepted principles for each type of financial transaction. The Cohen Commission Report states:

The public accounting profession has tried to develop detailed accounting principles to reduce the number of acceptable alternatives and to meet the changing needs of evolving economic conditions. Even so, there are many kinds of events or transactions for which authoritative accounting bodies have not specified one alternative as preferable or the circumstances in which each of several alternatives is appropriate. Thus, the guidance provided by detailed accounting principles in authoritative pronouncements is incomplete. In part, this incompleteness arises because authoritative accounting bodies have not always reacted quickly enough to changes in the business environment, to emerging practice problems, or to inappropriate application of existing accounting principles to new types of transactions and other events.

Adds an accounting professor: "Most of the brilliant financial minds of the past generation have gotten rich figuring ways to apply GAAP to absolutely unethical financial practices. Smart minds have found they can drive a truck through GAAP and get away with it. That's how flexible the rules are. In fact, the schemers use GAAP to justify their tactics."

In an effort to restrict creative accounting and to develop tougher guidelines, standard-setting authority was transferred from the AICPA to the newly formed FASB in 1972. Bowing to threats that the SEC might itself assume the standard-setting function, the accounting establishment quickly fathered the FASB.

Officially the board is a private-sector body administered by a wide cross section of interests and committed to the promulgation of objective accounting standards. Needless to say, there are more than a few skeptics. The Metcalf Report states:

The FASB's organizational separation from the private interest groups sponsoring it is the basis for the claim that it establishes accounting principles independently. However, the separation is one in name only. This study finds that The Big Eight accounting firms, the AICPA, and, to a lesser extent, the other sponsoring groups have control over the operation of the FASB. Such control is exercised in terms of money, personnel and organizational support.

Metcalf scoffed at the FASB's claim of independence, pointing out that the Financial Accounting Foundation, which has great influence with the board, is in turn tied to the AICPA:

An example of the special-interest orientation found throughout the FASB is the composition of the task forces which perform much of the work in researching and developing FASB positions on particular accounting issues. The memberships of such task forces are largely comprised of outside representatives from large accounting firms, corporate clients of Big Eight firms, contributors to the FASB, large investment firms, and big banks.

Critics take the SEC to task for allowing standard setting to remain in the private sector, whether at the AICPA or the FASB. In the Securities Act of 1933 and the Securities Exchange Act of 1934, Congress directed the SEC to protect investors from misleading financial reports. From this came the authority to establish accounting and reporting standards. Instead of setting its own standards, however, the SEC has relied on the rules established by the profession, except in those cases where it finds the AICPA or the FASB to be derelict in its duties.

In a strange and somewhat incomprehensible setup, the AICPA continues to issue some minor accounting standards in spite of the existence of the FASB. It is desperately holding on to the last vestiges of its power here. The atmosphere at the Institute's accounting standards offices is surreal: No one seems capable of clearly explaining what and why the AICPA does in this regard. The most one can decipher is that the staff issues standards on matters too small for the FASB to consider, but which are nevertheless important to practitioners in the field. Although the staff denies this, the AICPA appears to be terribly hostile toward and jealous of the FASB. "The king-stripped-of-his-throne" syndrome.

Metcalf found that the SEC policy on accounting standards plays right into the hands of The Big Eight. "The controlling influence of The Big Eight accounting firms in establishing accounting stan-

CONTROL OF THE "BIG EIGHT" ACCOUNTING FIRMS AND THE AICPA OVER ACCOUNTING STANDARDS APPROVED BY THE SEC

THE "BIG EIGHT" ACCOUNTING FIRMS

The "Big Eight" firms control of the AICPA.

AMERICAN INSTITUTE OF CERTIFIED PUBLIC ACCOUNTANTS (AICPA)

The AICPA Board of Directors has exclusive authority to elect and remove the members of the FAF Board of Trustees.

FINANCIAL ACCOUNTING FOUNDATION (FAF)

The FAF Board of Trustees has exclusive authority to appoint and remove the members of the FASB.

THE "BIG EIGHT" ACCOUNTING FIRMS AND THEIR CORPORATE CLIENTS

The "Big Eight" firms and their corporate clients, as well as all other independent auditors and publicly-owned corporations, are required to use FASB accounting standards recognized by the SEC when reporting financial information to the public.

SECURITIES AND EXCHANGE COMMISSION (SEC)

The SEC officially recognizes accounting standards established by the FASB as the only standards which satisfy the requirements of the Federal securities laws.

FINANCIAL ACCOUNTING STANDARDS BOARD (FASB)

The FASB establishes accounting standards, as well as determining the procedures used to establish accounting standards.

dards ultimately benefits the managements of their corporate clients by assuring that such standards will be generally acceptable to them. The Big Eight firms benefit because the present system enhances the value of their services to clients by permitting more flexibility in reporting financial results to the federal government and the public.

Unfortunately, accounting standards which permit corporate managements great flexibility in reporting the results of their business activities have resulted in many cases of inaccurate or misleading financial statements. Economic decisions based on such financial statements have caused substantial losses to investors, creditors, suppliers, purchasers, and others. To the extent that public policies have been based on inaccurate or misleading financial statements, the federal government has acted upon illusion rather than fact.

Both the SEC and the FASB deny this. The board insists that in spite of critics charges, it is fully independent from the accounting profession. For all the controversy that has swirled around the FASB since its inception, it is a rather tranquil place located in a corporate park. The senior staff is surprisingly relaxed and candid, exhibiting little of the fortress mentality that marks Big Eight officers.

"There's not a shred of evidence that we are controlled by The Big Eight," says board chairman Donald Kirk, a former Price Waterhouse partner. "The Big Eight and the AICPA have no special entree into our activities here. What's more, its preposterous to assert that The Big Eight talks with one voice and then tells us what to do. The Big Eight rarely agree on anything.

"None of us on the board have any affiliation with or obligation to the firms we were with prior to joining the FASB. I certainly disagree with Price Waterhouse quite often. People throughout the profession disagree with each other on hundreds of issues. Inflation accounting is one of them."

Attempts to reflect the impact of inflation in accounting principles goes back to 1969 when the Accounting Principles Board—the predecessor to the FASB—issued a statement suggesting that in addition to standard financial reports companies should also issue restatements of the information adjusted for inflation. There would be a comprehensive restatement of financial information in units of purchasing power. This was merely a request, and there was little voluntary action along the lines of the recommendation.

"The issue arose again in 1973, shortly after the board was formed," Sprouse recalls. "It was the time of the first oil crisis and of double-digit inflation. So the problem came right to our attention; it was an immediate concern. In December of that year our advisory council suggested that we take action immediately on the matter of inflation accounting.

"We issued a 'discussion memorandum,' raising the question of whether the adjusted information, as suggested by the APB, should be required in financials. We held a public hearing on the question in April 1974. At that time, the Financial Executives Institute asked for the chance to do field tests using the dual sets of financials with real companies. We agreed and over 100 companies completed the tests. They provided restated financial data for the most recent two years in their annual reports.

"Meanwhile, in the summer of 1974, the SEC came out with a proposal that instead of adjusting for inflation with the general-purchasing-power yardstick, we use specific prices for specific items. The difference in the two approaches is easy to explain. Let's say a company paid $5,000 for a truck three years ago. With the FASB's approach, we would apply the change in the consumer price index to the price of the truck. If the CPI went up thirty percent, we could apply that thirty percent to the price of the truck. The depreciation would then be based on the higher truck price. Our system focuses on the purchasing power of the dollar on general inflation.

"But the SEC said don't worry about the purchasing power of the dollar. Instead, let's look at specific increases. How much would it cost to replace that truck today? They said we should base depreciation on this replacement-cost factor. The SEC proposal was designed to more accurately reflect the impact of inflation on specific industries. In some industries, like computers and other high-tech fields, prices had actually gone down. The SEC wanted to reflect this."

With both sides seeing things differently, it's no surprise that the SEC and the FASB clashed over the issue. Believing at the time that it was too much of a burden for businesses to perform both types of revisions, the board deferred to the SEC, backing off while the commission issued ASR 190 in March 1976. This required that supplemental information on inventory and cost of goods sold as well as property, plant and equipment and depreciation be included in corporate 10-K reports filed with the SEC. The directive met with a good deal of hollering and screaming in the business community. Providing the revised financials, SEC style, posed a major problem. "Using the replacement-cost approach, the owners of a steel plant with an old blast furnace would have to come up with a figure of what it would cost to replace the plant today with new technology," Sprouse explains. "This is a very difficult estimating problem. The corporations were terribly unhappy with it.

"We took up the issue again in 1976. The SEC did not require the restatement of earnings, and this was what we believed users of financial reports really needed and wanted. What's more, our approach is much less complicated and, we believe, more accurate as well. Rather than trying to figure what it would cost to replace an old plant with new technology, it is so much simpler to apply a specific price index to inventory and property, plant and equipment."

Stung by criticism over ASR 190, the SEC was by now eager for a way out of the inflation-standard-setting fiasco. Commission officials purportedly made it clear to the FASB that they would withdraw their rule if the board issued a pronouncement of its own. Clearly, it was the SEC's turn to back off.

The board's exposure draft, issued in December 1978, gave management the option to choose between constant-dollar or current-cost accounting. Because many respondents did not want to make this decision on their own, the FASB required both restatements, issuing both Statement 33, which requires that earnings be restated in constant dollar, and current cost forms. As promised, the SEC withdrew ASR 190.

One look at the dual restatements is more than enough to convince the average investor to ignore them completely: They confuse things more than they clarify them. Which restatement is accurate? "As a stockholder you may be wondering how to measure the impact of double-digit inflation on your equity investments. There's a clue in this year's crop of annual reports. But you may need a calculator to sort out the meaning of the new, inflation-adjusted figures. . . .

"For instance, General Electric Company's 1975 dividend of $1.60 per share becomes $2.16 in 1979 dollars. While the company reported an average annual dividend growth of 14.5 percent using historical cost accounting, the increase comes to only 6.2 percent when it's adjusted for inflation."*

Clearly, most of The Big Eight prefer to work with the constant-dollar approach. As auditors to the nation's public companies, they do not want to incur the expense or responsibility of confirming replacement-cost estimates. This will drive up audit costs at a time when there is already great pressure on fees.

As of now, CPAs do not have to audit the restated financials. Although the board claims that this is in no way a favor to The Big Eight, there's no denying that the firms are pleased as punch to have it just this way. The accounting establishment has produced a wishy-washy rule that clouds the issue and that absolves the profession from responsibility for its shortcomings. Statement 33 appears to be little more than rulemaking for the sake of rulemaking— another effort at window dressing by an image-conscious profession. But this seeming nonaction is enough to satisfy the SEC.

"In partial response to this need for change in financial reporting, the FASB, in September 1979, issued Statement of Financial Accounting Standard No. 33, *Financial Reporting and Changing Prices;* its first standard to address the complex area of accounting for the effects of changing prices," states the SEC's 1980 annual report to Congress. "Considered by the Commission to be a significant break-through in the private sector standard-setting process, Statement No. 33 represents an important addition to the historical cost-based accounting model and, perhaps more importantly, reflects the willingness to deal with difficult issues requiring innovative solutions."

Business Week, May 5, 1980, p. 135.

Chester B. Vanatta, of Arthur Young, also sees merits in the pronouncement. "Clearly, it will be some time before all of the problems associated with inflation-adjusted data can be ironed out —certainly for several years of this new decade. In the meantime, though, I believe there are some pluses.

"For example, we are now seeing five-year earnings, dividend and share price trends adjusted to eliminate variations in the purchasing power of the dollar. The adjusted dividend data, when compared to adjusted earnings information, will help us assess whether, in real terms, capital and income purchasing power encroachment is taking place. And the adjusted rate of return on shareholder's equity will allow us to get a better perspective on a company's real earning power. The real cost to a company of replacing its inventories and plant, property, and equipment will become clearer. Financial analysts in particular view this information as a promising means of helping to predict future dividend payouts and as an important means of indicating a company's future cash needs.

"Of course there are difficulties. . . . But it is, in my view, a giant step forward."

Both the SEC and FASB point out that Statement No. 33 is a "test" of the dual restatements and that the board will review the matter for needed change by 1984. One observer, a former Big Eighter now a self-employed tax attorney, sees it another way.

"It's not a test; it's a stalling action. It's a way to buy five years. This accounting establishment has power, gobs of it. You won't get them to do what they don't want to do.

"You know what will happen in five years? They'll ask for five more. Inflation can bring the country to its deathbed, but the CPAs won't be pushed around. Oh, there'll be controversy—there always is. But so what? That never stops The Big Eight from doing what they want. Nothing does."

Index

Academy Awards, 1–2, 10–12
Academy of Motion Picture Arts and
  Sciences, 9
  See also Academy Awards
Accountancy Commission (proposed), 215–
  17
Accountants, staff. *See* Staff accountants
Accounting:
  definition of, 6
  as a multidisciplined profession, 177
  origins of, 3
  specialization within, 176–77
Accounting principles:
  Cohen Commission Report on, 226
  See also Generally accepted accounting
    principles
Accounting Principles Board, 229–30
Advertising, 44
Altman, Roger, 107
American Institute of Certified Public Ac-
  countants (AICPA), 219–20, 226, 227
  Auditing Standards Board of, 103–4
  Public Oversight Board (POB) of, 201,
    203–5
  SEC Practice Section of, 200–1, 217–18
Andersen. *See* Arthur Andersen & Co.
Annual reports, 99
Arthur Andersen & Co., 2, 8, 69, 117
  image of, 61
  Metcalf Report on, 134–35
  nonaudit services of, 61

Arthur Young & Co. (AY), 2, 117
  competition among firms and, 62–64
  fortress mentality at, 61
  image of, 61–63
  tax practice of, 148–50
Atwood, Robert, 129
Audit scope, 76–77, 93, 95
Audit staff, 77–78
  See also Staff accountants
Auditability, tests of, 80–82
Auditing (audits), 6–9, 66–105
  computer programs for, 79–80, 168–69
  definition of, 75
  interviews with client employees and, 82
  managers (supervisors) of, 78
  materiality criterion and, 93–95
  phase one of, 82, 86
  phase two of, 88, 90
  phase three of, 92
  uncertainty about future events and, 96
Auditing Standards Board, 103–4
Auditors:
  harmony between management and, 99
  selection of, 67–68
  See also Auditing; Partners; Staff account-
    ants
Auditor's reports, 99–105
  AICPA's proposal for revision of, 103–4
  explicit and implied messages conveyed
    by, 102–3
  standardization of, 102

[235]

typical example of, 100
Auerbach, Norman, 60, 74, 202, 203

Balance sheet, 76
Banks:
 Office of the Comptroller of the Currency
  (OCC) and, 126–33
 Peat, Marwick, Mitchell's "profit im-
  provement program" for, 110–11
Beery, Wallace, 10
Bernikow, Al, 155, 157, 163–64
Bernstein, Peter, 28*n*, 43*n*
Beyer, Robert, 54
Big Eight, The:
 auditing as most important activity of, 6–7
 government regulation of, 215–17
 independence of, 198–202, 209, 210
 as information bastions, 8–9
 international operations of, 69–70, 148–49
 Management Advisory Services of. *See*
  Management Advisory Services
 Metcalf Report on, 134–35, 198–201
 names of, 2
 national affairs offices of, 133
 overseas affiliates of, 59
 peer review by, 217–24
 small-business practice of. *See* Small-business practice
 tax practice of, 137–54
 testimony before government bodies by,
  133–36
 See also specific topics
Briloff, Abraham, 34–35, 68, 205
Budgeting, time, 86–88
Bureau of Indian Affairs, U.S. (BIA), 110
Burton, John, 203–4, 213–14

Cable Plan, 169
Cable-television industry, 167–69
Caltex Petroleum, 69–74
Capital contributions of partners, 30–32
Carter H. Golembe Associates, 129
Certified Public Accountants (CPAs), 6–7
 image of, 171–73
Chase, Chevy, 12
Chetkovich, Michael, 43
Chrysler Corporation, 106–8
Class-action suits, 93–94
Cohen Commission Report, 75
 on accounting principles, 226
 on auditor's reports, 99–100, 102–3

on college programs and faculty, 189–90
 independence of, 215–16
 on Management Advisory Services
  (MAS), 207
 on peer review, 218
 on time and budget pressures, 64, 86–87
 on uncertainty about future events, 96
Colleges and universities, 177–78
 Cohen Report on, 189–90
College students, recruitment of. *See*
 Recruiting
Colorado Division of Correctional Services,
 112
Competition among Big Eight firms, 47–48,
 62–65
 animosity created by, 59–61
 for consulting jobs, 115
 fees and, 64–65
 image and, 41–43
 for major audit accounts, 70–71
 Marcus on, 62–63
 proposals and, 70–72
 quality of work and, 63–64
 See also Marketing strategies
Compliance tests, 90
Comptroller of the Currency, Office of the
 (OCC), 126–33
Computer programs, 79–80, 168–69
Conflicts of interest, 133
 between tax and MAS work and auditing,
  208–9
 See also Independence of The Big Eight
Connor, Joseph, 25, 31, 57, 81, 207
 on image of Price Waterhouse, 41, 42
 personal characteristics of, 40
Consultants, 114–16, 120–26
 job demands of, 119–20
 power of, 123–26
 recruitment of, 120–21
 See also Management Advisory Services
Controls, internal, 88, 90
Coopers & Lybrand (C&L), 2, 8
 Caltex account and, 69, 72
 computer programs of, 79–80
 diary of a first-year staff accountant at,
  192–95
 image of, 60
 Management Consulting Services department of, 109–10
 marketing strategies of, 60
 price-cutter reputation of, 60